ACCLAIM FOR MARC HERMAN'S

SEARCHING FOR EL DORADO

"The trail from ancient myth to harsh reality is a fascinating journey." —*Maxim*

"A terrific dual narrative about how the whiff of gold can linger in a region for centuries, even when it's clear that extracting the stuff is no longer profitable. [Herman] writ[es] with casual, yet authoritative, flair." —*The Denver Post*

"The deeper into the jungle Herman gets, the more his story takes on momentum and life. . . . From these wizened miners and assorted hustlers, we start to get a different picture of El Dorado—or a different El Dorado, one whose analogues can be found in North American cities like Miami and New York, and not just in the Amazon." —*The Nation*

"Journalist Marc Herman has found ample evidence that what was unreal but nonetheless believable almost 500 years ago remains as unreal and believable today." —*Mother Jones*

MARC HERMAN

$\mathcal{S}$EARCHING FOR EL DORADO

Marc Herman's work has appeared in publications including *Mother Jones, GQ,* and *Harper's*. For his work
on *Searching for El Dorado,* he was named a Writer on
the Verge by *The Village Voice Literary Supplement* and
Newcomer to Watch by *Book* magazine. He lives in
the San Francisco Bay area.

SEARCHING FOR EL DORADO

A JOURNEY INTO THE SOUTH AMERICAN RAIN FOREST
ON THE TAIL OF THE WORLD'S LARGEST GOLD RUSH

MARC HERMAN

VINTAGE DEPARTURES

Vintage Books • A Division of Random House, Inc. • New York

FIRST VINTAGE DEPARTURES EDITION, FEBRUARY 2004

The Library of Congress has cataloged the
Nan A. Talese/Doubleday edition as follows:
Herman, Marc, 1969– .
Searching for El Dorado: a journey into the South American rain forest on
the tail of the world's largest gold rush / Marc Herman.—1st ed.
p. cm.
1. Guyana—Description and travel. 2. Venezuela—Description and travel.
3. Amazon River Region—Description and travel. 4. El Dorado.
5. Rain Forests—Amazon River Region.
6. Gold Mines and Mining—Amazon River Region.
7. Adventure and adventurers—Amazon River Region.
8. Herman, Marc, 1969–. I. Title.
F2372.H47 2002
918.8104'32—dc21
2002029034

Vintage ISBN: 0-375-72703-5

Book design by Deborah Kerner/Dancing Bears Design
Leaf motif illustration by Richard Waxberg
Map by Laura Hartman Maestro

www.vintagebooks.com

AUTHOR'S NOTE

Most foreign attempts to represent Caribbean English are at best embarrassing and at worst mocking. I've quoted speech directly only when the meaning would be transparent to any reader of any English, and in those cases quotes are verbatim from my notes and tape recordings. The rest I paraphrased outside quotation marks.

I have used North American spelling in quotations to prevent the story from devolving into a pointless exercise in transcription: the Caribbean patois "fuh" appears as "for," "fiah" as "fire," and so forth.

Caribbean literature written in local diction by local authors is increasingly available in North America and Europe. Peepal Tree Press, Leeds, U.K., is a good source.

— M. H.

The Spaniards have had a confused notion of this country, and have called it "El Dorado"; and an Englishman, whose name was Sir Walter Raleigh, came very near it about a hundred years ago; but being surrounded by inaccessible rocks and precipices, we have hitherto been sheltered from the rapaciousness of European nations, who have an inconceivable passion for the pebbles and dirt of our land, for the sake of which they would murder us to the last man.

– A LANDLORD SPEAKING TO **CANDIDE**

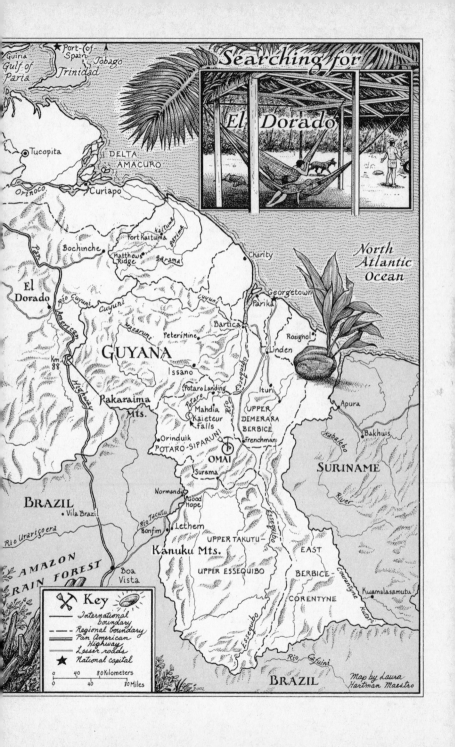

IF ALL OF US

MOVE TO ONE SIDE

OF THIS VESSEL

IT WILL CAPSIZE.

PLEASE DO NOT DO IT.

▶ ▶

— POSTED ON A GUYANESE FERRY

$\mathcal{S}$EARCHING _FOR_ EL DORADO

THE MYSTERIOUS
PROSPECTOR

It is a misconception that you sleep in a hammock with your feet
at one end and your head at the other. You'll fall out. The proper
way to do it is to lie diagonally across the hammock's width. In
southern Guyana, where they make some of the world's better
hammocks, people sometimes sit entirely sideways in theirs. The
best come from a group called the Wapisiana. The Wapisiana
make their hammocks with cotton twine woven back and forth
like a fishing net. Nothing special. But you could hang your entire family in one and it wouldn't break. The hammocks are also
nearly impossible to fall from because the design is a long, luxu-
riant oval that will catch you no matter how you move. An
example is in the British Museum and another in the Smith-
sonian's collection in Washington, D.C.

A North American hammock by comparison is small, tippy,
and not appropriate for use in the forest. So my first night in
Guyana I did not sleep well. I was hanging over the ground in a
hammock made from a few strands of crudely tied nylon. I had
bought it in ignorance the prior month at a sporting goods store
in Los Angeles. It proved too small to hold my legs and distributed weight badly. I also rigged it wrong from the poles in the

shelter where some local gold prospectors and I were sleeping. It hung too low.

I was tired from riding to the camp all day in the back of a truck so ignored the problem at first.

However: "This hammock not a jungle hammock, boy," a miner hanging to my left said.

He was only a few inches away but it was night and the shelter was very dark. Even when I shined a flashlight he was impossible to see through his hammock; rather than a net a miner's hammock is a large cloth rug, usually decorated with a colorful design, and the fabric obscured his head. He had a low, disinterested voice and his body was long and hung heavily.

"You want? Tie up higher, boy?" he said from the depths of his hammock.

"It's okay." I didn't want to interrupt his rest.

He rolled onto one shoulder, the ropes strained and he stuck his head over the edge of the fabric. I shined the flashlight. He was a young man sporting a wild pile of dreadlocks that pointed in many directions.

"Lot of snakes in Frenchman," he said. Frenchman was the camp's name, the legacy of two French prospectors said to have died in a cave collapse nearby.

People sleep tied to poles in a tropical forest rather than on the ground in tents because the forest floor is damp and filled with alarming creatures. It is preferable to hang at least a few feet out of reach.

"Okay. Okay," I said.

He got out of bed and showed me how to tie the ropes so they stayed as high as possible. He was a muscular young man wearing only some jockey shorts; he seemed sleepy and did not say much. He tied some loops into the ropes securing the hammock and nodded with satisfaction when it was hanging higher, then sat back into his own hammock and gave a two-fingered wave good night over the edge.

I had come to be in a gold miner's camp in Guyana as the result of a chance encounter.

A little over a year prior I had been living in a family cabin in New York's Catskill foothills when a storm hit. This was in 1994. Seven feet of snow fell, the furnace failed and my car died. By the end of the week it grew so cold in the cabin the water in the toilet bowl froze. It proved to be a long week.

But the previous Sunday's paper, which I dug from the snow and borrowed from the house next door included a chart of "lowest airfares." I scanned flights to the equator where it was warm. Venezuela's national carrier offered to fly from Miami, Florida, to Caracas, Venezuela, for only two hundred dollars. I had not planned to flee the cabin but suddenly it seemed like an ideal option. I had just left the first job I had gotten after graduating college and had yet to find a new one. Two days later I climbed over a snowbank that surrounded the house, walked down the hill, hitched a ride to the train station and as soon as possible connected with a bus to Miami.

From there I was in balmy, dirty Caracas the next day. Because in most of the world life is easy if you hold American currency, I figured I could afford to wait out the winter on Venezuela's Caribbean coast playing soccer and lying on the beach. That's roughly what happened in the end.

But.

Late in my trip I decided to head south by bus on a vague plan to see the Amazon forest. In North America the Amazon is associated most often with Brazil, sometimes Ecuador and Peru. However its north edge reaches into Venezuela and Guyana as well. Some of the jungle's least-known corners are across those borders. The first paved road from Venezuela to Brazil only went through as recently as 1991 and no road to speak of exists from either country through Guyana even today. Three days later I got off the bus at a town named for its milepost: Kilometro Ochenta y Ocho, Kilometer 88. I debarked to a clearing by the road's shoulder to get some lunch.

Halfway through lunch a man and a woman walked out of the trees. The man was large and white. He looked bad: his shirt was covered in mud; a potbelly strained it; he wore a two-week beard and his hands were pink with abrasions. He had not bathed in some time. His shoes were foam shower sandals, and insect bites and welts covered his feet. He was one of those men whose age could have fallen anywhere ten years to either side of forty-five.

The woman who walked with him was young enough to be a daughter but seemed by their manner to be his girlfriend. She was Latin, presumably Venezuelan. I said hello to them in my halting Spanish. The young woman appeared not to notice. The man said hello but was unfriendly. He wouldn't give his name.

They ordered lunch from the tin-roofed barbecue where I was eating; a tired-looking young woman on the other side of the restaurant was cooking chickens over a fire in an oil drum. While the couple waited for their food I asked what they were doing in Km 88.

The man said—reluctantly, and in English—that he was a gold miner in Guyana. The border was across the street behind some low buildings, he said.

Km 88 was obviously not an official border crossing. It consisted of a hotel with an aggrieved toucan shrieking in a cage, a small dry-goods store and a cinder-block garage. The town seemed too small to be more than a highway stop, but the man said it was a supply outpost for a few thousand gold prospectors.

The surrounding forest was full of them he said. A gold rush was underway in that part of the forest. One of the world's largest gold mines was under construction in the trees a few miles east of town and another was scheduled to open within a few months on Guyana's side of the border.

He leaned on the card table where I sat. It strained. The young woman with him had wandered off to gossip with the chicken cook in Spanish.

The forest around us held five, ten, twenty, maybe fifty billion dollars in gold he said. Thousands of people local and foreign were looking for it. His camp had only a few men digging so far. He had been there a few months. But if they discovered enough traces of gold he planned to head north to the United States, talk to bankers and find backing to return with larger tools. Then he could hire more employees and mount a proper exploration effort. When he found enough gold he would make a claim with the government, sell the claim to an international gold company for millions of dollars and retire to the Bahamas. That was his plan.

After a few minutes he took a paper plate of chicken from the woman cooking over the oil-drum fire, paid her a dollar in local bills and walked back across the road with his companion. They disappeared around the hotel and into the forest and crossed back over the border to Guyana.

When I got back to the United States a few weeks later I went to a library. It took about an hour to confirm the prospector's story. Geology journals and stock market reports—not anything in a respected newspaper, but those breathless newsletters Wall Street fetishists read for investing tips—were full of articles on gold discoveries in that part of the northern Amazon.

It took longer to find out how outsiders had even known of

the gold there. It turned out they had followed a very old trail. History books said that four hundred years ago the part of the forest where gold was turning up was also the last presumed location of El Dorado: the city of gold from conquistador myths.

How a golden city came to be located in an obscure patch of rain forest on the Guyanese border appeared to be a matter of some argument.

The story was five centuries old. El Dorado had been a person at first, not a place. A few years after Columbus a story had emerged in South America of what was likely a Chibcha or Muisca Indian king living in what is today Colombia. This king would cover himself in sap or oil to which he adhered a layer of golden dust. Thus the name El Dorado—"the gilded one" or "the golden man."

All aglitter, El Dorado would be the image of a god walking the earth. On ceremonial occasions he would hurl gold and sometimes himself into a lake. The gold would wash away and the next morning he would cover himself in more from an apparently inexhaustible supply.

The Spanish heard the story and decided Lake Guatavita in Colombia was the site of the ritual. They tried to drain a number of Andean lakes; to do this required cutting away the stone on one side at great effort with hand tools, perhaps the first foreign attempt to excavate a piece of South America to recover something valuable. This was in the 1520s. Nothing came of it. (Modern archaeologists, however, have found gold artifacts at the bottom of some of the same lakes.)

The Spanish were happy for their agents to start looking elsewhere for the gold. Indians in Colombia had many golden objects, so the Spanish presumed there had to be a gold mine somewhere. This was the germ of the eventual misapprehension that El Dorado was a place and not a person: that there was a single source for South America's treasure.

The effort to find this source drove the first European expansions through South America. Also North America. The word "California" comes from a similar Spanish myth of a utopian land of riches. The Seven Cities of Cibola, which the conquistador Coronado presumed to exist somewhere in what is now the American Southwest, were mythical cities of gold as well. De Soto was looking for something along the same lines when he first saw the Mississippi. Other utopian myths existed concurrently. Francisco Pizarro seemed to think a gold land was adjacent to an equally miraculous land of cinnamon, or was itself a land of cinnamon. Spices were nearly as valuable as gold at the time.

Hundreds of searches got underway from the Colombian coast. Most went sharply awry. The explorers would hack into the unknown forest and get lost. They were facing the Andes Mountains and the Amazon jungle, both basically impassable. Before long they had to ask the people living nearby for directions. Some of the locals cooperated; others had every incentive to send the invaders charging toward a rival village, over a waterfall or slugging into some forest of no return. Within a few weeks the explorers and their helpers and slaves would bog down in the mud and grind to a halt. The expeditions would fall into mutiny and disarray. Boats sank, horses died, disease spread. The resources on hand soon ran out and from there the only options were to straggle back defeated or never be heard from again. Both occurred.

The rest of the story is well told and central to the conquest of the Americas. The conquistador Francisco Pizarro packed a small expedition over the Andes in 1532 and arrived at the court of the Incas at Cajamarca. There he made a deal in bad faith with the Inca ruler Atahualpa and took him hostage in an ambush. Atahualpa offered a roomful of gold as ransom. Gold poured in from every corner of the Inca empire. This dazzled Pizarro and lent more credence to the possibility of a nearby gilded kingdom. The Spanish took the gold and killed Atahualpa anyway; Pizarro and his various brothers proved to be glorified thugs, and in due time several succumbed to treacherous deaths themselves.

Most of the gold Pizarro saw in Peru existed as religious or architectural objects. But there was still no gold mine apparent and still no source. The Spanish satisfied themselves with looting what the Incas had, melted the objects into ingots and loaded the ingots on galleons back to Europe. It was waste. Archaeologists still lose sleep over the destruction of artifacts; economists, notably Peter Bernstein in *The Power of Gold,* point out that all the seized treasure did not help Spanish finances very much in the end anyway. The discovery of silver mines in Bolivia soon stole Spanish attention: they offered a way to dig up wealth from its origin and not just get it by sacking.

The myth of a golden empire persisted anyway. Its presumed location tended to move every few years to whatever part of South America was least mapped and most mysterious at the time. By then the continent's northwest was far better known to Europeans than the east. So suspicion began shifting eastward. In 1541 the youngest Pizarro brother, Gonzalo, decided he would make an expedition east from Quito, Ecuador, to find the lost empire.

He and his lieutenant Francisco Orellana headed into the western Amazon forest with hundreds of men and slaves. Before long the effort stalled in the forest as usual and the two men split. Pizarro waited upriver and Orellana headed off downriver. Pizarro eventually got tired of waiting for Orellana's return and went back to Quito. Orellana had gotten lost and unintentionally navigated the whole of the Amazon, crossed South America, followed the Atlantic coast past Guyana and finally ended up in Venezuela. He did not find any gold empire en route but did stumble onto the world's largest river and cross the continent west to east. Information from Orellana's journey and others reached Spanish governors, who continued writing guesses as to El Dorado's nature and location for the next century. Some already believed the golden city lay closer to the Atlantic than the Pacific—in the eastern jungle rather than the western mountains. Another theory suggested that the northern Amazon in Venezuela was the Incas' ancestral home, and that's why no one had ever found El Dorado across the continent in Peru.

The Inca gold: was it El Dorado? There is certainly plenty of gold nearby. In the late 1990s, Denver's Newmont Mining Corporation, an international gold mining company, developed one of the world's richest gold mines in Cajamarca near where Pizarro killed Atahualpa. Speculation continues that a mysterious cache of Inca gold remains hidden in the Andes, in a lost stronghold of the last Inca. A Reno, Nevada, amateur archaeologist named Gene Savoy claimed to have found what he termed El Dorado in 2000 in the Peruvian mountains. There was no gold there, but Savoy, who has discovered several important pre-Columbian sites, believed the ruins he found could have been the seat of an El Dorado kingdom. More academically minded archaeologists are skeptical. Attempts to drain Lake Guatavita in Colombia continued for centuries meanwhile, the most recent in 1965; and the capital of the Brazilian Amazon today is the city of Manaus, presumably Manoa, another common name for El Dorado.

Most of the Spanish efforts ended by 1600, and the myth would have likely died with them. It didn't because England took up the search in the person of Sir Walter Raleigh. In 1595 Raleigh parked his ships off Venezuela and headed into the maze of swamps at the mouth of the Orinoco River. The Orinoco is the continent's second-largest river after the Amazon. Its delta is hundreds of miles of marshland and confusion. Today cocaine smugglers hide there. If you wanted to hide a golden empire, it would be a suitable place to do so.

This was not the first attempt at El Dorado from the Caribbean side of the continent. A Spaniard named De Vera had also tried it, among others. But Raleigh's effort is the one people remember today because he wrote a successful book about the adventure after surviving. He intended to find El Dorado for Queen Elizabeth. He thought it was a mountain of crystal.

After making it a third of the way up the Orinoco and back over a few months, Raleigh returned to England and wrote the book describing a paradise he claimed to have found: *The Discoverie of the Large, Rich and Bewtiful Empyre of Guiana*. His deputy Lawrence Keymis made separate journeys and added his own diaries, which are less well known, but include the first known descriptions of trips along the jungles of the still-obscure Essequibo River in Guyana, a north-flowing waterway halfway between the Orinoco and the Amazon. In both cases the explorers faked plenty of details—dog-headed mermen; headless tribes—but the claims made for good reading. V. S. Naipaul, who wrote a history of the region, notes that Raleigh had his skeptics. The gold Raleigh had returned with from South America—his proof of El Dorado's existence—was not gold at all, according to the Royal Mint at the time. Naipaul also notes the title of Raleigh's book was much longer than it has become in its modern incarnation, and argues the title's length made it seem like a credible report, and not the fantasy it was. Raleigh and Keymis alleged El Dorado lay somewhere in Guiana. (Guyana is the modern nation; Guiana is the region encompassing parts of Venezuela, Brazil, Guyana, Suriname, and French Guiana.)

Raleigh was a celebrity in England at the time. This and the claims of knowing where a mountain of crystal was did not prevent him from ending up in prison on unrelated matters upon returning home. Released twenty years later in 1616, he sailed off again quite unadvisedly to South America and undertook a last search for El Dorado. A septuagenarian by then, he was not strong enough to go up the Orinoco himself. His deputy Keymis and son Wat went in his place. Upriver a month later Keymis and Wat broke an English truce, senselessly attacked a Spanish camp and all ended up dead: Raleigh's son killed in the fight, Captain Keymis a subsequent suicide in his stateroom, Raleigh his head lopped off after returning to London.

With all this tragedy it is somewhat surprising that the myth of El Dorado survived the next four hundred years as a story of a utopia and not of a curse. But it is perhaps somewhat more surprising that at the end of the four centuries a gold mine finally turned up. Local prospectors had found something, and then North Americans had come with money and bought the right to build the largest gold mine in South America.

Five centuries after Columbus, nearly to the year, treasure maps in old history books and geological maps in modern investment newsletters were identical. The people who searched for El Dorado had been right all along. About the time I was sitting down in the library, a billion-dollar gold mine was opening for business on the banks of the Essequibo at a spot of jungle called Omai. Raleigh's deputy Lawrence Keymis had passed the site in a longboat four hundred years prior, noticed nothing, and continued on his way blithely unaware.

In 1995, a little over a year after meeting the gold miner at Km 88, I went back to South America. I had not gotten much of a job after returning home after all and the story of the gold had stayed with me. I was also calling myself a freelance reporter by then, based on some odd jobs at a newspaper in Montana and an apprentice job in New York. In truth I was not reporting much of anything and was "freelance" only in the sense of being unemployed. Still, I had kept up with the few reports I could find out of that part of South America, and I went back intending to write down what I saw. My plan was to head farther south of where I had met the miner, continue to the Guyanese border and catch a ride through the gold mining areas the stock newsletters suggested existed on the far side of the forest. The capital, called Georgetown, was just north of that forest on the Atlantic coast.

In Georgetown I could arrange to visit the gold mine discovered on the Essequibo at Omai. It was the largest gold mine in South America at the time and was located four hours south of Georgetown. Before leaving I called the American and the Canadian firms that owned it, but representatives of each said I would have to talk to the mine managers in Georgetown if I wanted to see the gold mine. I headed south, fittingly I suppose, on speculation.

From Caracas it takes a day by bus to reach the Orinoco River. The river bisects Venezuela into its urban north and frontier south both literally and psychologically, in much the same way the Mississippi divides the east and west in the United States. From there the highway leads for two days into the gold-bearing areas. Once you're that far south it is possible to cross into Guyana as the miners do: directly from Venezuela by river in a small motorboat. But this requires bribing or ducking the patrols. Crossing is officially illegal because of a border dispute.

The dispute is a century old and also has to do with the gold. Venezuela is shaped like a mushroom on international maps, but the local maps show an additional piece of land dangling from the southeast side of the country. Rather than note the rivers and towns there, Venezuelan cartographers mark this tail with yellow stripes like crime scene tape and label it the Zona en Reclamación—Reclaimed Zone or Zone Under Recovery. The area is a swath of jungle beside a high plateau and officially constitutes half of neighboring Guyana. Control of the land there means control of billions in gold as well as pricey timber and access to a potentially valuable Atlantic port: the mouth of the Essequibo. Unfortunately the argument over the area has no easy resolution. Europeans drew the contested border somewhat randomly in the 1800s. Venezuela probably lost the land unfairly. But Guyana was a colony when the original deal went through. The current government had nothing to do with it, and the Venezuelan claim amounts to half the smaller country. Also, it's the rich half. The result is a stalemate with occasional hard words tossed back and forth between the governments.

Rather than get mixed up in all that I detoured farther south and dipped into Brazil. From there a bus ran perfectly legally to the Guyanese border. The bus was a four-wheel-drive, high-riding thing: a cartoonish vehicle with knobby balloon tires like a child's bicycle. I was the only one on board after a stop in the first half hour. There had been forest to either side of the road in Venezuela, but it had receded on the Brazilian side. The bus drove a dirt road that crossed a dry plain wide enough to see the curve of the earth on the horizon.

After two hours the bus reached a dusty town of a few hundred people. Nothing was there but some goats and a few old men and women playing dominoes in a hot plaza. The driver said this was Bonfim, gruffly hurried me off—you don't make any money carrying a single passenger one direction—and pulled fast out of the plaza back the way he'd come.

There was no border in sight. I asked the people playing

dominoes where to go. An old man in a baseball cap spoke a little English and directed me two miles out of town to a narrow river called the Takutu. The Takutu was the border, he said. I picked up my bag. It was afternoon and the sun was high as I walked.

At Bonfim the Takutu is an unimpressive, shallow gully, and most people wade across. In the rainy season it swells just enough for a woman on the south bank to make a few dollars ferrying passengers in a motorized skiff. She charged one Brazilian real to putter the launch across the river to a cracked plank set in the northern embankment. I stepped out of the boat and walked up the plank and was in Guyana.

I stood on the bank for a moment with my passport ready waiting for a border guard to appear. When none did, I put my passport away and followed some goats across a yellow swale toward Bonfim's sister town just past the river. It was called Lethem; it said this on the wall of the post office at the bottom of the swale. It was a shack with a window made of chicken wire. An elderly man was there. I asked him how to get to Georgetown. He said there was no road to speak of, but an old cattle trail once existed to drive herds from southern ranges to slaughter on the coast. The remnant of that trail ended at Lethem and headed north. Other than that the mail plane was the only way across the country from Guyana's south, and the mail plane had already left that day he said. He was a slender man who was stooped and walked unsteadily. The goats milled around him, and when one bumped him he yelled and shooed them off, and they retreated with the sound of the small bells tied with yarn around their necks. I headed off crosstown on the mailman's direction. A barn and a runway were visible about a hundred yards away. Some low bungalows sat a little closer. I walked up a dirt road toward the barn.

The border area had seemed on maps to be entirely within the Amazon forest. The region was colored green on my map. But the sagebrush plain that had begun in Brazil continued across the river. The plateau was a large area but bordered by mountains on two sides and the rain forest on the rest. To the west was a wall of mesas called the Pakaraimas. Opposite the mesas, across the plain, was a range of smaller, green peaks called the Kunukus. Most of the area appeared uninhabited and unmarked by roads. There were no power lines or crops visible. Anthills covered the plain. Beside the mesas were clouds twisting like dropped scarves. Few have any reason to travel to the south of Guyana but its history and appearance recall the American West. The scant population is Amerindian and descendants of cattle ranchers from Europe and North America. The spring rodeo is a popular event. The region looks like parts of Wyoming, and would feel like Wyoming but for the Amazon behind the mountains. The vines—a reminder that this is still the rain forest basin—are visible cresting the distant ridges on the Kanukus.

There was a dry-goods store inside the barn and a green cargo truck parked outside. A few men were just past the shop's screen door playing dominoes. They slapped tiles down with violent slams on a card table and did not pay me any attention.

A woman named Shirley Melville was behind the store counter. Below her most of the front half of a goat sat bloodily in a display case beneath a butcher's scale. The store had a pungent smell. Melville was a stout person with a direct manner. She said she could arrange transport for the next morning leaving at dawn and named a price, and I accepted. It was to be with the truck parked outside. She went back to some bookkeeping and brushed me off.

The next morning I headed north across the savannah in the

back of the truck, and that was the night I rigged my bad hammock in the miners' camp at Frenchman.

There are two kinds of gold mines in the northern Amazon forest. They are easily distinguished. The first kind is the local mines. They are subsistence operations run by a few men with crude tools; the men who stay at Frenchman and dozens of camps like it work at these mines. The second type of gold mine is a large-scale, internationally financed operation. These are enormous factories producing gold with advanced geology and chemistry and millions in heavy equipment. Omai, the mine I sought to reach, was a large mine.

But on the cattle trail I was first amid the small ones. After sleeping a few hours in Frenchman we left early the next morning in a convoy of three (two other trucks had come late in the night). The savannah was behind us by then. The prior night we had crossed into the jungle behind the Kunuku Mountains. The trail that had been a good dirt road on the plains was now a ditch hardly wider than the truck. Five miles per hour was a good speed on the rutted trail. To each side was a wall of forest: an indistinguishable mass of vines and leaves that reached close and sometimes brushed the truck loudly with a branch as we passed. From time to time gold mines were dimly visible behind the trees to each side as we went. The prospectors were in side creeks and in narrow swaths of cleared forest.

The cattle trail was their supply line. We stopped at every few mines, picked someone up, dropped someone else off to work and delivered spare parts as we picked our way north.

The gold miners worked in teams of five or six. When on the creeks and the river they used rafts made from scrap metal. The rafts were slow, square vessels that floated low in the water and looked questionably seaworthy. They were perhaps twenty feet long. The crew lived cramped in hammocks strung from poles that held up a roof in the center. The rafts looked like cruder versions of the puttering houseboats vacationers rent at holiday lakes. In the center was a loud engine and a pump. A fat black hose went over the side and a diver took it to the bottom to suck up the silt and soil on the riverbed. The diver breathed through a small rubber hose gripped in his teeth. The pump pulled the dredged bits of riverbed to the surface and dumped them in a steel hopper. There the other members of the team treated the mud with mercury, the liquid metal most called quicksilver. It is simple chemistry: the mercury bonded with the gold and formed heavy nuggets that dropped out of solution in the mud. The miners strained out the nuggets and dumped the rest of the mud back in the river. Other men recovered the nuggets. Another man stayed busy pumping oxygen down to the diver.

The gold mines on land were similar. The miners would cut away a patch of trees beside the road with chain saws and machetes and dig holes ten or twenty feet across in the forest floor. They cut the trees haphazardly, and many of the clearings still had a few feet of tree trunk sticking up around the clearing here and there. The trunks were cracked in half jaggedly. The clearings had an uneven, violent look to them, as if a bomb had gone off a few feet above ground. In the center of the clearing a few men would usually be in the bottom of a shallow crater wetting the dirt down with water from buckets or hoses. Others sifted mud from the hole with wide pans like Chinese woks. When they found a promising amount of gold, and if they had the right tools—some fire hoses and a pump—they streamed greater amounts of water at the pit to blast away at the ground until it filled up to their knees with mud. They hauled out the mud in buckets, dumped it in a long box with metal sides and mixed in a pint or so of mercury from a heavy bottle. As on the boats, the mercury bonded with the gold, and the miners strained the mud, pulled out the nuggets of gold and mercury, and dumped the rest of the muck they'd made somewhere off to the side.

When they had several pieces of gold they put them in a metal pan. Frequently they used a pan from the camp kitchen. One man heated the nuggets with a blowtorch. The mercury boiled and floated away into the air. Often the miners breathed in some mercury during this step. It was severely toxic but few did much to protect themselves. Some would put a rag over their mouths, but rarely. When all the mercury was burned away, the gold was left in the bottom of the pan like melted butter and so-lidified into nuggets as it cooled. They would squeeze the last bits of mercury in a rag and reuse what was left. The gold nuggets were asymmetrical and flat. They were quite small usually, per-haps the size of a tiny earring.

It was hard work. The men were muscled from fighting the currents in the river, lifting the buckets of slurry, and hauling hoses all day. There were also no police in the forest and they had to keep their treasure close at hand. Some kept it inside their mouths: they had gold teeth that glinted when they smiled, plus large rings, often one for each finger. Many of the men lacked shoes or shirts but had a fat piece of jewelry somewhere on their bodies. This was their bank account.

It took two days to cover the hundred miles from Frenchman to Georgetown. The road improved the farther north it went. For most of the way it was hardly a road at all and more like a trench. It amounted to driving down a creekbed. We hauled the twelve-ton truck up muddy hills with a winch on the front bumper con-nected to a steel cable. The driver tied the cable to the trees and dragged the truck like a sled, sometimes for hours at a time. But after two days of this the truck reached a good dirt road, a few hours later macadam, and finally a two-lane highway. It arrived in Georgetown by early evening and pulled past some wooden churches and squat government buildings into a square near a wharf. It was just past dark.

The capital was a shock of noise and activity after the days in the forest. Thousands of people were shopping at a night bazaar. There were jewelry shops with currency traders idling in front, thick wads of local bills held cavalierly in their hands. Minibuses with their destinations through the city painted on their hoods waited nearby in a line. Crowds pushed through narrow avenues to wooden market stalls selling clothes and electronics. The bazaar was audible throughout much of the surrounding area. The most modest watchmaker or seller of plastic kitchen implements had a public address system to raise his or her stand's profile above the din. Speakers were stacked to wobbly heights and blared trilling Hindi music from Bollywood musicals if the shop's proprietor was of East Indian descent, fast soca or American R&B if the owner was black. The music blared and mixed badly at volumes sufficient, I was sure, to cause the tropical birds for sale nearby to fall dead from their perches in small wooden cages.

When the truck stopped at an intersection I hopped over the tailgate with my bag, pushed through the crowd and forced open the door of a cab. It was waiting in a line of mule carts along one side of the market square. We headed across the capital to a wooden hotel called the Tropicana I'd had recommended to me in Lethem. It was a few rooms in a third story crudely added to a family home above a karaoke bar. The proprietor was an East Indian man who greeted me barefoot and bathrobed in his living room with a newspaper in one hand, scowling at having been interrupted from his reading. He fetched one of his daughters to take me upstairs to a wooden hallway. I took the first room offered and dropped my bag just past the threshold. It was a spare chamber made of unpainted wood planks with a sagging bed in the center. I was exhausted from the ride north and did not care where I slept. I lay down in my clothes.

I could hear the bar through the floorboards. The singers were not bad but seemed to be competing with each other, so sang the same songs over and over in indistinguishable renditions. The most popular were Billy Ocean's "Caribbean Queen" and Larry Graham's "One in a Million You," and soon I had the lyrics of both memorized.

The cattle trail takes as long as two weeks to travel that time of the year, because of rain, so four days from the border to the capital was not bad. But it was still four days in the back of a cargo truck. I was exhausted. I passed out on a mattress that looked and felt like a piece of sodden plywood.

A DISASTER

The offices of Omai Gold Mines Ltd. were a two-story stucco cube half a block from the Tropicana. The next morning, my first day in Georgetown, I walked down the road and encountered an armed guard at a white gate who asked my business. I said I was a reporter—becoming a freelance reporter is as easy as calling yourself one—and wanted to see the gold mine. He told me I had to speak with someone named Seeta Mohamed. She was the company press officer. I left my number at the Tropicana and waited for most of the afternoon, but Mohamed did not call. In truth, I was glad. I was still tired from the trip through the forest. My clothes were ruined with mud, grease, and oil, and I needed the day to gather myself before trying to talk to someone at the mine the following morning.

But the next morning, again, Mohamed did not call. I decided to go back to Omai Ltd. and hang around until someone noticed me, but first walked downtown to have breakfast. I went to a cafeteria in a department store by the wharf and an hour later headed back toward the Tropicana and the gold mine's office.

Partway there I became caught in a brief rain on a palm-lined avenue. I ducked under an awning by the Bank of Guyana to wait out the squall. A woman there sold newspapers from a wooden tray, and I bought the capital's two thin dailies to pass the time: the nominally independent *Stabroek News* and the government-associated *Chronicle*. I leaned against the building, figuring the storm would only be a minute, but kept an eye on a nearby sewage canal—open sewers are the bane of the capital—and watched it swell with rain and garbage. I noted a higher spot to move to if the sidewalk flooded over.

I looked at the *Chronicle* first. The back page was full of timorous debate over the fate of the West Indian cricket team. The letters page contained the usual high drama over civic slights.

But when I turned to the front page I saw an enormous headline and a photograph of the Essequibo River turned an odd shade of red. I had crossed the river in the truck on an old ferry earlier that week; the water had been a coppery color tending toward black.

The story with the photo said the previous night part of the gold mine at Omai had collapsed. A reservoir for toxic waste had ruptured, and the contents, which the paper said were mostly cyanide, began spilling into the river. The cyanide was still spilling by sunup. Residents downriver, who used the water for cooking and to bathe, were advised to stay away from it. The government and mine officials gave no indication when the spill might be contained. Millions of gallons of the cyanide waste was exiting the burst dam.

In a country of rivers, the Essequibo is by far the grandest but not the one nearest the capital. It is about an hour east of Georgetown. There is another called the Demarara that is closer. The Demarara was nowhere near the accident, so the water was fine in the capital and the city was not in a panic. Reaction to the spill on the street tended instead toward slow shakes of the head and rueful discussion through the early morning. No one had even mentioned it in the cafeteria.

When the rain squall ended I walked to Omai's office. The company had locked its gate and the security guard was not answering questions. I went back to the Tropicana and tried calling, but Omai was not answering its phone.

I headed a few blocks away to the *Stabroek News* office in Lacytown. Lacytown is a shopping district by day and a criminal area by night. The street was already crowded with sidewalk vendors and minibus porters yelling their destinations at intersections. I leaped over a sewage canal and walked into the front office, where a young, well-dressed woman with a severe gaze agreed to speak with me only reluctantly. What I wanted to know was what had happened in the hours since that morning's newspaper went to press. She was willing to tell me a quick summary of what they knew. The photos in the paper had come from a chartered plane at first light, but that had already come and gone, she said, and no new photos were in yet. There were no injuries at the mine. The cyanide was still spilling and had been for about eight hours by then. No one knew how to make it stop, but that was under discussion with engineers at the mine and the hope was to have something figured out before nightfall. Guyana did not have the technicians or the money to evaluate the toxicity of the water or figure out any way to contain it, so had called for help from the international community. I asked if there was any way to reach the mine. The young woman said the road south was closed (this was false), and even if it was open there would be no way for anyone to get inside the company property unless he was there already or approved by the company.

She was helpful but brusque and in a hurry. Thank you, she said. She turned on her heels and left the room through a door behind her. An icy puff escaped from the air-conditioned room through the door.

I decided to head toward the river. From the newspaper office it was ten minutes' walk past some wooden government buildings to the market. It was possible to get the right minibus there; I'd seen it the night I arrived. When I got to the market the vendors were setting up their tables—eggs, plastic shoes, limp vegetables—and word of the spill had begun to spread more widely by then. Some of the vendors speculated about what was happening south of town. They slid poles together and tied blue tarps above their card tables. No one knew anything. At the edge of the main bazaar I climbed into a minivan with about a dozen other cramped-in souls and headed toward the river.

The van pulled out and filled with music. Songs from that year's carnival in Trinidad blared from two enormous speakers in the back of the van. The van bounced along toward the river to a tune of delirious celebration. It was cramped and uncomfortable in the seats and we stared glumly forward. I asked if anyone else was going to the river, and no one was. Most were heading to towns partway along the coast. They had not heard anything new about the spill either and only shook their heads when I told them what I'd learned at the newspaper office.

To reach the Essequibo from Georgetown takes one hour's drive past the rice fields along the coast to a town called Parika. There is nothing in Parika but a pier with a few dozen high-prowed, wooden speedboats hiding in the wharf's shade, and some hawkers selling vegetables where the pier meets the land. There are also a few farms and a hotel. The town's main function is to serve as a terminal for boats heading up the Essequibo into the forest or across the delta toward the country's northwest coast. The Essequibo runs through a part of the forest with no roads, so the boats from Parika are the only way to get to the towns upriver. Usually there are crowds on the wharf forming lines into the boats. But no one else on the minibus was going to Parika that morning. It was slow going. The bus stopped often for passengers to get off partway at farms and coastal towns. When we reached the river I was alone with the driver.

I got off the bus, paid my three dollars and walked to the end of the long wharf. The water becomes brackish and turns a muddy brown color at the Essequibo's mouth. It was running fast and choppy with the usual churn of a delta. The red plume from the newspaper photos was not anywhere to be seen. No one was making announcements or testing the water, and no one on the pier—some men lingered at the edge—claimed to have seen anything unusual. The longboats were not running. I walked to the other edge of the pier and looked for any boat to hire. I wanted to go one hour upriver to a town called Bartica. It was the largest town in the interior. The newspaper had said there were worries about the water there and some complaints of shortness of breath. It was seventy miles from there to the site of the accident.

The speedboat pilots were all waiting and talking in a clump along a gangway. None of them were leaving the dock upriver, though a few were venturing the other way to the coast. The upriver boats left only when they were full anyway and there were not enough passengers—none—so far that morning. The longboat pilots were all young men in shorts, barefoot, eager to go back to work but hesitant to go upriver once word of the cyanide spill spread. I waited three hours asking officers on the wharf what they knew and looking for town officials, but by noon no one had told me anything except to stay out of the water. Parika was a dead end.

After I returned from Parika it was clear that I was not going to get anywhere without access to Omai, and to get that required being more than a reporter in my own mind. I went back to the Tropicana and began making phone calls to North America. I had contacted several newspapers and magazines before leaving, sent writing samples and so forth, and received thin encouragement to call in the unlikely event anything of note happened in Guyana. So I called. A man at a magazine in New York asked if anyone had died. I said I did not think so, but a large river in the Amazon appeared to be full of poison, with people living downriver. He said to call back if anyone died.

I made more calls. I left a few dozen messages and made no headway. I gave up. In the end the spill would be widely reported outside the United States, particularly in Canada and England, but received comparatively little notice in America. In general it did not meet the threshold of interest for most foreign news pages. The *New York Times* managed to get someone upriver after some days, and the Denver-area newspapers gave it unusual attention, focusing on one of the mine's parent companies, Golden Star Resources. The company offices were located in a Denver suburb. But for the most part the spill passed without much notice.

Personally, after returning to the United States some weeks later I did get a chance to report on the spill for a few small magazines, government newsletters, and pamphlets of the sort read by about a half-dozen obscure bureaucrats and the odd paranoid. Those stories finally gave me an excuse to ask questions about what had happened, and after a while I was able to piece it together. Here is what had happened to cause the cyanide to spill into the river.

Sometime around midnight of August 19, 1995, a passing truck driver at the mine four hours south of Georgetown noticed some liquid running across a dirt service road. He sent word of the problem back to the main office and within an hour a crew came to inspect what figured to be an annoyance.

After looking only a moment the inspectors discovered a crack in an earthen dam that formed one side of a toxic waste reservoir beside the mine. The reservoir—really just a deep pit constructed beside a creek—held cyanide waste thrown off by the mine's gold-processing machines.

The workers continued to look in the dark and not long after found a more serious hole widening on the other end of the dam and a mix of water, silt and cyanide flowing out very forcefully through the hole. By then enough time had passed for the waste in the open reservoir to be drawing visibly lower and the cyanide to be exiting by thousands of gallons a minute.

The reservoir was full of cyanide because the chemical is essential to finding gold on a large scale, using a cryptically named procedure called "cyanide leaching."

Cyanide leaching means exactly what its vampiric tone suggests: sucking the gold from rocks with cyanide. The gold in your wedding ring or jewelry was likely produced this way. The process requires blowing chunks of stone out of the ground to make boulders weighing several tons each, carrying them out of a pit in dump trucks to a mill, and pouring them into that mill. The mill consists of spinning cylinders several stories tall. They look like outsized versions of the rock tumblers kids used to buy to polish stones. They spin so fast they are nicknamed "cyclones."

Once the cyclones have ground the stone into sand, the miners make piles of it the size of buildings and pour cyanide over it. The cyanide does the same thing mercury does in the small, local mines. Like mercury, cyanide possesses chemical properties that cause it to draw (or less attractively "leach") motes of gold dust into identifiable nuggets. Because Omai was in the middle of a rain forest they did this in a large tank rather than just in a pile on the ground, which is the usual practice. But in both cases the cyanide drew the gold out of the mud.

Developed in the late 1800s and greatly refined in the 1970s, the cyanide trick works spectacularly well for isolating gold from stone and makes gold mining vastly more profitable when done on a very large scale. The technique can recover gold traces as scant as a few grains of dust. This means that rather than picking around for visible nuggets, miners can wring the earth for every last bit of metal in every shovel of dirt and get more gold out of the ground.

The technique became industry standard in the 1970s and revolutionized jewelry production. The only drawback was that the new mines were jarringly expensive: the Omai gold mine cost $260 million to build, and another planned nearby in Venezuela, Las Cristinas, would cost nearly $600 million. But they recovered greatly more gold than ever before, and by the 1980s the technique got so good some mining companies were able to stop looking for gold at all. Instead they would rework old mines where they already knew the metal existed, find gold left behind by older technologies, apply the cyanide procedure, and make the mine profitable again. This had been the case at Omai. Two companies had already mapped the area, one a German team in the early 1900s and the American Anaconda company in the 1950s. Golden Star Resources, the Denver firm that discovered the mine, had gotten hold of Anaconda's maps and just dug in the same place.

In the 1990s, foreign miners took these techniques to several obscure corners of the world with unusual intensity. The Cold War had ended and new land was open for business; creative financing schemes were available; environmental and safety regulations were squeezing profits in the industrialized countries; it was a good time for a gold rush elsewhere. In return for turning over land to a foreign miner a host country would receive jobs, a small cut of the earnings, and the collateral benefits of the gold mine: modern facilities that usually came with hospitals and good roads. Often the miners went so far as to build schools, sponsor health clinics, string electrical wires and sponsor scholarships as part of doing business in a host country.

Omai was a typical effort for the time. Geologists knew the soil there held millions of ounces of gold. If recovered with the cyanide technique it was worth billions. And Guyana did not have enough money in its treasury to dig its own gold mine. It was two billion dollars in debt. So the country offered to sell the mining rights to the gold in exchange for the imports of technology and jobs the mine brought. Then it charged the foreign company corporate taxes and a small royalty and figured to make millions off the mine.

Once the deal was in place the actual work proved more difficult than anyone had figured. Even with cyanide, the rock formations that held the gold at Omai were billions of years old and among the hardest on earth. The gold was definitely there. But it required expensive processing to gather it from tens of millions of tons of worthless, intransigent rock.

Still, confidence was high. Omai was not an unusual project; it was one of roughly a hundred such efforts under way in the world. Mining companies had intensified their searches for gold in the late 1980s. At the same time Omai was getting under way, cyanide mines were under consideration, or construction, across the South Pacific, West Africa, Borneo, the Philippines, Australia, Canada, the United States, Russia, eastern Europe, Turkey—everywhere. This was a gold rush of sorts, but a quieter one than usual, and very different from other gold rushes the world had experienced every few hundred years. Usually gold rushes mean thousands of individuals rush to one place and start digging. In this case a small group of companies—gold mining is a tiny industry, worth about twenty billion dollars total, which is small by corporate standards—had rushed to many places and were digging in all of them. Omai was one of the early successes in South America. After several years of geological tests and contractual negotiations, it opened to great optimism in 1993, assumed to be the first of many large investments and literal treasure hunts in a cash-poor region.

In the early 1990s, as mining companies began building large cyanide gold mines, environmental pressures increased on them from governments and ecology groups to do so with minimal pollution. Local newspapers often covered the arrival of a gold mine. Many of the richest mines were to be located in inconveniently fragile places: the Amazon, the rain forests of Borneo and New Guinea, and along rivers in Europe and Asia. It is difficult to build, much less operate a strip mine in such a place without killing a lot of plants and animals and worrying the nearby people. Miles of forest have to be cut back and the soil scraped down to the bedrock; water becomes suspect and roads are built through otherwise uninhabited forests.

One of the most common worries, fairly obviously, was introducing millions of gallons of cyanide into these places. The rivers were often used as drinking water. Birds tended to mistake the cyanide tanks for lakes and land in them and die.

In Guyana, representatives of Golden Star Resources and the mine's majority owner, Cambior of Canada, maintained to the host government that cyanide would not be dangerous or poisonous if handled correctly. This was a common argument: two gold mining lobbies, the Gold Institute in Washington, D.C., and the

World Gold Council, based in New York City, have each argued repeatedly for cyanide's safety on behalf of their member companies, which together comprise the majority of the industry.

The idea seems appalling at first glance—a perfectly safe lake of cyanide. But the miners have a point. Cyanide's weirdest property, other than making gold appear out of sand, is that it subsequently disappears without a trace. The toxin decomposes when exposed to sunlight. Mystery writers sometimes use this peculiarity in their plots. Cyanide is a murder weapon that vanishes: if you put a few drops of the poison in a cup of water and take a drink, it makes your lungs stop working and you suffocate; but if you put the cup of water out in the sun for a few hours the poison disappears, leaving the glass of water perfectly benign. I am not suggesting you try this yourself.

Mercury, by comparison, which the local miners used, is classified as a heavy metal. This is a literal description: mercury is a metal and it is very heavy. Once introduced into soil or water it stays there virtually forever and climbs the local food chain. Before long it settles into people and the entire system of life in a region suffers heavy metal poisoning. This is a gruesome, ghastly fate. Neurological disease and skeletal deformities can result, and once in a region the problem never really goes away. Gold mines are notorious for poisoning water permanently. Mercury dating to the California gold rush still circulates in rivers in the Sierra Nevada and remains a persistent public health issue in San Francisco Bay. Anglers try not to eat what they catch inside the Golden Gate more than once or twice a month. Rivers in nearby San Jose, California, which pass the sites of old quicksilver mines where forty-niners sought mercury for gold prospecting, still suffer persistent pollution problems today.

Mercury's toxicity meant rather than a handicap, cyanide became a political advantage for the large gold mining companies hoping to work in rain forests. Promising to use safer cyanide instead of mercury meant large-scale foreign operations could grab the public relations high ground from the cruder local miners. The local miners couldn't use cyanide themselves because they could not afford it: they did not have the means to build enormous factories with cyclone machines and dump trucks. Mercury also disables you slowly over years, but can be held and used without special equipment, where handling cyanide can immediately kill you. So the locals found it very difficult to work with cyanide even in small amounts, though some tried.

The peculiar debate over the relative safety of cyanide and mercury evolved into an argument for taking land from local miners and granting the rights to the gold there to the foreign miners. It was a perverse argument at a glance—digging a massive hole in a rain forest and filling it with cyanide was the environmentally correct choice. But it was true. From an environmental and a public health standpoint, if a gold mine was inevitable, a single, massive cyanide gold mine was greatly preferable to fifty teams of untraceable small miners using mercury throughout the forest.

In the case of Omai the argument was even easier because few local miners were working that particular patch of ground anyway. The stone at the site was far too hard for them to work with their hoses and shovels. The company would have to level three square miles, admittedly, but the damage would stay contained there and would be worth it for the billions of dollars to come.

When Omai opened in 1993 after two years of construction, it delivered what it promised. It was virtually the only foreign investment of any seriousness in one of the continent's poorest countries. It employed about a thousand Guyanese but otherwise was invisible to most of the country. The mine was located in the jungle away from the population and unaffected by its surroundings: it was a city-state of gold, a self-contained island of technology in the trees surrounded by a country without roads or reliable phones. The only ways to reach it were by air or on a company-built haul road. It might as well have been an oil platform in the middle of the sea for its isolation. It had its own electricity, telephone system, airport, police department, fire department, hospital, commissary, machine shops, and road system. On one side was the Essequibo and jungle surrounded the rest. The first year of its operation the country's production of gold went up 400 percent. Omai exported most of the gold. The second year the gold mine accounted for nearly a quarter of the government's income on taxes and royalties alone. It was a huge success. Then the third year the dam cracked.

What had happened was basically a failure of civil engineering. A culvert, a pipe in the dam, buckled. Eventually water got into the dam's inner structures. That weakened it at critical spots, and soon a crack developed. The inevitable failure was surprisingly undramatic for how catastrophic it was. The dam didn't burst so much as slump apart in a kind of calm, resigned collapse. Picture a fallen soufflé. The water and waste rushing out the resulting hole was greatly less calm. Tropical storms—unfamiliar to the North American engineers who designed and built the dam— may have accelerated the erosion. The soil around the dam was wet, and the lake of waste itself brimmed from a heavy rainy season. The rushing waste soon made the compromised wall too weak to support its own weight, and it failed. There was some question about who was responsible. A few weeks after the disaster, when I was back in the United States, I called Golden Star Resources to ask about the construction of the dam. The receptionist said the company board was at a meeting in the Bahamas.

I got the number in the Bahamas, which turned out to be a small party at someone's house. The company's vice president at the time, a man named Rick Winters, was there, and he said he didn't know who had built the dam. He also didn't know who was going to rebuild the dam. This was unconvincing; it is a little like not knowing who is building your house. Winters insisted he had no idea. (Two companies had built the dam. One was Knight-Piesold of Vancouver, Canada, and the other was Golder Associates, also of Canada. Neither claimed responsibility. Some attention later fell on Omai's directions to these companies, specifically an unusual decision to raise the height of the dam as the waste in the reservoir behind it increased. This is not considered a sound engineering practice. In the end everyone blamed everyone else, which ultimately had the effect of no one's having to take full responsibility.)

There were other problems typical of complicated projects in small countries. The dam was to have been built to standards required by the state of California. But there was no way to enforce those standards. Government inspections were not common. Inspectors had little training and little authority anyway. The country had never had an environmental safety law, no construction codes to speak of, no liability laws, no fines for bad faith—in effect, no way to explain or punish mistakes or ensure what the company called "North American standards" was as evident in practice as on paper. Calling the spill an accident was inaccurate, said a Guyanese government inquiry afterward. The mine was flawed from the beginning and the disaster foretold in the blueprints. But no one outside the company was qualified to notice that or do anything about it.

Not surprisingly, none of this comforted the people living downriver at the time. What they knew was that one morning the Essequibo's normally dark current was a peculiar shade of ocher. Contrary to some reports the color was not from the cyanide. It was dirt and clay carried out of the dam, "suspended solids" in the technical argot. Tests downriver by the Pan American Health Organization and chemists from Canadian and Brazilian agencies confirmed the Essequibo's massive current was diluting the poison and the water was safe. But local perception was a different matter. A river had changed color overnight. The drinking water had millions upon millions of gallons of cyanide in it, the active ingredient in suicide capsules and a psychological twin to arsenic. Echoes from the People's Temple suicides at Jonestown—where the victims had famously died from drinking cyanide-laced fruit punch—created a particular strain of horror and a terrible sense of déjà vu. At the very least it is unnerving to drink water that is not a color water is supposed to be. Much less when the color is red. Villages closer to the spill had less allusive problems. They did not trust the fish or the water supply, and some people began complaining of mysterious rashes. Rashes are not typical of cyanide poisoning, but it was unknown what else had come out of the containment and suspicion of the river ran very high. Complaints continue of mysterious headaches and rashes since the spill. Mine officials call this opportunism. Lawsuits continue.

Guyana was a fertile place for suspicion. Omai had never enjoyed clear public support. There had been a smaller spill once before and the company had not announced it for several days, even to the people living nearby. A treatment plant designed to weaken the poison before it went into the reservoir had never gotten built despite appearing in the mine's original plans. The mine's operators argued after the spill—David Fennell, Golden Star's CEO at the time, was one who argued this to me by phone—that treating the water was never necessary, because the composition of the soil and the effect of the sun would take care of the cyanide better than a treatment plant anyway. This again became a conflict of science versus perception. If true it was hard to explain locally why the water treatment plant had been in the mine's plans in the first place.

The terms of the original deal for the gold mine, which gave 95 percent to the outsiders and 5 percent to the locals, had always looked bad also. The country's government made much more from taxes and royalties on the mine's operations than it did from its small ownership stake. But keeping a scant nickel of every dollar still had the air of a deal made over a barrel. The idea of clearing miles of trees in an otherwise remote, intact piece of forest and importing poison was distasteful at a first glance as well.

So when the dam cracked, every street in Georgetown—the rum shops, the domino games, the beauty parlors, the markets— became a forum for discussions of the disaster by the next afternoon. The more details of the mishap emerged, the more public patience with the company's explanations appeared to wane. Calls to shut Omai down and kick out the foreigners came swiftly on the street. Some came from inside the parliament. By late afternoon the picketers outside the company office were holding signs reading "Omai is Jonestown."

In the end it took four days for all the waste to drain into the river. The company had dug a trench to divert some of it, but despite all efforts most of the toxic waste had ultimately gotten loose from the containment and into the river by week's end. Debate continues over how much spilled. The United Nations Environment Program recorded the spill as nearly a billion gallons. Golden Star said ten million. In either case it was the largest such spill in history. The mine officials, chiefly Fennell, have used that fact to make the point of cyanide's safety yet again: a total failure, the largest spill of cyanide in history upriver from a populated area, and no one died and people drink the water in the Essequibo today and eat the fish. This is true.

Several of Guyana's neighbors used the spill to settle political scores. Venezuelan newspapers ran editorials demanding a final redrawing of the border. The claim was that Venezuela would have never let such a thing happen. Caribbean partners temporarily suspended trade for the small country's few products. They cited worries about poisoned cropwater and tainted fish.

Within a month of the spill's end the mine directors informed the government they would resume digging up gold within half a year. The company would lose a million dollars a month sitting idle.

Once back in business the mine would have to release cyanide into the river in small batches. This would keep the waste area from failing again. The company explained it would only release a little cyanide at a time and it would be perfectly safe. This was probably true if done correctly but public concern remained and trust had disappeared.

An inquiry into the cause of the accident took the rest of the year. Engineers began rebuilding Omai pace for pace with the investigation, before it was known what had happened to cause the accident. No one could stop this except the Guyanese government, which didn't. It still needed the money from the gold mine. Permanent questions remained over the river. The water was fine, but no one had tested the soils in the bed and no one knew what might have settled there. Still, the emotional impact of the spill appears to have been greater than the physical impact. When I left Guyana for home some weeks later, the local newspapers, the riverside villages, the parliament, and the rum shops were still full of argument and recrimination and the river was perhaps still full of something. The gold mine was open again by spring as promised.

In early 1997, a year and a half after the cyanide spill, a magazine offered to hire me to write an article about the gold rush. I flew to Caracas for the third time and boarded the now familiar bus south. I intended to follow the same route I had before: down the Venezuelan side of the border to Brazil, north to Guyana, and then to Omai, where I would finally have a way to get inside—I was official now.

At the sandy Orinoco River I transferred to a minibus full of Venezuelan miners. The minibus was a pleasing light blue. There were about a dozen wiry young men on board heading south. The bus pulled out before sundown and drove a narrow stretch of the Amazon highway through yellow rangeland for two hours; the driver played a tape of horrible Venezuelan pop music at high volume as we went. It was supposed to be a day to Brazil from there.

But a few hours south of the Orinoco the bus stopped at a roadblock. Five or six teenagers in national guard uniforms and severe haircuts stood behind a white gate. They looked purposeful and menacing. They held automatic weapons. It was night.

There are many roadside checkpoints in southern Venezuela, but the guards are not usually so heavily armed. They also tend to be playing cards or watching TV rather than standing at attention. The oldest boy waved the driver to a stop and another soldier boarded. He said everyone had to debark and motioned us off with his shotgun. He was short and slight, but the weapon allowed him to act cruelly. The barrel was thick as a lead pipe and he liked to point it at people. Each passenger slid his bag from the badly welded luggage racks above the torn seats and filed meekly off the bus. The miners carried their few things in gym bags and school backpacks.

We were made to stand against the bus. Three of the soldiers lolled their machine guns vaguely our way while two others used badly trained dogs to search us. The miners' bags proved to be filled with dirty clothes and greasy tools: nothing threatening. Here and there a soldier would find a box of crackers or a half bottle of alcohol that hit the dirt hard when he upended it onto the ground. But after several minutes of searching bags and frisking the passengers a little alcohol was the extent of the contraband. It was unclear what the soldiers were hoping to find.

The oldest one, perhaps twenty-two, approved the inspections. He was smallish but armed like the others. We could reboard the bus, the young captain said. But anyone heading to the town just ahead would have to walk. The bus could not drive down the spur to it. The passengers gathered their things from the dirt.

I approached the captain while the others boarded and asked the reason for the searches, but he would not explain it. We spoke in Spanish. I am not fluent in Spanish or even particularly competent but I do not think that was the reason the young captain would not explain the roadblock. He wouldn't explain it to anyone; one of the other men also asked. He would only say that there was a problem down the road and we should move along. He waved me toward the bus with the end of his gun.

The town nearby was a gold mining outpost called, notably, El Dorado. It had been the site of several large gold and diamond discoveries in the early 1900s. Thus the name. It used to be the last milepost on the road; now it was the first mile on the highway's extension. I had stopped there briefly on the way back north in 1994. It was a dirty little town. It was surrounded by gold mines and named after a utopia but had a rough history. The nearest landmark was a prison on an island in a river and a penal colony. The Venezuelans had briefly held Papillon there. More encouragingly, just west was a national park containing the world's highest waterfall: Angel Falls. After the road extension a few tourism operators had set up shop in El Dorado with hopeful offices promising jeep tours and a better future. But so far they had done only so-so. The drunk prospectors around the plaza tended to dissuade the few tourists who got off the bus there from staying long. The town's two hotels were brothels. I had made the mistake of staying overnight the previous time I had passed through—alone, thanks—and the rooms had been furnished like cells. A plastic trash barrel filled with water for both drinking and bathing stagnated in the corner of each room. Mosquitos and their larvae sat like a film on the water's surface. The rooms were windowless and black. The floor was slanted toward a drain in the corner; the night I had stayed there the drain was not working and there had been two inches of water on the floor. The light source was a naked bulb hanging from a wire. You had to screw the bulb in to turn the light on, but the water on the floor made it unwise to touch the socket without something to stand on, for risk of electrocution. El Dorado was surrounded by gold and diamonds, per its name, but from there the name didn't hold up: it was not a place easily associated with abundance or riches.

Most of the miners reembarked but two remained on the side of the road with their bags. I asked one of them, a man about thirty with a narrow face and curly black hair, if he knew what had caused the guards to close the road. He laughed, said the search was normal and put his bag over his shoulder. He was walking to El Dorado to work at one of the mines near the town limits. Another man with long hair and a green canvas backpack said the same thing.

It seemed odd. Against my better judgment, I decided to head into town with the men. If nothing unusual was happening it would only be one night. The guards did not seem pleased to have people walking into town but did not stop us. Their job seemed to be searching the bus, not sealing the town. The two men and I waited on the dirt shoulder while the youngest soldier leaned on the gate, a white pole weighted at one end like a phonograph arm lifted and the bus left us behind. We watched it go.

We walked east for half an hour on a concrete road through dry shrubland until we reached the plaza. The town was deserted. It was a few hours past dark.

El Dorado had first become a gold prospectors' outpost early in the twentieth century. The forest had been slowly filling with prospectors for several hundred years then. African slaves from the Dutch and English plantations on the Caribbean coast had fled south into the forest in the late 1600s. Some had panned the rivers for subsistence. When they found gold and diamonds, more prospectors came before long. Brazilian prospectors struck gold in the forest north of the Amazon River in the 1700s. In the notable year 1849, Venezuelan prospectors found another seam a few hundred miles north near the Orinoco. Both finds led to brief gold rushes.

The rubber boom in Brazil brought more people into the forest in the late 1800s. Many of the rubber tappers worked as gold miners on the side. By the 1920s a string of frontier towns had emerged in the border area and a semipermanent presence of at least a few thousand miners—a census is nearly impossible—moved into those towns.

El Dorado was one of the busiest frontier hubs then. It was near two of the richest rivers: the Cuyuni and the Caroni. The town's population grew through the fifties, the sixties, and into the seventies. By 1980 it crested during the largest gold rush so far known.

In 1980 the world was suffering from a long string of financial problems. Gold is a common investment during such times of uncertainty and inflation. The United States was also off the gold standard by then; that meant anyone could buy or sell gold, whereas before governments controlled the trade in it. The combination pushed the price of gold to its highest value ever. An ounce of gold cost $850 in 1980 after costing $35 in 1971.

When the price of gold rose to such ridiculous heights, five hundred years of searching for an El Dorado compressed into a decade of mad thrashing through the forest. In Brazil, hundreds of thousands of men—high estimates said a million—rushed from South American cities with high unemployment into the forests to get rich. Guyanese and Venezuelan miners rushed south from their own cities. More came from the nearby Caribbean islands. Most all of these men had limited options elsewhere: they were individuals or small groups with a few tools and a little bit of start-up money if any at all.

That was when North American miners—the big mines—had first recognized a business opportunity. The high price of gold meant investors and banks saw profits in backing gold mines. Canadian and American gold exploration companies were soon able to obtain millions of dollars, easy credit, and cheap loans to go exploring. By the mid-eighties North American and later other foreign geologists and financiers (often the same person) were arriving in the northern Amazon for the first time in decades to take part in the late-eighties gold rush. Money and better technologies—from the very esoteric, like ground-penetrating radar, to the fairly pedestrian, like affordable helicopters—let them find much more gold than the local miners could with only picks and shovels. The foreigners looked intensely. By then it was assumed there was gold throughout the forest: a prospector's axiom says that where there is gold, there is more. This was true in that part of the forest, and the North American companies found evidence of billions worth by the mid-eighties.

Besides Omai there were eleven million ounces of gold at a spot near Km 88, called Las Cristinas, which a Vancouver company called Placer Dome hoped to operate. Then Omai's developers found more gold at a site in Suriname, a few hundred miles northeast. A mine went in just north of Km 88 a few miles from the town of El Dorado. Several more expanded in Venezuela farther north near the Orinoco. Among some North American miners, the southern highway to Brazil took on the nickname Billionaire Alley.

But there was a conflict. The small South American miners had been there first. The newcomers had been there only a few years. Usually a gold mine belongs to the person who discovers it. But the small miners had no formal claims on the land they were working and were not allowed to own it in most cases. This problem was most acute in Venezuela. The government controlled the land there. When they leased it to foreign companies the small miners had to move.

Sharing the gold was not likely in most cases. The foreign mines used cleaner, more profitable, more efficient techniques—cyanide—and paid millions in taxes to the national government. The small miners used mercury, dumped silt in the rivers all day, and worked almost entirely under the table.

But for the local miners, there were few other jobs in the area, and those that existed did not offer the possibility of instant riches. As the foreigners arrived, the local miners stayed put. Before long, in Venezuela, the government called in the national guard and troops began evicting the miners by force.

The buildings around the plaza were deserted and locked. El Dorado's central plaza has along its sides the two brothels, a disco built on a deck over a silently murderous river called the Yuruan, a bar, a path to a jail, several concrete homes of modest but humane dimensions and two small grocery stores. An empanada cart sits on one end most days. It is not advisable to eat from the cart. It is a petri dish serving a mix of pastry, liver fluke, and hot sauce. Other than some men in the bar across the plaza and the woman running the empanada cart there was no one in sight. The only activity was a pack of dogs with bloody fur roaming after scraps.

Just off the plaza a row of money-trading shops were empty. They were tin-roofed buildings with dirt floors. All the stores down that side alley were closed also and the doors barred with gates locked with heavy chains. The two miners I had walked into town with said good night and headed down a side street together. I headed back to the plaza and walked into the hotel; I woke the attendant from a cot behind the desk and took a room, left my bag, and went back outside to the bar.

There were people in the bar. Two young men in running shorts played pool on a warped table. They marked complicated scores on the torn green felt with white chalk. I played a few minutes and then asked the men where everyone else was: they said there was a strike. A strike on what? They wouldn't explain. They kept playing pool.

A man in pink hot pants, ballet shoes, and a blue halter top came from the back of the bar then and asked me to buy him a drink. He had bleached his curly hair white with peroxide but left his mustache black.

"No, lo siento," I said. Buying rounds of drinks seemed like an entanglement to avoid.

"Una Polarcita," he said, asking again. The local beer was called Polar. It had a polar bear on the label; it came in under-sized bottles so you could drink it before the tropical air turned it to hot tea. (Cold seemed to be the key selling point; the northern Brazilian brand was Antarctica.)

I thanked the others for playing pool with me and went to ask the bartender, a boy about fourteen, what had happened in town. The bleached man in woman's clothing followed me. He knew what had happened, he said. He and the bartender explained that the national guard had attacked a group of miners north of town the previous day and thrown several into the El Dorado jail. The miners had all fled town into the forest afterward. The rest of the town expected the miners to riot in response, so had locked themselves in their homes. Other than that, some women were at the lockup trying to get their husbands and brothers released. The attack had been an ambush.

"Por qué?" I said. Why had the guard attacked the miners, and why would the miners riot in their own town? My rudimentary grasp of Spanish was a constant embarrassment, but what they said was very simple. No one knew the precise reason for the attack but it had occurred at a place called Fosforito. It was not far from another prospecting area called La Camorra, and the assumption was La Camorra might be next. A few dozen guards had been involved. They had fired tear gas and attacked the fleeing miners with shotguns and long strips of flexible steel.

I asked where the nearest hospital was.

"San Felix," the blond man said. It was a city two hours north on the Orinoco.

I bought his beer and left for the lockup a few blocks away. There were no soldiers anywhere in sight. The jail was a few yards down a malodorous alley. It was a concrete bunker with a steel door and a thick deadbolt across the front. The walls were covered in hateful graffiti painted in red spray paint. Most were obvious slogans: "The Mines Are Ours," that sort of thing. A dozen or so men and women were outside screaming insults and curses at the jailers. The jailers appeared to be locked inside with the prisoners. The people at the jail repeated a version of the same story the bartender and the bleached man had told. They described a surprise attack. No one there knew where all the miners were either, just that they were "on strike." What it meant for them to be on strike was elusive. The miners had simply disappeared and weren't working.

After an hour of listening to insults shouted at the jail I left for my room at the larger of the two hotels on the plaza. It was a two-story cinder-block building. A narrow entrance led to a courtyard with a stagnant fountain. I tried asking the clerk downstairs what he knew. He was a gruff, shirtless man who had again been asleep on the cot behind the desk. He said everyone was on strike and left it at that. He handed me a padlock for the shackle on my door (I'd used my own so far), a key, and a lightbulb.

The next morning I woke a bit groggy and ravaged by mosquitoes. I came out of the hotel and saw perhaps twenty men filling one end of the plaza. They all had backpacks and bundles of metal pans and tools. A few were holding machetes and long steel prybars. Near the bar two large prostitutes watched the crowd from the diseased empanada cart. A few men leaned on the wall outside the hotel. The rest of the businesses were still locked down behind steel gates. The tour guide shop was closed and its vehicle, the best jeep in town, was gone.

A boy in a security guard uniform several sizes too large stood outside the hotel. The uniform did not look big on the boy so much as the boy looked diminished in the uniform. The cuffs on his pants had split from his standing on them and the white shirt hung over his shoulders like an absurd cape. He wore a fat blue polyester tie loose as a stethoscope. He had a small pistol in his hand for want of anywhere else to put it; he said he was guarding the bank next door. From whom? From the gold miners, he said, and raised his eyebrows toward the other side of the plaza.

Across the plaza an old man in a beaten leather hat was shuttling sweet coffee, in plastic cups the size of shot glasses, from the empanada cart to the miners. It was seven-thirty in the morning. I walked across the plaza and asked one of the miners what they were doing there. He was an older man, short, with powerful arms. He said the boats were due at the landing on the Yuruan and they intended to leave for work when they arrived. He was putting me off: four of the river pirogues were already beached at the landing within sight of the square. They were narrow wooden boats that held six or eight people each. Another was on the water, where the driver made a preposterous show of spraying water in a rooster tail over the river. None of the miners would say why they had not left yet. They clammed up and began giving me displeased stares, so I retreated across the square.

At the hotel two men stood against the wall behind a white jeep. One of the men looked Guyanese and the other Venezuelan. The nearer fellow said his name was Ramón Castillo. He was unhealthy and looked to be in his forties. He said he was a tour guide for the national park and spoke five languages including English. He spoke to me in English. He seemed a little drunk and coughed when he spoke. I asked him what the men across the square were doing.

"These men, they are waiting for something but they do not know what," he said. The miners usually gathered at the landing to catch the boats to work but were not sure whether or not to leave that morning, he said. The guard could be waiting at the mines downriver, or might be coming to town, or might not be coming at all. It made everyone indecisive.

Castillo had a bottle of beer in one hand. He took a drink and he coughed again.

"What do you think?" I said.

"I don't know," he said, and shook his head equivocally.

Castillo produced the local paper from under his arm, *El Correo de Caroni,* "the Caroni River Mail." He let me look. It had published photos of the attack the previous day. I had not seen any other newspaper around. Castillo said the copy had made it to town with some miners arriving early that morning. In the photos men fled clouds of tear gas, and soldiers chased them with shotguns. One picture showed a man with his back bloodied by what appeared to be buckshot. Another, more gruesome photo showed the back of a miner whom the soldiers had caught and whipped with a flat metal spring.

The newspaper did not give a full explanation for the attack. It only said the national guard had been ordered to clear illegal gold miners from a land concession north of El Dorado after the miners had refused to leave.

The other man leaning on the hotel saw me rummaging for a camera.

"Don't take out the camera," he said.

He was a Guyanese of Portuguese background. He said his name was Patrick Silva. He looked prosperous: he was well dressed in clean clothes and the truck turned out to be his. The jeep was old and full of rust holes but it ran. He stepped farther into the cover behind it and waved me over to him. I was white and had an expensive camera, he said; it would appear I was photographing miners for the soldiers to track down later. This was unwise.

"They will think you are a spy for the company," he said.

He seemed serious about it. I asked what he meant by "the company."

He straightened up. He said "the company" meant one of the foreign mining companies digging for gold in the area. There were several companies working up and down a fifty-mile stretch of road, and each had to deal with this issue. The nearest to El Dorado was Monarch; it owned La Camorra, the mine closest to El Dorado. The previous day's attack had happened not far from there. (Monarch was a smallish gold concern headquartered in New Jersey, traded on the Canadian stock exchange, and incorporated in the Bahamas. Many mining companies are incorporated offshore for tax purposes. Monarch later approached bankruptcy and an Idaho mining company called Hecla bought its holdings.)

Silva owned a dredge boat moored nearby. He was a medium-scale gold miner: better off than the men across the street working their small pits, but still small enough to be harassed by the guard. He said it was unwise to be associated with "the company" because that suggested an association with the soldiers as well. The guard protected the borders around the mines at La Camorra and elsewhere and controlled the road. This meant it provided de facto security for the foreign gold mines. It set up checkpoints along the road and searched the miners aggressively—this is what had happened the previous night on the bus—and evicted them from land when necessary.

Silva was a river miner but had docked in town that day to repair his boat. He claimed soldiers had boarded him and disassembled the mining equipment a few days prior. They could do this whenever they wanted because it was technically illegal to mine gold in much of the area. On the rivers the prohibition was for reasons of environmental protection, he said, and on land because many of the several foreign companies working in the area tended to lease sections of forest much larger than their actual mine site, to leave open the possibility of finding more gold later. A large part of the guard's job was to keep the local miners from working on land that was already leased, or from settling in too seriously on land that might be available for lease to foreign companies later. The upshot, Silva claimed, was that he had to pay bribes to keep working. The guard let the mines stay open to keep the bribes coming; Venezuelan soldiers don't earn much money. The checkpoints on the road, for example: they looked like a way to search the miners for explosives or other contraband tools, but they operated more like tollbooths, he said. (These bribes are commonly discussed in the region and denied by the guard.)

Castillo listened and drank from the bottle of warm beer. It was early but he was pretty drunk already.

The soldiers were not always stopping the miners. They needed the gold mines to stay open for the bribes to flow. A slow simmer kept everyone happy: the local miners got to keep their jobs; the soldiers got a cut of the gold; the foreign gold companies got to operate without the local miners stealing too much of their land or equipment. Attacks on the miners were not usually public or broad.

So the previous day's attack had been unusual in its severity,

Silva said. It was upsetting the balance. There was nothing but rumors to explain it. He said the story in town was that it had been a disagreement over a patch of scrubby forest scheduled for logging. There was gold there as well, and local miners had been digging for it recently. They were reluctant to leave because there was a lot of gold there and they had spent months and hundreds of dollars digging their mines. So they stayed, but when it was time for the logging to begin, the guard ran them off the land violently.

Another theory, to which Castillo was partial, was that a regional guard commander north of town had demanded a large percentage of the gold at the mine to let the work continue. The miners had balked. So the commander had ordered them attacked and would install more cooperative miners before long.

From El Dorado there was no way to find out the truth of what had happened. The only witnesses were two hours north or in jail, and the equivalent to the regional mayor, the alcalde, was nowhere in town. The regional commander who had ordered the attack was two hours north as well, and there seemed to be no working phone in El Dorado; the three at the phone office on the far end of town had been pulled out of the wall, I discovered later. The town was operating on accusations and guesses.

By eight we heard motors approaching. Two green military trucks careered through the plaza. They skimmed close to the miners before stopping in front of the hotel. The trucks had unusually high plywood sides. The wood made the number of soldiers in the back and how heavily armed they were impossible to determine. The driver in the lead truck was a stocky man in a green camouflage uniform. He wore a cap low so his eyes were not visible. He turned off his motor and opened the door. A second soldier in the passenger seat waited with one leg out his door and a shotgun across his knee.

The second truck of soldiers pulled a little straighter into the center of the plaza. The twenty or so miners had been milling in clumps or sitting on their packs, but now they got up and stood in a wide mob that filled one side of the plaza. The older man who had been carrying coffee scurried off behind a building. Everyone else ran out of the plaza.

Each side stayed where it was, and a standoff resulted. The driver of the second truck kept racing the motor so that the truck would lurch forward a few feet toward the miners. One or two miners would take a step forward toward it to show they weren't intimidated. Just before the truck collided with the miners the two sides would back off. It happened a few times. In between there was a lot of hard staring but nothing decisive. Minutes passed and neither side would back down. Before long five minutes had passed with the two groups both claiming the plaza but neither moving toward or against the other; then fifteen minutes had passed; then twenty.

Finally, inevitably, a half-dozen young soldiers waiting in the back of the truck popped up with shotguns visible over the truck side. I do not know why they did this. I suspect they were nervous or just wanted to stand up. The truck had just missed, perhaps slightly hit, one of the miners a little so that he fell, and some other miners leaped forward more aggressively than before. But it certainly looked like the soldiers were readying to aim the guns at the miners.

The women at the empanada cart ducked into the bar; the boy guarding the bank, Castillo, and I ran inside the hotel. The only person who stayed in the plaza besides the miners and the soldiers was Silva.

There was a lobby in the hotel with a window on the second floor. The windows were the type with slats of glass that opened with a handle slid on a rail. I had to pry it open to see out. Ramón

Castillo came upstairs for a moment, then went back downstairs and peered around the side of the doorway into the plaza.

When I got the window open, Silva had done something that seemed to me quite brave. He was walking across the plaza. The soldiers let him cross. Everyone watched Silva. Castillo took the opportunity to scamper from the hotel door and out of the plaza to safety. I watched him walk in quick steps along the wall of the hotel and disappear around the corner. After a moment's conversation with one of the miners, Silva seemed to have decided it was time to leave. He crossed directly back to his truck, piled two friends in the back, climbed into the torn driver's seat, and started the engine. He looked through the windshield to the hotel window and waved for me. I looked from the miners to the soldiers. There were perhaps fifty feet between them. The guns were still halfway up and halfway down, and the plaza felt very uncertain. Silva threw open the passenger door; I ran down the stairs and got in the truck. It sped out of the plaza.

Silva's boat was moored a few blocks away. It was maybe a hundred yards from the plaza. I sat in the passenger seat. We bounced past the jail. He said the miner at the plaza had told him they had agreed not to leave until the guard did first. That meant it would be a while, or the guard would have to attack the miners. A fight in the plaza wasn't in anyone's interest, but tempers were high. When we pulled in, his dog, a slender Doberman, ran to defend the boat from me. One of the men who had ridden in the back got out of the truck, collared the dog, and whispered something in its clipped ears. He was an employee of Silva's. He was a large man in a white T-shirt and shorts and worked as a diver on the boat. The dog did not calm down but was content to strain against the man's arms and let the rest of us debark and pass.

The boat was an open-air raft with pontoons along the side and a motor in the center. The motor was disassembled. The two employees who had ridden with us from the square got about working on the motor within a few minutes. A third man waved from the far end of the deck. He ignored the work and lay back in a hammock tied between two parts of the boat. It was his day off, he said, and closed his eyes. He hung over the ends of the pontoons in his hammock, and below him the boat was open to the river.

The three men were miners who worked for Silva. They were older than most of the miners in the square, in their thirties, and were all Venezuelans from north of El Dorado. Neither of the two who had been in the plaza was worried about the situation there spreading further, the one who had held back the dog said, but it would keep them from working for a few days, and that was a concern. Their pay from Silva was a percentage of the production: no production, no pay.

Silva had taken a seat on the corner of a piece of machinery. He watched his two employees start hoisting parts of the engine together with a pulley and chain. The boat smelled of oil and grease, and a loamy scent from the moss along the side of the river.

Silva had been working on the river for thirteen years and was one of the more successful gold miners in town. He was a fit man in his late forties with graying hair. He had made a lot of money finding gold in the 1980s. In addition to the jeep and the boat he had a generous house on the river; it was visible behind him, a low white building with a flat roof. I asked him what he thought of the morning's events. He was, of course, partial to his own cause, and thought the problem was foreigners.

"The *ambiente* [environment] is an excuse for the foreign companies to come in and take the gold," he said. "They clear hectares of land. They dig enormous holes and use cyanide and they have accidents." Meanwhile he was banned as a polluter, which he felt was hypocritical. "There is mercury in the canals in Scotland and in Florida. But then you come here and I am not allowed to work because I use mercury."

The two other men were struggling with the hoist. Silva rolled the sleeves of his oxford shirt up and helped them. He steadied part of the engine as it rose.

He worked illegally but could usually get away with it, he said. Once they had fixed the boat he would wait for tempers to cool around town and then go back out on the river. He and the crew would look for gold for a few months. They would probably get away with it for a while longer because the forest was large and the guard enforced the law unevenly. But eventually, of course, they would get caught. Then they would have to bribe the soldiers or have their operation disrupted again. Most likely it would be a little of both—pay just enough bribe to stay in business, but watch the soldiers do some small amount of damage, like disassembling an engine, for appearances. Then they would repair everything and start the cycle all over again. One of the other men heaved on the chain, and Silva and the first man fitted some pieces of metal together.

Few events alter a landscape as fast and completely as a gold rush. Some of the changes are positive. A better road appears, a restaurant along the road. But a brothel arrives as well as an uptick in smuggling. Or a fishing village no longer has any fish. A town that happens to be located inside the borders of a gold field must relocate. Malaria returns where it had lessened; so does AIDS. Miles of land are cleared down to the bedrock. If local miners make a new discovery in the forest, thousands of miners arrive and impinge on the existing villages. If a foreign company follows after that, the relationship flips and the local miners are now fighting invaders. All of these problems became the daily news of the northern Amazon when a gold rush just south in Brazil stretched north. The bad news outweighed the good news, and the local miners took on a reputation for lawlessness and violence.

They came by it honestly in many cases. The most infamous incident, in 1993, involved the massacre of nineteen men, women, and children in the village of Haximu, Venezuela, allegedly by Brazilian miners, part of a terror campaign designed to scare the villagers off gold-rich lands. The bodies were mutilated and burned, according to Brazilian reports. To date there have been no convictions. The Haximu incident, though the worst and highest-profile such attack, only suggested the broader problems.

A clearer picture finally emerged more publicly, if still quietly, in numerous studies of the Yanomami, a group of Amerindians living in extremely remote portions of the Venezuelan Amazon. The Yanomami and an even more obscure group called the Kayapo had very little contact with the outside world but had long been familiar to anthropologists. But they became a sort of celebrity tribe as a result of the gold rush's impact on them. They eventually appeared in travel brochures and coffee-table books and received goodwill visits from the likes of British pop star Sting. They happened to live in a gold-rich part of the forest. As much as 15 percent of the group's population died between 1988 and 1990, with the bulk of the deaths attributed to diseases introduced by Brazilian gold miners—chiefly malaria and dengue, called "bonebreak fever." Others died in fights with miners over access to land. A similar problem affected lesser-known populations throughout the forest. Red Thread, a Guyanese women's rights organization, has noted a sharply greater incidence of sexual assault in towns and villages near mining camps. Evidence of toxicity sufficient to cause Minamata disease, mercury poisoning, turned up in both the Brazilian and the Guyanese Amazon, and symptoms of the disease were found in Brazilian riverside towns in the early 1990s.

It was a peculiarly quiet issue for the times. In the 1980s and 1990s, rain forests had become an environmental cause célèbre in wealthier countries without rain forests themselves. "Save the rain forest" had replaced "Save the whales" as bumper-sticker shorthand for environmental concern. But save it from whom? The common answer in North American politics was loggers and subsistence farmers, who chopped down trees very visibly in relatively accessible areas. Miners worked mostly unobserved and often in extremely remote places. Their activities were nearly impossible to track, and their impact was difficult to describe in concise terms. Logging, for example, is a fairly straightforward thing to describe. There is a forest, then you log, and the forest changes, with both positive and negative consequences. A gold rush does not have an analogous, descriptive event like a tree falling. The effects can't be easily measured, and what is measurable tends to be hopelessly technical. It was a difficult story to tell. The conclusions were often ambiguous. The events were chaotic, and the effects equally a matter of public health, personal security, economics, environmental science and national sovereignty. None of the issues fell at the top of anyone's particular agenda: environmentalists did not have an answer to the human rights matters, human rights observers did not have anything to say about the need for local employment; economists had nothing to say about toxic water. In the end no one said much of anything about the gold rush outside the region. Though miners were arriving in the Amazon at a time when the forest was brightly positioned in the world's spotlight, the gold rush received comparatively little international attention.

There *was* a local debate. But in Guyana and Brazil the small miners were nearly impossible to stop and in most cases encouraged, because they created jobs for rural populations. (After the reports surfaced on the Yanomami casualties, Brazil cracked down on its miners, but many just fled across the nearest border; the Guyanese government wrestles constantly with the need to evict Brazilian gold smugglers.) In Brazil the miners grew so confident for a time that they built their own airstrips along the border with Venezuela and virtually ignored national boundaries. They gave the runways off-the-cuff, fanciful names like Banana and Saddam Hussein. The remote border there was too thickly forested to patrol and was a long-standing smuggler's route already. An anthropologist who lived with Brazilian gold miners at the time, Gordon McMillan, writes that the borders were so ignored Venezuela finally had to send in the air force. A Venezuelan fighter shot down a Brazilian plane on a supply run to a mining camp somewhere in the jungle in 1992. This did not have much permanent impact except to drive the miners back to traveling by land and boat.

Between the desire to limit illegal border crossing, the need to defend the local population, and disputes with foreign mining companies over land, skirmishes and tension between local miners and security forces was nearly constant in the northern Amazon for much of the 1990s. It was worse in Venezuela and Brazil than in Guyana, which had no army to speak of anyway, plus more land and few miners competing for it. But even they had problems: Omai's private security force had shot local miners stealing things like dirt from the mine—the small miners wanted to sift the big miner's waste for trace gold—on at least one occasion; thefts were common and there were armed guards patrolling the forest around the mine.

The violence proved to be an industry problem, not a regional one. The gold rush was global. In southeastern Africa, Amnesty International reported a 1996 incident in Tanzania: security forces allegedly bulldozed a local mining area without warning, burying as many as fifty men alive. The gold miners claimed to have been protesting their displacement by a Canadian company, Barrick Gold. Barrick Gold denied that the miners were attacked by security forces on its behalf and may not have been attacked at all. The incident is still disputed. A case in Indonesia alleged that an American gold and copper mining company was involved in human rights violations by the local military. "Indonesian security forces based around the Freeport mine had committed human rights violations widely publicized in the mid-1990s," according to Amnesty International. Pollution at the same mine led to sanctions from the U.S. government against the New Orleans company that owned it, Freeport-McMoRan Copper and Gold. To Guyana's east, Golden Star Resources (Omai's discoverer) planned another gold mine and demanded the forced relocation of a village of five hundred located near the mine site; years of confrontation followed. In Kilometer 88 the disputes became serious enough that the foreign company working there, Canada's Placer Dome Inc., eventually had to work out a compromise with the local miners and let them work on some of the company land. But such compromises were rare.

In the northern Amazon, as in many places, this was all a new and complicated problem. You couldn't just outlaw gold mining. There was interest in gold, and the local governments had a right to do business. They needed to give people jobs and sell their resources. But property rights were unclear. No one knew what to do when local miners continued to work on land leased to overseas miners, short of shooting at them. In El Dorado the lack of answer meant standoffs, beatings, shootings and tear gas. There were constant skirmishes and tensions around the mines.

We had not heard anything from the plaza for an hour, and I decided to head back to it. It seemed possible to observe events from the side alleys. I thanked Silva for his help and left him to his work on the boat. He was in a crouch beside the motor working with some tools. He looked over his shoulder and suggested I get out of town soon. I thanked him again and he turned back to his work. That was the last time I saw him.

I walked down a gangplank past the growling dog. By the time I got back to the plaza it was greatly calmer than before. There were townspeople returning slowly to the center. One of the grocery stores had unlocked its gate. The bar was open again. The miners were still on their side of the plaza but stood in a looser group, in less of a nervous huddle, and some were hanging around the boats a few yards from the plaza. I waited by the bar and watched things ease. Within an hour the guard trucks drove out of town, leaving a few soldiers behind patrolling with clubs.

I found Castillo in a squat against the hotel wall. He had sobered up a little. It was about noon and getting hot outside.

"Hi, Ramón."

"It's safe now," he said. He gave a nod and a quick look around.

A pickup with a gabled-roof structure like a doghouse was parked in the square, and about a dozen miners were loading into the back. I asked if he could show me the way to the mines. I still wanted to talk to the miners about the strike. Castillo would make me a less suspicious presence.

"Okay. Yes." He stood up. "Thirty dollars," he said. "Translation."

I offered twenty.

"Dollars or bolivars?"

"Dollars."

"Yes okay, twenty," he said. "But now give me ten more also."

"What?"

"We need to buy things first. You have bolivars?"

I relented and handed over the equivalent of ten dollars in bolivars.

"Wait here," he said.

Castillo took the money and walked in short strides to a dry-goods store across the plaza. He returned a few minutes later with a pack of cigarettes and two bottles of American whiskey. They were in his pockets and bulged from his shirt absurdly. He looked like an artless shoplifter.

He had gone to the smaller of the two stores on the plaza. The larger one was closed and locked and no one was around. Everything else in the plaza was returning to normal: a man started the coals at the chicken restaurant; a line formed at the dispensary where a boy pumped gasoline from barrels with a hand pump into gas cans for the motorboats; a teenage boy wrestled some speakers into place at a disco near the river.

I asked Castillo why the larger grocery store had not opened yet.

"They are afraid still," he said. We walked toward the little truck with the gabled roof. He explained that store had a contract to supply food and liquor to the guard station on the main road. The miners looted the store on occasion as reprisal after attacks, he said. The store would probably wait another day before opening just to be safe; it usually did.

The steel box over the truck's bed had benches along each side. But ten men took up all the seats, so Castillo and I stepped on the bumper and hung off the back. Two more miners shared the bumper with us. They were short, thickly built men, wearing baseball hats in the sun. We pulled out abruptly, and one of the men had to lunge for his grip to avoid falling off. Everyone in the back laughed at his inattentiveness. The metal roof was too hot to touch, and we had to keep moving our hands around to keep a grip. Fortunately it was only a few minutes up the spur to the main road. We turned sharply into what appeared to be a wall of trees and passed through with the branches whipping the sides of the truck. On the other side was a dirt road with rows of tents down each side.

"Here," Castillo said and let go of the roof.

He fell from the truck holding his stomach as if cradling a baby. The whiskey bottles were rattling around in his shirt. The leap surprised me and the truck was going pretty fast. I hesitated, dropped off late and had to walk back a few dozen yards through a cloud of dust. The truck kept going with the miners laughing. When the dust settled I found Castillo standing in front of one of the tents. It was a thatch shelter with open walls; a blue tarp was pulled over the thatch structure, which was bound together with twine and gray duct tape. Half a dozen men sat around a square hole in the ground: five Venezuelans and a Guyanese man. Castillo made introductions and offered one of the men the whiskey bottles.

The Guyanese man was named Ricky. He was a head taller than everyone else; the Venezuelan prospectors were strong but compact. No one was working—the strike continued. I asked Ricky about it. I said I was an American reporter and wanted to know about the strike for a magazine article. Ricky agreed and said he would speak for the group both because he was fluent in English and because he was the group's unofficial foreman.

The strike was still going on, with only few exceptions. He cast an arm down the road toward the other tents. They were empty or there were similar groups of men sleeping on benches or sitting around talking. One team right alongside had gotten back to work and were bagging rocks in burlap sacks. It was not a traditional strike; there wasn't a union. But the miners had agreed to stop working to demonstrate that they were unified against the guard. The abject point seemed to be that if the guard attacked them the miners would counterattack together, though Ricky was skeptical and hoped that wasn't tested anytime soon.

The camp had a hole in the center. The rock near El Dorado was too hard to work with pans and water hoses. At El Dorado there was rock all the way to the surface. So the men had to build long shafts straight into the earth and lower themselves on ropes. La Camorra was a row of these shafts, each with a tent over it. Some of the shafts operated like independent businesses, like Silva's dredge boat: a boss owned the tools and paid the miners a percentage of the gold they recovered. Others operated like small cooperatives, with the miners working in teams and splitting the profits and costs. It was harder work splitting the rocks in El Dorado than working in the soft ground elsewhere, but there was a lot of gold in the rocks. Usually they dug with hand tools, but in some cases they could rent a jackhammer together from a wealthier miner in town.

The gold mine Ricky worked was a square opening in the dirt floor three feet wide by two across or so reinforced at the edges with stripped tree branches. It descended a few dozen feet straight down. Normally it was illuminated with a lamp run off a battery in the bottom, but with no one working the lamp was off that day and the hole pitch black. A winch made of pieces of tree trunk and thick rope, the parts glued together with tar, sat across the mouth of the hole. It took two men to lower the others and their tools into the shaft. One or two, sometimes three, miners could work in the bottom at a time, Ricky said. The ventilation system was a household desk fan blowing into a duct made of black plastic garbage bags. Overhead the tarpaulins lashed to a trellis of wooden poles kept the sun off the winch operators and rain from flooding the mine.

A row of these holes ran down each side of a dirt road for a mile. Ricky said we were on the North American Monarch company's land, but it depended whom you asked. (Monarch said by phone later that we weren't.)

Each gold miner knocked out sixty, on a good day one hundred, pounds of rock from the floor. They bagged them in a burlap sack and the people above hauled the sack to the surface on the wooden winch. If a particularly large boulder came loose they winched that up also and smashed it aboveground; there wasn't always room below to swing a sledgehammer hard enough to split a really big boulder. They had to haul most of the rocks out to keep enough space to work, but once on the surface they could see the gold in the rocks and separate the ones with a lot of visible gold in them from the ones that looked less promising.

Ricky retrieved a sample from a rice sack nearby. He handed it over to me. The gold was visible as auburn flecks here and there in a gray substrate. The entire stone was about the size and shape of a shoe and had red and black sections. I turned it over in my hands and saw more small bits of gold like shiny blotches. They were mostly on one side of the rock, and scattered, not a seam or a vein as I'd imagined.

When they had a bag of rocks they took it by truck to one of the wildcat mills nearby. For a percentage the mill owner crushed the rocks down into sand and extracted the gold with mercury.

So why didn't the guard just shut down the mills? Why were the men still in business if gold mining was illegal? There was some discussion in Spanish, most of which I understood but some of which Castillo translated for me. They agreed with what Silva had said earlier in the morning: the mines were an essential part of the local economy. Ricky claimed their mine shaft existed at all because of the guard's presence; they had gotten some of their tools from the guard. The most important was dynamite. Only the guard had access to explosives, which were necessary for making a gold mine in hard rocks. It was illegal to possess dynamite.

"But we need dynamite to blast in the hole," he said. "So we get the dynamite from the guard."

"You buy it?"

"Buy it, yes," Ricky said. "Sometimes with a little gold, money, whichever. But then when you leave the soldier calls to his friend and they set up a checkpoint a little way along the road. And they stop you there and look in your car and take the dynamite back because it is contraband. To get it back you must buy it a second time." (Guard soldiers denied this.)

Ramón and Ricky translated some of the conversation for one of the other miners. He was a young Venezuelan miner with no shirt and a complicated hairdo that made him look like a heavy metal guitarist. He passed the conversation on to the rest, and there were nods and some side talk. The rest of the men sat on a plank between two barrels listening, nodding if he translated for them, some adding a word now and then, others gossiping in pairs about unrelated things. Castillo sat with the men and smoked.

I asked them, through Castillo, about the standoff. The man with the distracting hair said he had not worried much about it. It was an ambivalent strike. He had been among those who went into town to confront the guard, but most of the miners had not. There were a few thousand of them and only twenty or thirty went to the square, he said. Everyone else knew the mines would not be shut down long anyway, because Ricky was right: they were the entire local economy, and everyone, including the soldiers needed the mines running. The guard commanders could take a longer stoppage. But the regular soldiers would go broke relying on their forty-dollar-a-month wages and all the shops in town needed the miners' business. So the miners would all be back to work by morning, the longhaired miner said.

Ricky said once that happened they would be back to worrying about other miners and not the guard. Since none of the miners had clear title to their mines, and the guard wasn't about to resolve disputes among the miners, the camps sometimes ran on frontier law. Most of the time the miners cooperated with each other, but when they did not it was a serious matter.

"You put a line down," Ricky said. He was reluctant to talk on the topic and did not translate it for the others. "And you have to respect that line. You work on this side and the other man on the other side. Okay, sometimes people cross the line. Sometimes if there is a good find, a group with a gun will come and take that mine." And then there were reprisals, and counterreprisals. "And then a few days later maybe you see that person in town and they are a little drunk. . . . These things do happen," he said. I asked him to name the last time that had happened but he refused.

The sun was getting higher and it was warming under the tarp that covered the mineshaft. The men were smoking and passing around the whiskey despite the heat and the early hour. A few dozen yards down the road the other team had gotten back to work already around a neighboring shaft. Ricky spoke in Spanish with the long-haired miner about whether to start back to work themselves. They decided to wait until the next day as previously decided and not worry about the neighbors. They thanked Castillo for the whiskey. Ricky had not drunk any but said to me it had helped the others decide about taking the rest of the day off.

The guard never showed up in La Camorra that day. I left the camp after a few more hours. Castillo and I caught a truck back to the plaza. The buses were not running into town yet, so I walked to the main highway, the same way I had arrived the previous night. Castillo felt obligated to come some of the way—I had paid him for a full day as a guide—but after a half mile or so said maybe he would take a nap now and headed back. I thanked him and wished him luck. He had drunk a fair share of the alcohol we had brought for the miners. He gave a tired thumbs-up and turned back toward town with his shuffling walk.

I reached the road and within a few hours had flagged down a bus full of tourists heading to the national park. At the spur a small sign I'd not seen the previous night pointed back toward town: "El Dorado." It seemed like a cruel joke: the city of gold was a tense, dusty frontier town. I boarded and the bus pulled onto the asphalt. There were more spurs off the main road as we went south that led to more mining towns nearby but out of view. The gold mines were invisible from the road, as were the soldiers. It is possible to float right past El Dorado and not notice it still, though there is a sign now. The bus headed south, and I continued on my way to Guyana and Omai.

Two days later I reached Lethem on the Guyanese border and bought a space on a cargo plane to Georgetown. It was a boxy prop plane with canvas walls and jump seats made of cotton webbing. We flew up the Essequibo for an hour. The range of mesas along the Venezuelan border was visible to the west out the window. The plane slithered sideways more than it traveled forward but landed in Georgetown two hours later on an airstrip fringed with palms. The taxi from the airport drove into Georgetown weaving around cows and horsecarts in the road.

I had called Omai from North America about seeing the gold mine but not gotten any response. But being in the country helped. Two days after landing in Georgetown I was in an ante-room in Omai's office sitting across from Seeta Mohamed, the person I had failed to reach a year and a half prior. She was Omai's press officer: a slight, thirtyish West Indian woman with short black hair and a direct manner. She sat at a small wooden desk frowning at a fax from my boss in North America. The fax confirmed my assignment and requested I be granted access to the gold mine. Mohamed put the fax down on her lap and stared at me with a glare of unmasked irritation. Her face was thin. She did not like reporters but couldn't think of an excuse to not let me see the gold mine. Okay, she said, and read over the fax again. I could come back in two mornings and join a tour she had arranged for some high school students. I thanked her and fled before she could change her mind.

Omai's office sat catercorner to the national botanical garden, a beautiful spot by day that no one will walk past after dark. Two days later I walked there at eight in the morning and joined a crowd of children and teachers. We waited outside a school bus idling in the office's front. The kids were not Guyanese. An acad-emy for the children of foreign diplomats had arranged the trip to Omai. I shared my seat with two American boys about sixteen years old. The boys pushed and punched at each other. They cadged pens and papers and other small objects back and forth with the jerky, panicked energy of squirrels. Soon Mohamed and a driver boarded without a word. The bus traveled four hours south into the interior on the company road. It was a wide dirt highway unlike any other in the interior, a red carpet through the jungle. The dirt road had been built as wide as a three lane high-way by the mining company for its fuel trucks to travel. The for-est overhung the edges in spots. A line was visible where a machine had trimmed it back recently. The soil was red in that part of the forest and the road was the color of bricks. A cloud of dust the same color covered the bus's back window. Green cargo trucks ferrying local miners passed on one side or the other every few minutes. Most disappeared soon onto trails the miners had constructed off the main road. At curves we could see the forest spreading out to each side of the road in its usual green endless-ness. The kids ignored the view and either clapped and sang or complained most of the way.

Mohamed rode in a front seat and kept to herself—organiz-ing company papers in a folder, ordering her day. After the first hour I walked down the aisle to the front of the bus and at-tempted to introduce myself again. We'd spoken on the phone and in person only a handful of times. She was not encouraging. She handed me company pamphlets and told me to start with them. She went back to organizing her papers. I returned to my seat with the boys and read pamphlets for the rest of the trip without learning much.

The only other adults on board were a few weary-looking teachers and a young man from the Guyana Environmental Pro-tection Agency. The Guyana EPA was a hopeful little office created in the wake of the cyanide accident: perhaps the best-intentioned, least powerful collection of earnest ecologists in the hemisphere. Its staff consisted, and still consists, of a handful of junior chemists and biologists with recent degrees from European universities, a few underfunded professors, a couple of assistants, and a roomful of outdated maps. The EPA man was just back from college in England and only on the job a few weeks so far. He had come south of his own initiative and not for an official in-spection. He had come to see the new toxic waste pond but ad-mitted, in a low tone, that he was not certain what he was looking for and did not know what he might do back in Georgetown with what he learned. The staff barely would have stuck pins into the maps back at the office on the University of Guyana's tattered campus before running out of money to do anything else.

By noon the bus arrived at the Essequibo. Mohamed ordered everyone off to a ferry dock. Soon a boat churned our way from downriver. Mohamed, a bit of a disciplinarian, kept the teenagers herded in the pier's corner, snapping her voice like a snare drum.

"Stay with the bus. Stay with the bus. With the bus," she said.

A boy behind her ignored the order and stepped away from the group to film his friends with a videocamera. Mohamed noticed him and seemed to consider saying something, then turned away and compensated by corralling the remaining children more tightly against the pier's railing. In a few minutes the boat arrived, kissed the dock, and the group headed onto the river. Some single students watched the water and others pretended to toss each other over the deck rail. It was only a few minutes until they were across and in the gate and shepherded to a new bus, blue and white, driven into the mine.

This seemed to be Mohamed's cue. She stepped into the aisle and leaned on the back of the bus driver's chair noting points of interest out the window. The forest lined both sides of the road for a few hundred yards up a slight rise. At the crest we emerged into what looked like a desert. It opened below us. It was a bright orange field and looked a half mile wide. The soil was scraped away and the entire area graded with bulldozers. It could have been a suburb under construction, a new housing subdivision in the woods east of Seattle or some mid-Atlantic pine barrens. Along the side were tall cones of dirt like the mounds of sawdust that pile beside Oregon lumber mills. Each cone was perhaps a hundred feet high and sat in a flat area of cleared forest about a quarter mile across. The adults all nodded along with Mohamed's commentary. The children were not finding anything to hold their interest and went back to trading small objects and notes. The bus rounded a curve. A series of flat buildings were to the left and to the right what looked like a refinery. The landscape around the buildings was broad and low and designed to the needs of machines. There was no one and nothing moving in sight. The clearing had a feeling of evacuation. I asked Mohamed where everyone was. It was against the rules to walk on the grounds without reason, she said. We pulled up to a field house and stopped. Mohamed said we were going inside first to eat lunch and see a film. Everyone debarked.

It was about noon. A half-dozen mine employees were inside the cafeteria dressed in blue jumpsuits and new, expensive work boots. They carried hard hats in coded colors under their arms. Mohamed kept up a constant narrative and hurried the group through the cafeteria: the mine operated twenty-four hours a day, seven days a week, she said. The men slept in barracks on site for three weeks at a time. They worked ten-hour shifts. That added up to the best jobs in the country, she said. They were the best-paid and were offered the most skills to learn. I asked to speak to some of the employees while we ate but Mohamed said such a thing was impossible. I asked why. She ushered me through the food line—chicken, red beans, and rice, smelling excellent—and to a seat far away from the children.

"Aren't you going to eat?" I said. I put down my tray on the bench.

"No." She was scanning the area. Some miners were sitting at the other end of the lunch table. I introduced myself, but Mohamed looked at them and they did not respond beyond brief hellos. She was much firmer with me than I expected. She put a hand on my shoulder with an unpleasant tightness and said *please*, do not speak with anyone in the cafeteria. Then she offered some lists of rock-milling statistics and financial statements from her folder and asked me to write down comments on national prosperity due to arrive at some vague point ten years in the future.

I had not figured on her being a full-fledged minder. She kept on: the men had health care provided free of charge.

"How is the rice?" she said when I turned back to the men a second time.

"Fine, thanks," I said.

There was an insistent air in Mohamed's voice: the miners earned wages ten times the national average, as much as four hundred, seven hundred dollars a month, she said. This was enough to put them on easy street in Georgetown.

"May I ask them about that?"

"Unfortunately not."

The EPA man was gone. I asked Mohamed where he was. He had gotten permission to see a chemistry lab, she said. I did not see the young government man again for the rest of the day.

After lunch Mohamed led us into a conference room dolled up like a small museum. The walls had photos of the mine's construction, and there were rocks on tables with bits of gold in them. There was a movie screen in front: she dimmed the lights and played a blaring promotional video. Cyanide became gold in the movie: step one, step two, step three. Mohamed passed out accompanying dittos. The teachers flipped through them and seemed to be losing their ability to feign interest. The sheets were technical schematics with titles like the "Cyanide Circuit." By this time it had been five hours since we had left Georgetown, and even the most interested of the kids had grown restless. A few became bold enough to wander around the room. The tallish boy with the videocamera seemed to be the ringleader. He attempted to photograph a rock sample on a table off to the side, part of a geology display. Mohamed noticed him away not watching the movie and she lunged his way in a sudden rage.

"Is that a videocamera?"

The boy acted perplexed. Of course it was a videocamera. He was a little taller than Mohamed and about double her girth. Everyone looked their way. Mohamed grabbed for the camera, but the boy was too fast and slung it seamlessly over his back by a strap. The teachers seemed happy to let Mohamed enforce her own rules. The movie was nearing its climax. A man in protective gear stood before a raging furnace and tipped a crucible. It was thick-walled and scorched black. Sparks and islands of flaming slag and brilliant yellow molten gold drained from a spout into what appeared to be a loaf pan. When it cooled, there it was: a bar of gold, 500 ounces, worth $150,000. And that was a day's work at the Omai gold mine, THE END. The children, urged by their teachers, clapped politely.

Mohamed was simmering and wanted to hurry outside. "Okay, back to the bus!" she said.

She passed out hard hats in candy colors: bright shades of yellow, orange or blue. The kids immediately began trading with each other to match their clothes. The fussing went on for some time. Children adjusted their hat sizes and tried them backward and forward. Some checked their looks in compacts. The teachers had clearly turned the students over to Mohamed and taken the day off. They sat in the back of the bus and gossiped among themselves. The bus followed a dirt road to the edge of the hole and stopped at a rise, where Mohamed marched everyone off. The rise overlooked the gold mine. It was an immense crater, looking about half a mile around. The walls of the hole were cut away in descending steps like a negative of a ziggurat. The scale of the pit made it difficult to remember the land had once been level there and covered in trees, and that the hole was man-made and not carved from a canyon. A road circled the pit. Beyond the road more land had been denuded and looked dusty and dry. The only way to keep a sense of scale was to look at the power poles lining the road on the far side of the hole. Each looked like a pencil held at arm's length. Visible in the distant bottom, dump trucks and steam shovels looked the size of a thumb. They chipped away at tall piles of stones. They did not help keep the hole's size clear. The yellow trucks were three stories high but looked like wheelbarrows. The digging itself going on in the bottom of the pit, though unearthing millions in treasure, could have been any other construction project. Bulldozers quarried away at the floor, smoothing the slopes and making dents. Very far away we could hear the warning horns beeping when the machines backed up with loads of rocks held high on bent arms. The tools were too far away to see the humans sitting in them. The bottom of the hole was flat and clean as a drained swimming pool and had the peach color of some Florida motels.

From the overlook at the edge of the gold mine the gross volume of missing land created a sense of vertigo. A warm wind rose from the chasm. It was oddly quiet: only distantly a pile-driving machine meted out blows with a metronomic *ping* and now and then a diesel truck passed loudly behind us.

Mohamed ordered everyone back on the bus for the ride to see the new toxic waste pond. The pond caused a buzz of excitement among the kids. They were interested in seeing a cyanide-flooded canyon. The bus climbed a rise in the dirt road and crossed a bluff. The pond was open below us. It looked like a good place to go water skiing. It was a placid, self-contained lake, except that the color was all wrong. The waste had a cinnamon cast like Mexican chocolate. It lay beyond a black pipe. We debarked. None of the kids had any questions. One of the adults went and sat on the pipe that carried the cyanide toward the pool. She cleaned her glasses. Mohamed made some halfhearted comments about how much better the new pond was than the old one that had cracked and spilled the waste. We didn't stay long.

She led us up the side of the mill where they mixed in the cyanide. It seemed unwise to stand so close to the tank where this occurred, but Mohamed assured us it was safe. She led the way up a metal stairway bolted like a fire escape to the mill's exterior. A light, warm drizzle was lingering, the sky a foggy gray, and she cautioned the students to be careful as they walked. The metal catwalks were slick, and we were several stories up. At the top we stood above the tank and looked down through a grate in the floor. Below was what looked like a taffy machine, armatures inside other armatures, with a rotor spinning a gray soup of soil, cyanide, gold, and water. It was not possible to breathe in the cyanide, Mohamed said. It was only dangerous with contact or by drinking it. The catwalk was only a few feet over the tank. It would have been possible to dangle a toe into the liquid.

The catwalk was the highest point around, higher than the hills—mines, of course, tend to go down, not up. It provided a view of the surrounding forest from above the canopy. The trees looked inexhaustible and the mine was only the most minor imperfection, enough to catch the eye but not detract, like a thin scar. In the foreground more trucks for moving the rock sat parked heavily to one side in a semicircle. The black cyanide conduit ran to the waste pond from the nearby mill, a tower of steel and keening verticality, to the cyanide lake. The lake looked nearly, but not quite, small.

The Omai pit was at the time still the largest, or maybe third-largest, or arguably sixth-largest gold mine in South America and somewhere between tenth- and twentieth-largest in the world.

The number was difficult to peg because it depended on who did the boasting. Size could mean the richness of the gold deposit, the depth and breadth of the hole, the project's cost, or the amount of land involved—there were as many different opportunities for heroic description as were necessary to interest potential investors. It was easy to find some way to claim the mine to be somehow the "biggest" or at least "at one time the biggest." Practically it didn't matter whether the hole was the first or twentieth biggest pot of gold on earth. In order to create economies of scale and turn a profit, gold mines like Omai had to be gigantic. Omai certainly was. Even the children were quiet for a moment when we passed it a last time. Mohamed gathered us together and rose to the meat of her presentation; she had been holding out on us with the biggest and best numbers: tons of rock dug in a typical year (twenty million), tons powdered in the mill so far that year (seven million), ounces of gold recovered the previous year (roughly 300,000, ninety million dollars' worth or so before expenses), the cost to build the mine (a quarter billion U.S. dollars), the price of new tires for the earth-moving trucks (seven thousand dollars each). She had brought a small bullhorn from the bus for this part of the presentation. It did not work correctly and issued painful squeals when she pressed the button to talk.

The kids gave the pit another glance and resumed their fidgeting. Mohamed disregarded them and finished her speech. Past the edge of the road, behind her, treads from a bulldozer had turned the clay over in foot-wide sections like a tilled field. El Dorado, in the end, was real, had been discovered, and was a pile of dirt.

WASEER
AND DOTSON

The last time I went to Guyana was in the fall of 2000. I went because I was given an opportunity to write this story, and because the gold mines were going bankrupt. The price of gold was crashing and gold mines were closing down. Omai was barely holding itself together as a business. Across the border in Venezuela, the mine at Km 88 that had caused so much conflict was now being cast aside by the company that had worked to build it; it wasn't worth the trouble and expense. Omai's geologists were not looking in the forest for more gold, because they couldn't make any money at it.

I did not take the southern route and the cattle trail this time. I flew directly from North America to Georgetown. The city had not changed much since I had first seen it five years prior. Perhaps the homes on stilts along the river had sunk farther into the swamp. The main road to town was still washed out and broken. Downtown, horse carts still blocked traffic. They were made of axles and rubber tires salvaged from junkyards, little rolling tragedies, where all the miracles of the industrial age had added up to just more work for the horse and an inferior way of moving chattel around than existed in the year 1000. The carts still carried anemic cargos, a few boards of lumber or a few stalks of sugar.

I took a room at a guesthouse called the Rima. It was a family home up a narrow stairwell and the friendliest place to stay in town. The proprietor was a soft-spoken woman of grandmotherly manners named Mrs. Singh. After checking in I attended to some spots that had suddenly appeared, painlessly but disconcertingly, on the inside of my right arm. Then I headed out to dinner at a bar called the Palm Court. It was half a block away down a quiet avenue, Middle Street.

The Palm was close to the Rima but also to the embassies, and so received the bulk of the city's foreign clientele. This was in part because other dining options inflicted greater amounts of karaoke music on their patrons, plus the Palm had the strongest drinks and the best roti, which in Guyana is a curry burrito and better than that sounds.

The place was mostly empty. A white foreigner was there, on a stool beside the security guard, and at the other end of the bar two East Indian locals. The young men were conducting some kind of business. The guard was an older man with a thin face. He was not guarding anything. He and the foreigner watched television.

I took a seat beside the guard and the other foreigner. The bar was hardwood shaped in a half-moon. It sat on one end of an outdoor patio under an awning that mostly kept out the rain. If a Guyanese bar had a television, there was usually a cricket match on. The rest of the time the TV played a popular, ghastly public-access listing of the day's obituaries. The latter was on at the time. I'd seen the show before: viewers paid a small fee to post a photograph of their deceased loved one. Then they composed a biographical text that scrolled down the screen, naming the person's relations and hobbies beside the photo. A thumping soca beat or a pop hit accompanied each death announcement. The blaring music and dancing video letters combined to make the show at once both cheerful and macabre.

We watched. The name of a woman in her forties was on-screen, in puffy blue letters outlined in white. Beside her name was a grainy blow-up of a family snapshot. She had short hair and looked impassive. The dead woman's picture hovered, spectral, above us. Her biographical information scrolled past. She had a large family and every name was there: daughters, sons-in-law, aunts, nephews. They all seemed to live outside the country; most were in New York City, Toronto, or London. The names and foreign cities gave an impression of a woman who had died abandoned, and I found it a horribly depressing television show.

"They love it," the foreign man beside me said. His accent was American.

"That so?"

The bartender, a stocky man in a tropical shirt, said sure, it was all right, like he never paid it much attention, and took my drink order.

The American sipped his beer and I introduced myself. He said he was a logger. He had worked in five countries hugging the equator and rattled them off. He was in Guyana working for a Malaysian company. I asked if he liked being a logger. He said it wasn't bad but people gave him grief often.

"You go to a cocktail party back home and someone asks you what you do, and you say, 'I manage the rain forest.' So then they say, 'So you log the rain forest?' and you say yeah, *that's* what I do, I log the rain forest. I cut down the rain forest."

The bartender wandered away to take an order at the other end of the bar: two men in excessive ropy gold necklaces and bright silk shirts, like low-level mobsters.

The logger was a fit man with red hair.

"I have a guy comes down here," he said. "Some agronomist, or agricultural economist." He said this with his voice arcing toward sarcasm. "Who never raised a crop for profit in his life. Some environmentalist. Tells me one of my guys should fell the tree this way"—he karate-chopped the air, a bit startling—"not that way. They have no idea how the job works. This tree not that one."

He swiveled his stool and heaved an imaginary object held by an invisible handle across the bar. He pantomimed moving a heavy weight: strain.

"Know what I do? I say, 'Here. Here's the chain saw.' You want that guy's job? Because I don't think you would do that guy's job." The logger smacked the bar with his palm, making a small pop. "You want this bartop made out of plastic and glue? Fine. But most people don't. They want to make it out of wood." The rant turned poisonous. "There are consumers and there are producers. And the consumers always try to tell the producers how to do things. And what, I don't know shit? I have advanced degrees. From good schools."

He may have been drunk but he probably wasn't. It was almost impossible to get drunk on Banks beer, which was watery and tasted faintly of chocolate. He turned back toward the bar.

"You know how much diesel they use at that gold mine?" he said. He was talking about Omai.

"No."

He did. "I know a guy there, went down there once."

The bartender was staying at the far end of the bar now talking to the other men.

"Yeah?"

"Yeah. Fifteen thousand gallons. They have to truck it in every day," he said. "But it's worth it. Know why?"

"Uh, no."

"Activity. Otherwise nothing happens. These countries, any-thing you can do to create activity is good."

He drank and argued for a while about activity for its own sake. It didn't matter if the mine made a profit before it ran out of gold, he said—this was my question; certainly logging wasn't an easy way to profit in South America either, he said, but it was something to do. "A country has the right to use what it has, to feed its people," he said. "We logged the entire Southeast." He meant the American South, not Guyana's, which was barely touched at all by outsiders. "We plowed under the whole Mid-west for farming, and then some environmentalist comes down here to tell these people they can't do that too? Countries have a right to feed their people."

The bartender wandered back.

"You using?" He slid the menu across the bar. Food was not eaten in Guyana, it was "used," like an implement.

"Yes." Use dinner, not take away, I said. I ordered some food.

"It's their Wild West," the logger said. "We had a gold rush, they have a gold rush."

The bartender brought another drink without my asking for one. I took it and paid.

"Have you ever flown over this place in a plane?" the log-ger said.

"This morning."

"Well, did you look down? It's like looking over a bunch of broccoli. There's ninety-five, ninety-seven percent of this place untouched," he said.

I agreed with most of what he said, but returning to the city still gave me pause. The mine had brought hundreds of millions of dollars in gold out of the ground, and Georgetown was still a holy mess anyway. Across the bar, Main Street and the taxi stand were visible in the patio lights. A few drivers waited for fares and gossiped with the sentry, who looked bored. The buildings across the street were faded and ramshackle wooden mansions slowly rotting into the swamp. The sun had set. No one walked at night past them. Not even a few yards. It had been this way for decades and was not improving. The crime was worsening in some neighborhoods. There were home invasions now, Mrs. Singh had said. She had many locks on the Rima's door. Rich families and foreign businessmen like the logger often had a guard with a gun overnight in front of their homes the bartender said. The other 300,000 citizens in the capital shackled their gates and turned the streets over to bandits each night, waiting the darkness out behind fences topped with broken glass or, in the better neighborhoods, concertina wire.

Those were the places where people could protect themselves. In the worst quarters—Tiger Bay, Lacytown—or near them the capital ran itself like the inside of a prison: people traveling in groups if they had to go out but the groups avoiding each other's eyes. It was a woeful city. The market was full of dozens of orphans sleeping on cardboard boxes. Near the airport people were squatting in the garbage dump. The plumbing still didn't work. The hospital was a nightmare. There was no adequate psychiatric institution to speak of, so downtown a handful of half-clad men and women in need of hospitalization sat on Main Street waving scrap-metal machetes at their demons, shouting threats and obscenities. (The latter is true, to be fair, on Market Street in San Francisco.)

The logger paid his bill and left, refused the taxi, and walked down the street over the security guard's protests. I took a cab the half block to the Rima. It appeared nothing had changed.

A week later, intending to confirm this, I took a minibus to the banks of the Essequibo, where I transferred to a longboat upriver.

I was going to a town named Mahdia. Mahdia was a gold camp that dated back to the 1930s. It had been a good spot to find gold for most of a century, peaking in the seventies and eighties, but the sense in Georgetown—at least as I heard it later that week at a bar called the Demico, a madhouse where some of the miners got snot-flying drunk after coming back from the forest—was that Mahdia was running dry. Still there were said to be thousands of men working there, and if the gold rush was ebbing, Mahdia would be the clearest place to see what people were doing in response. The rumor was they were all moving into diamonds and striking out for areas deeper in the forest. It's not as if they could come back to Georgetown and get a different job. There still weren't any.

To get to Mahdia required a ride up the Essequibo into the forest to the town of Bartica. An old road began there. A newer road built by a logging company a few years prior went direct from Georgetown, but the road from Bartica passed through richer gold areas. It was the traditional miner's route.

It was a long trip. From the bazaar in Georgetown a minibus went to Parika, and from there the longboats waited lashed to the pilings beneath the wharf. The longboats were wide and long and open to the sky. Most were painted in bright reds and yellows and greens. The prows stuck up a bit in the dark water from the weight of the massive engines in back. It was shady and pleasant waiting beneath the wharf on the boat's bench seat. The seats filled with people and goods. In half an hour the pilot climbed over everyone to his small space in the rear and started one of the engines.

The boat caromed off the pilings and withdrew from beneath the wharf, and the sun walked its way down the hull. The light hit us suddenly and was painful, like hot oil poured on your head. There were reactions all over the boat when the passengers realized, a little late, that we were on the water and there were things we had forgotten to do to prepare. We all winced and searched our bags for hats, then hunkered down, pulled our chins to our chests, and laced our fingers over the backs of our necks: cheating into the shade of the seat. The boat turned toward the wrong way, toward the shore; some of the passengers packed on their benches looked frustrated and, depending on individual curiosity, turned fully around or just swiveled an eye to investigate why the pilot had not headed upriver. The explanation came into view: more passengers waited on a narrow ledge along the wharf's side. Farther back on the pier, unhealthful barefoot boys arrived with additions to the cargo. The boat was already filled by then. But the people and merchandise came on board anyway. A porter took on puffy bags of rice; a new American chain saw still in the box; cases of dried macaroni and cheese; cheap suitcases full of dresses and pants bought in town. The porter pointed at the least lucky passengers and ordered them to give up the spare inches around them. He hid boxes underneath feet and behind seats, in the small cone of space in the tip of the bow, beside the outboard motor; he strapped a box down on the back bench where the pilot should sit. In ten minutes of furious geometry he had packed the boat and not refused anything passed to him. He looked back toward the stevedores hopeful for more paying cargo, though the boat was clearly sinking by then.

The pilot was cautious backing out from the dock. But as soon as we slipped clear of the pilings his wrist twisted, goosing the motor, and the boat reared back in the water. The spray climbed the hull and peeled away in a widening arc as the boat picked up speed. The bow pranced in front of us. We leaped over waves, around driftwood, and between islands very fast. The river narrowed and greenery rose taller on each side.

Shipwrecks lay on the banks walled in by mangroves. The

edge of the forest had infiltrated the ships. Trees grew from the portholes and shattered the wooden decks; vines covered the hulls sagging like fishing nets. We bulleted south for an hour. The motor buzzed rather than roared, the only disappointment: it made a cloying falsetto like a kazoo. But in only an hour Bartica was suddenly upon us.

At Bartica the river bulges. Two other rivers flow from the west to form a wide confluence. Bartica is on the west bank. Four thousand people live there. The majority of the boats do not travel much farther upriver than the town; there are only a few small villages beyond Bartica and then a rapids called the Itanami Falls. Itanami is the biggest rapids on the Essequibo, and before motorboats existed gold miners attempted to shoot it in canoes. They pulled upriver with overmatched paddles. There is an old gold miner's song about the experience marked by a likably frank tone of utter panic. It is reprinted in a government tourist pamphlet, despite there being few tourists to read it:

> Captain, captain, put me ashore,
> I don't want to go anymore.
> Itanami gon' frighten me,
> Itanami gon' wuk me belly.

Guyanese maps use large letters to mark Bartica's location on the river. It is considered the capital of the forest interior. It is nevertheless a very small place. I stepped from the boat to a wooden landing along a dirt street running north-south. There was a post office that seemed to do little but display a government poster advising the symptoms of foot-and-mouth disease. Next door to it was the Bartica school, a wooden field house two stories high, long and narrow. Primary students played outside in their uniforms. The market was a rickety grouping of wooden stalls covered in tin roofs and wire, like a chicken coop built to human scale. Weary women sat behind tables piled with wan, undersized eggplants and toddlers' singlets. The dirt airstrip was at the end of the road; the presence of a red windsock, hanging sad and limp in the heat after the rain, was the only indication it was not just a field. Other than this main street there was a secondary avenue, some outlying houses, and that was most of the town.

Bartica is the only settlement of any size in the interior and an important place for the miners. It is advantageously located. It was the first settlement established when Europeans came and could have become the capital, but the crops failed in the thin soil and it never became much more than a gold camp. It currently has some pretensions toward tourism but most of the people there are still miners. The town is on maps for the sole reason that it is the trailhead to everywhere else.

I met the man who would take me the rest of the way south in a few hours. This is not a small thing. Transport is random south of Georgetown. I was lucky. I took him for a miner. He was a twenty-five-year-old East Indian trucker named Waseer Mohammed. I was waiting on the main road asking the street vendors how to get a ride south when he and another man crashed a heavy green cargo truck into a ditch behind me. The truck did not have brakes. He was not muscular or particularly imposing like many of the men who did outdoor work in the interior. But he had a sense of impatience about him when I first saw him. He looked at me with an unfriendly squint, dropped from the cab, and crossed to a wooden shack selling takeout chicken. His round face was covered in black stubble and his head was shaved nearly bald. He barked something at a second man, who had disappeared beneath the truck's fender and was investigating some mechanical mystery. Only the backs of the second man's legs were visible; when he came up for air after only a minute he was a slender Afro-Guyanese man of medium height also looking about twenty-five. He walked slowly away from the truck, wiped a dark engine fluid from his palm to his knee, and joined the driver.

"Hey, Waseer," the apparent mechanic said. He slapped at his friend. "Hey, Waseer boy."

Waseer's voice was angry for no visible reason. He barked something I did not hear at the other man. I crossed the road and waited by the cargo truck while they bought rice and chicken, packed in paper boxes to take away. They noticed me but did not say anything until they returned to the truck with the bag lunches. They ignored me.

"Mahdia?" I said.

"Yeah, boy," said Waseer. He was curt. "We go Mahdia today."

To ride with them would cost twelve U.S. dollars and they would be in Mahdia the next morning.

"Okay."

There was a cream-colored two-story building near the river, Waseer said. The truck would pull out from it in two hours.

Gold miners work in remote locations and getting supplies to them is, by local standards, a big industry. Arguably the gold mines are the less important part of the system, and the snack stands and tool vendors, prostitutes and drug dealers that support the digging are the real business of the mines. This is nothing new. A California gold rush–era maxim holds that if you want to make money on gold, sell shovels. It's usually a good scheme. (This expression survives with modern technology companies, which sometimes claim to produce the "picks and shovels" for computers and communications.)

But when the miners move on, the support systems do as

well, and quickly. Waseer's truck turned out to be one of the last making the Mahdia run down the old road.

It was a ten-minute walk down the center of the road to the cream-colored dry-goods store. Waseer, the mechanic, and a small teenager with a large bandage on one finger were in a dirt yard around the back loading supplies—hundred-pound sacks of rice, pieces of engines, barrels of diesel fuel. The truck rested heavily in the dirt. Someone had bolted a small clown horn to the flat hood and bent it off-center like a broken nose: encouraging.

Waseer and the mechanic were heaving some machinery into the truck. When I called up to them a shirtless East Indian man in his forties came from the back of the store and called from behind me. He waved me over and we went inside to pay the fare. He gouged a little extra over the deal I'd made with Waseer and counted the money twice with his thumb. He stretched and rubbed each bill between his thumb and forefinger like a tailor testing fabric and worried the bills into a wooden cash box underneath the shop counter. Outside the store a row of red and white hibiscus bounced in the river air. Outside was pleasing and elegant. Inside the store was dank and cold. There was a clammy breeze from a fan. The walls were made of crumbling concrete block and in need of repair. There were no windows and it was shadowy inside.

When the supplies were loaded we waited out a rain squall and got into the truck. The boy was named Lionel and rode in the back amid the cargo. The mechanic rode perched on the roof of the cab with his legs dangling like a mahout. I got the passenger's seat, which was a metal basket made of sharp springs. Waseer started the truck and drove eight feet before the engine complained in a high register and shut itself down. He dropped his hand beside his hip to the ignition and tried the key again.

The motor strained, coughed, gave one optimistic ker-piffle sound and fell silent. He stared at the gas pedal and gave it a few experimental squeezes.

"Dotson?"

So the mechanic's name was Dotson. His voice came back through the metal roof.

"Waseer?"

"You finish brakes?"

"They leaking bad." His heels bounced idly against the windshield.

"You fix starter?"

Dotson got tired of yelling. His heels disappeared and his hand appeared on a stanchion attached by the window. Only the front windshield still had glass; the windows in the doors were gone and open to the air. The mechanic dropped from the roof.

"No start, Dotson," Waseer said.

Dotson stood outside the window fingering the brim of his cap, a shredded flap of nylon advertising a basketball team.

"Just now," he said after a moment.

He disappeared beneath the cab and soon there were creaking, pops, and something spinning under the floor. Then several sharp bangs.

"Waseer?" Dotson said. His voice came from the same place as the noises.

Waseer twisted his wrist and turned the key beside him. The engine gave a hopeful chirp. It seemed vaguely interested.

More banging.

"Again," said the voice in the floor.

It caught on the fourth try. Waseer raced the engine. Puffs of cottony exhaust bloomed outside. Dotson staggered from under the truck looking for air.

"You fix brakes?" Waseer said.

The mechanic's face appeared at the side window. His mouth was a flat line and he looked to be losing patience. "I *saying* they leaking bad, boy."

Dotson stashed the tools and kicked himself back onto the cab roof. His legs hung over the windshield again and his heels thumped idly against the glass. Two yellow sandals flew through the window onto the floor in front of me: Dotson's shoes. In the back Lionel had yet to make a sound or was inaudible over the motor if he had.

The road led out of town past some shacks. On the edge was an open-air dance hall made of rough-milled planks. The DJ was under a broad tent roof preparing for the evening. He stacked his speakers into unsteady towers many times as tall as he was and looked busy guying them steady with tarpaulin cord. The road climbed past some fallow fields. Soon the town was hidden behind a hilltop's round cap. The road crested, and as the pavement fell away the forest was visible fifty feet below. The road dropped down the hill below the level of the canopy and we drove into the shade of the leaves. The light turned indirect and the air cooled. We were in a tunnel of young trees with narrow trunks. The trees led to more trees. The slimmest rectangle of blue sky was visible above, in a gap in the canopy caused by the presence of the trail.

Transportation over mediumish distances is a constant problem in that part of the world. The trucks were not much of a solution. Waseer said ours was rumored to have been left in Guyana by the British army on their way back from the war in the Falkland Islands. Whether it had been in the war or not was irrelevant to its condition. It was at least twenty years old and spare parts were scarce. Its condition was typical. Many of the supplies in the forest went by these old, unreliable trucks via terrible roads. Even the new dirt roads foreign companies—miners and loggers—built, which were excellent, would not be maintained after the mining or logging ended, and would not stay excellent for long in the tropical rain. This road had never been flat in the first place. The dual problems of a seventy-year-old road and a limping, twenty-year-old truck rarely allowed us to top ten miles an hour. That was when we were moving; often we weren't. The first breakdown came two hours south of Bartica.

We stopped at a wide spot in the trail with smoke pouring from the gearshift and into the windows. The cab reeked with a cancerous odor, asbestos or burning Teflon or something like that. We sat for a few minutes in the cab after Dotson had leaped again from the roof.

"What happened?" I said.

"The wheel," Waseer said.

"What about the wheel?"

"The wheel break," he said. We got out.

Dotson sat on an upturned block of wood hammering at the nub of an axle's inner workings. Something had flown apart, he said. *Bang.* It was serious. *Bang.* Lionel stood behind him passing up tools and scraping away bits of mud from the undercarriage. His scraping had the inattentive patterns of someone trying to look busy. The repairs were going nowhere. Dotson gave up.

"Waseer boy, we need some things," he said.

Waseer seemed unconcerned. He was at the truck's rear checking on a land tortoise he'd captured crossing the trail earlier in the day. We had stopped for a moment while he leaped out and snatched it from where it was trying to pull itself out of a tire track. The creature was about the size of a bowling ball. Waseer had pinned it against sacks of rice and tools in the back. When I had gotten to the back of the truck Waseer had the dismayed creature locked in the crook of his elbow and was coming back over the tailgate with it. The creature gave a frown of complaint and withdrew into its shell.

Waseer had told me some of his history before the breakdown. Like most of the men in Bartica, he and Dotson had both worked as gold miners. They had worked farther down the road, Waseer as a river diver and Dotson on land. But neither of them had lasted long. The work was hard and dangerous, and when the opportunity to move to the supply truck came they had each taken it to get out of the mines. He had been three years driving the truck, Waseer said. Dotson had been on another crew for a while and joined his more recently. Recently things had slowed down, and there was some possibility they would both be out of work eventually, Waseer had confirmed. The new road carried most of the miners to Mahdia and the areas in between seemed to have fewer miners and less need for supplies.

For now we were stranded. Waseer heaved the tortoise at Dotson. The animal pinwheeled through the air and Dotson managed a football catch. They were going to cook it for Waseer's uncle when they got back home in a few days, Waseer said. Lionel leaned on the truck following the tortoise's flight.

"I like wild meat. Turtle, wild deer," Waseer said. He liked to cook and was good at it. Dotson tossed the tortoise back and Waseer cradled it against his chest. Then he heaved it back again.

"Powas," Waseer said. It was a large flightless bird like a grouse. "Labba," a ratlike animal. He could cook anything, he said. The turtle arced over the trail spinning. The sky was darkening through the trees.

"What about the truck?" I said then.

Waseer gave an irritated glance at me and at the truck and then me again.

"We walk back. Come back with cruiser," he said. A cruiser was a small pickup.

"Walk back to Bartica?"

"Yeah."

"When?"

"Just now."

"How far is it?"

"Thirteen mile."

"Walk back thirteen miles starting now?"

"Just now," he said. Just now meant a minute or a week.

After a few minutes Waseer got bored with catch and put the tortoise back in the truck under some rice sacks and heavy tools. It made pathetic swimming motions on the floor, which was made of wooden slats. Then it would rest for a moment; then give another heave. Every few tries it moved part of a centimeter. For several minutes it kept at this grim progress.

The road was deserted. We had been stuck there well over an hour. Gold miners had traveled the road for seventy years by then, but no one had passed that evening. Dotson in a burst of optimism or boredom returned to work on the hopeless repair. He was not going to get anywhere before running out of light, though. Lionel kicked at a tree. Waseer ate some of his bag lunch. The tortoise struggled; I watched it with empathy but did not offer assistance. The forest was deserted. The day ended badly for everyone.

At last light Waseer and Dotson headed off to Bartica for help.

Dotson turned back immediately.

"You stay here. This road here," he said to Lionel and me, who were both near the back of the truck. He pointed one hand at his feet and said "here" again as if berating a bad dog. Lionel and I leaned on the tailgate.

"Yeah, Dotson," said Lionel. He said it slowly and made his disinterest plain.

He had the obligatory bearing of a teenaged boy receiving a lecture. His hands clasped and unclasped and clasped again and he bounced on the balls of his feet in his foam sandals.

"This bush here?" Dotson said. He pointed to the vegetation at the side of the trail. "You go out into it, you turn once, you turn twice." He pivoted on his heels. "You can't find your way back. Only a few paces away, you can't find your way back to the road."

Waseer was nearly gone around a curve down the trail.

"Dotson, you coming?" He waited fifty yards away.

The mechanic had his back to Waseer. Dotson gave a slight tic with the corner of one eye, the only evidence he'd heard the driver.

"If you go in there you must break off the branches as you go, and you must go with a cutlass," he said quickly a last time. He turned and chased after Waseer. Before long they were gone around the curve back to Bartica.

A cutlass is a machete. It is shaped like an old-fashioned ice-skate blade: a swoosh with an upturned tip. Everyone carries one in the Guyanese forest, perhaps as city people carry wallets.

Lionel and I watched them go. The sun was already set. The forest was becoming hard to see beyond the first few lines of trees.

So: we would be camping. This was not unusual. Most of the local mines came and went in a few months—the miners dug, took what was there, and moved on to the next patch of forest— and towns did not have time to grow up around any but the largest. For the duration of their work the miners camped near their mines and returned to a supply town like Bartica when they needed supplies or for a break. After a few months they might go all the way to Georgetown and sell their production to a currency trader or a jeweler there.

But much of the time they slept in the forest when working or in transit. So our breakdown did not mean the night passed in any unusual way; only our location was unplanned.

"Let me ask you something," Lionel said.

We were leaning on the side of the truck with our arms folded listening to the forest sounds.

"Sure."

"In America, you ever go there on *The Price Is Right*?"

I had not ever gone on *The Price Is Right*, but wouldn't rule it out, I said.

"You gotta pay a lot of money to go on that?"

"I'm not sure."

"No?"

"Well, I don't think so."

"You at least gotta put a little down payment on them things you win, yeah?"

I considered telling him the U.S. government would tax him if he appeared on the program and won a refrigerator or a new car. But I tried to think of something more useful to say. He let it drop and stood with his arms still crossed tightly over his narrow chest as if he were cold.

"You like television?" he asked after a minute.

"Sure."

"I like *Wild Discovery*," Lionel said with a little pride.

It was a nature program pirated from American cable.

"Why that?"

"Not many animals here. Better animals outside."

"Outside" was the local term for places beyond Guyana, encompassing all of the rest of the world. "I never go outside," Lionel said, which sounded absurd to me at the time, the forest leering around him.

The first evidence of sundown in the forest even before the

darkness was a steady increase in noise. During the day the primary sound is a faint crinkling like a constant drizzle. It is not actually rain; it is millions of leaves dropping continuously from the trees, bouncing off each other and settling into the floor. It's lovely. But nocturnal creatures greatly outnumber daytime animals. After nightfall the sound of leaves is subsumed beneath a far louder din of hoots and screams. Within half an hour of sundown the sound grows louder until it is something physical and close, like a passing train. By an hour after sundown everything was awake and shouting at once.

Some of the animals were visible from the trail. Bats the size of hawks massed in a cloud of black at the treetops. Columns of birds about the same size shrieked back at them with defensive, hostile noises. Very nearby something else hollered as well. I did not see the animal but only the tree shaking under its weight while something rushed from the scene through a clump of vines.

Waseer and Dotson had been gone two hours. Waseer had offered some hope they would be back before morning, but it was unlikely. Lionel and I leaned on the truck listening to the darkness for hours.

I don't know what time it was when Lionel and I decided to give up on them and go to sleep. Lionel climbed in the back and started arranging his things for the evening. I got my hammock out of my bag.

Lionel slept with the cargo on bags of rice. He offered me a spot nearby. But the back of the truck had a plastic tarp over it and was a hotbox even at night. It felt like being stuffed inside a plastic bag, then put in a stove, and needless with so much open forest. I dropped from the back of the truck, got my hammock from my bag, and tied one end to a tree off the trail. I walked a few steps into the trees to find a second place to tie up. I put down the end of the rope and turned a few times looking for a suitable tree and that was enough to lose the location of the road. A hammock is about twelve feet long end to end, so I was probably three steps from the trail. And I had a flashlight. But Dotson was right: I had to take up the end of the hammock again and follow the fabric to get back to the trail. I tied my hammock to a different tree so it hung parallel to the trail and so I could see the truck from where I hung. I kicked off my shoes, hung them from branches, and got in bed.

I had one of the wide cloth models of hammock by then; it was luxurious and warm. I pulled the extra cloth over myself to form a snug cocoon and keep off mosquitoes. I lay back and listened to the animals roaring.

After a few minutes I was so pleased with my accommodations I got out of bed and went to the truck to ask Lionel if he was sure he didn't want to tie up nearby. There was a spare hammock behind the seat in the cab, I said. I climbed up the tailgate and shined the flashlight into the back. He was still arranging the sacks in a crawl space between two piles of engine parts. A flashlight in his teeth lit his long face. The tortoise was beside him on the floor still trapped under machinery and rice. No, no, Lionel said: he was staying put for the night. But it was fine if I wanted to stay outside. As he said this his voice caught in such a way as to indicate concern, but he said nothing else. I offered a good night and lowered myself down.

"There's tigers," he finally said.

I pulled myself back up the steel tailgate. "Tigers?"

"Yeah, boy."

"Tiger" was the local catchall for jaguars and ocelots and the rest of the forest's wild cats. They used the trail to get around. But they are extraordinarily rare and attacks rarer; from what I had heard in Georgetown the most recent case of jaguar attack had actually occurred in the city. The previous month a zoo-keeper at the Georgetown Zoo had forgotten to feed one of the four cats in captivity there. By the time he opened the cage door the animal was hungry and took the first food it saw—which was the zookeeper, who died of his wounds. But of the forest there were only rumors. Comments about jaguars in the northern Amazon rang similar to stories of shark attacks or grizzly bears elsewhere: the odds of a jaguar attacking someone on any given night were roughly zero. But it was still worrisome to people who traveled the road frequently, because every once in a while it actually happened. Lionel was a bit terse on the topic and became more so the darker it got outside.

While I walked back to my hammock a sound like a maraca began in the trees. It was sharp and a new sound.

"What's that?" I asked. I yelled it through the tarp.

"Creature," he yelled back.

"What kind of creature?"

Lionel said a parrot.

"A parrot?"

"Par-*rot*," he corrected. I went back to bed. Maybe it was a parrot. It was difficult to parse the noises among the thousands clattering nearby: there was a deep ribbet that repeated twice; a *skreek, skreek* that voiced three times in succession then once sharply; there was a wet scraping like a washboard in a jug band—*rruck-uk-uk, rruck-uk-uk;* a little rarely there were honks like Canada geese. There was also a familiar tweet, thumps of heavy walking, a retching noise, and farther off broken moments of thunder that sounded like growls. Very frequently there was a sound exactly, dislocatingly similar to a modem connecting. A soprano bird call went *heh-keh-keh* and repeated without pause; there was a trembling whirr like a steel desk fan, which I poked my head out of the hammock to find was a hummingbird the size of a cat. Every few minutes came a call-and-response among what were possibly mammals, certainly less nasal than birds that featured long melodic verses and a chorus of "khak-ra-*hah*, khak-ra-*hook*." This seemed to be a celebratory noise, because a sound of great weight bashing against trees followed immediately after.

Beneath all of this was a steady pulsation: crickets. The pulse sounded less like a multitude of insects an inch long than a single, monstrous cricket of the kind in atomic-age movies, straddling the forest just above with its fluids thrumming.

At daybreak a man named Joseph arrived on foot. He was on his way up the trail. He worked at a nature resort a few miles away and claimed to have walked from Bartica that morning. He must have left earlier than Dotson and Waseer, because they were nowhere to be found yet.

"You have a breakdown," Joseph said.

He was an Amerindian man about forty standing with his arms crossed; he was barefoot, in well-kept jeans, and carried a walking stick. A wide-brimmed canvas sunhat was pushed back on his head.

"Do you have some water?"

"In there," I said. I pointed to my bag hanging on a tree.

Joseph rummaged around in the bag, found the bottle, and took a swig.

"You have any problem with the tiger?" he said.

He capped the bottle.

"What?"

"She walks this road."

"A tiger?"

"Yes, yes."

"One in particular?"

"Oh yes."

I said I had not had any problems with the tiger.

"Are you a Christian?" he said.

He leaned across the shrubs and extended a hand.

"Joseph."

I introduced myself. Joseph said a tiger had walked the road nearby and pointed toward the trail's vanishing point to the south.

"I saw her just there. Two times I have seen her. This time she begins to play."

He pantomimed a jaguar: rode his clavicles together and rotated them seductively, creeping through tall grass. His fingers extended into claws.

"She puffs up her shoulders so. Then she advances."

"When did this happen?"

Joseph stayed with the impression of a jaguar advancing on his prey.

"I back up but she still advancing," he said. "So I look for a tree, like so." He indicated with his walking stick toward the larger of the two trees holding my bag. They were only saplings eight inches around or so: far too weak to have a grown man climbing more than a few feet up their trunks.

"And I climb with my cutlass," he said. "And I start thinking of how it is I will kill her? With slashing the head?"

He pretended to hack at his own ear with the side of his hand.

"Or a slash at the legs?"

He bent at the waist and sawed the other hand viciously at his right knee.

"What happened?"

"She didn't come."

"You're lucky."

"Yes, yes." Then, again: "Are you a Christian?"

There were still a lot of missionaries in the interior. I asked where he was heading. Joseph said he was on his way to a religious camp a few miles farther up the trail. It was beside a waterfall. There were no guests there yet, but the management was hopeful, he said. There would be a ministry as well. Joseph had a job there through the church and was due for lunch. He had already come thirteen miles that morning, all the way from Bartica, he said, but had seven more to go. His legs looked strong; it seemed possible.

He took a last sip of water and huffed carelessly away into the forest with a brief blessing and a warning about the tiger.

The forest had gone quiet after sunrise and the rescue pickup was audible a long way off. Lionel had been awake for a few hours already. He waited, turning small circles in the dirt.

"Morning," I said.

"Turtle get away," Lionel said.

"Wha?"

"It get away."

"No way."

"Yeah."

"You're sure about that?"

He nodded four slow nods with his eyes fixing a point in the mud. I voiced more doubts: the truck's tail was high and made of slick steel. The tortoise would have needed to get out from under about a quarter ton of rice, make its way through a maze of cargo, then scale the wall, leap eight feet to the trail, and crawl into the forest without Lionel's hearing anything moving. It seemed more likely to be hidden in some dark corner of the supplies.

Lionel dropped to a crouch and pointed under the truck. Two tortoise-sized turds sat there.

"It get away," he said curtly.

The red pickup approached up the trail. Waseer was in the passenger seat and Dotson in the back standing up and leaning on the top of the cab. There were two other men with them—the driver and a man in the back with Dotson. A soundtrack from an Indian musical issued in thumps and bleats from the pickup's speakers. They were badly blown out. The music sounded like cardboard flapping.

Dotson did not seem to care personally about the lost tortoise. He threw a few insults at the boy in a pro forma sort of way: mostly unnecessary comments about Lionel's mother. Then he left to begin the repairs. He and one of the newcomers dug through the scrap metal in the back of the red pickup and pulled out spare parts.

Waseer was angrier. The turtle was supposed to be for his uncle, who liked to use them in soup, Waseer said. He clouted the back of Lionel's head with his palm. He had marked the shell with an *X*, carved with the cutlass for good luck. Now that luck was gone too, he said. He clouted the boy again.

"It get away in the night," Lionel said. His patience for Waseer's bullying had long waned but he was much smaller than the driver and did not have much recourse.

In two hours they had put the wheel back on, but the truck wouldn't start because of a cat in the engine.

"There's a cat," Dotson said.

Waseer was in the driver's seat turning the key to no avail.

"A cat?" he said.

The two Indian men from the cruiser crawled underneath the truck and looked as Dotson pointed. They crawled back out.

"Yes, a cat," reported the older of the two men.

Dotson told Lionel to get a stick.

Lionel took the cutlass from the passenger seat, hacked a

switch from a tree, and shinnied under the truck. He poked at re-
cesses behind the wheels at Dotson's direction. In a moment a
large, hairy black cat dropped onto the trail. It posed for a moment in a stance of feral panic, its limbs wide. Then it went
bounding away into the trees.

Everyone watched the cat gallop off.

"There she go," said one of the cruiser guys.

"There was a cat in the engine?" I said.

"Yes," the other man from the cruiser confirmed.

"Cat," said Lionel.

Dotson banged on the starter with a hammer and Waseer
turned the key.

"It dead in this bush, boy," said the other man from the
cruiser.

There was a rattle beneath us like a box of rocks. The motor
caught. The other two men headed back to Bartica.

In a few hours we felt far from anywhere. We drove through a
green tunnel of trees. A dragonfly with red stripes on its wings led
the truck from the front. Emperor butterflies a gaudy satin blue
flew in front of Dotson's perch on the roof. I climbed partway out
the side window, gave the mechanic a wave and asked how he was
doing. He returned a thumbs-up and a wide smile, but as he did
was ducking and weaving to dodge branches that tried to sweep
him off the top of the truck. It seemed best not to distract him. I
slipped back into the cab. A flock of black powas birds pulled out
in front of us. Waseer tried to run one down. They looked like
large quail; they sprinted before us in an imbecilic panic for ten or
twenty yards before the lead bird ducked them back into the underbrush. Not long after, a reptile three feet long and blue hurled
itself into the trail and turned toward the truck's grill. It stared
Waseer down. Waseer mashed at the gas pedal and steered down

the middle. There seemed to be nothing in the forest he did not consider worth trying to capture and eat. Most probably are worth it. The creature stood its ground with its scales catching the light. They changed color when the animal made slight movements, from blue to a thin red, then from red to deep green. The truck made its ten miles an hour with the pedal floored. When we were nearly upon the lizard it spun and ran away, swiveling its tiny hips. The comb on its head tilted high and gave it a startlingly haughty bearing for a lizard. It threw itself clear of the trail and stood at the edge looking back over its shoulder at us, and as we passed it flipped its tail and strolled off into the forest with an air of victory in its gait.

"You see some weird things," Waseer said. "You see some weird, weird, weird, weird things."

It was midday. Light hit the canopy and filtered through the leaves, tinting the air yellow and green. The wheels flushed a caiman, a small alligator, from a puddle; it skittered to higher ground and struck a pose with its chest puffed out. When it breathed its body rose and fell so that it appeared to do push-ups on a fallen tree.

"You know labba? Labba have very sweet meat," said Waseer, thinking about cooking again. It was a beautiful forest.

Several hours later, Dotson had taken over driving and we reached a fork in the road. The places along the road had no names, but their distance from Bartica identified them. The fork was at Forty Mile. The trail to the right headed to a mining village called Issano. Dotson knew the place.

"I work gold miner at Forty Mile," he said. "Few month. I do good, man. Lot of gold at this Forty Mile. I make four, five carats diamond too."

"Why'd you stop?" I yelled. The motor was loud through the floor with Dotson driving, something about his choice of gears.

"It hard, hard work," Dotson yelled back. "You go back-dam for months, sometimes six month you go." Back-dam meant the backcountry. "Back in the bush." He lifted a finger to indicate the passing trees. The truck swerved and he put his free hand on the wheel in a hurry.

Waseer said he had been a miner in this same forest as Dotson but the two had not worked together. He sat comfortably on the passenger seat's bare springs. All that was left of the chair was stiff wire woven in a grid. I perched in the space between the seats. This required affecting a crabbish crouch on top of the empty toolbox. Dotson's preference for the roof made sense after that.

Waseer said he had actually gone to the interior to find diamonds, which offered greater profit, but gold had proved to be steadier. Diamonds were difficult to recover; you did well when you found them but it could be weeks without a payoff. Gold was there every day. "Steady money," he said. He had made four, five U.S. dollars per day or more at times. It was a good income for the area. (He was likely exaggerating. Most miners make one to three dollars per day.) He had been a diver on a dredge boat looking for gold in the river, he said. There were fewer dredge boats since he had done the job a few years prior, though. The rivers were mostly worked out. All the good mining had moved to the land. There was still plenty of gold there. Even in Mahdia, he said. Rumors of the old mine's demise were false. There was endless gold out there.

"This is a rich country." He waved at the passing trees. "Rich trees, diamonds, gold."

"Uranium," Dotson said.

Dotson let his attention lapse and the truck fell hard into a hole filled with water, an opaque, dirty color that masked its depth. The impact made gallons of mud and water jet through rusted spots in the floor. The truck fell sickeningly sideways and seemed to think about tipping before dropping back level. The force threw Waseer out of his seat and into the door and piled me on top of him. I clambered back to the toolbox. Waseer righted himself and seemed untroubled.

"Uranium," he said. "Fish. Timber. But gold and diamonds best. You make a lot of money all at once. Make money fast. Boom!" He slapped his knuckles into his opposite palm.

"And the mercury?" I said.

"You gotta mix it up, like this," Waseer explained, as if to a child. He leaned forward in his seat, reached toward the floor and moved his hands in a kneading motion.

"It catch the gold . . . you cook it after. It poison," Waseer said. "Doesn't make you sick for years later. But few years, takes your nature."

"Takes your nature," I said.

"Can't be no good for service properly," Waseer explained. He made a few lascivious thrusts of his hips.

"Takes your nature, boy," Dotson agreed. He gave a grave tilt to his eyebrows. This was why he had quit, he said.

"One man, took his nature, I say no more. It affect your mind, make you stupid. But later, later."

"Women, they use it some for no have a baby," Waseer said.

I had heard rumors of mercury use for both contraceptive and medicinal purposes. There is an ancient but surviving tradition of drinking mercury as a spiritual curative in some Caribbean cultures. (The magical properties of quicksilver include an ability to pass from the mouth through the body virtually immediately.) But I had only met one man who claimed to have done it, in Bartica a few years prior. There was no documented evidence available in Georgetown to confirm the contraception rumors, but doctors I'd spoken with there had said the general use of mercury in the mining areas meant that many did not consider it threatening. The lack of symptoms was convincing, said Waseer. He had needed convincing himself. Minamata disease—named for Minamata, Japan, a town poisoned with mercury from factory runoff in the first half of the twentieth century—takes years to develop. Few miners notice its effects accruing, or they overlook them amid other diseases that kill or addle them first. Patrick Silva's claim in El Dorado years prior that mercury poisoning was a myth, perhaps one concocted by outsiders to run the locals off the land and gain control of the mines, was a popular notion.

Others realized the risks but considered it the cost of doing business. Waseer fell into that camp. He had not quit mining because of the health risk, he said. The work was just not worth the money. To make a steady profit required too much wheeling and dealing. The wages were low when he mined for others—he had worked for a man who owned a dredge boat. The owner kept 70 percent. For a team of six that meant splitting the remaining 30 percent of the week's gold six ways, and they might have found only a fraction of an ounce. He often made only a few dollars a week working for someone else. He had found himself selling his percentage of the gold on the black market to get by. I asked how that worked.

"You sell [the gold] to the government," he said. The Guyanese government was designated the official buyer of all gold produced by the citizens, through an office called the Gold Board. "But outsiders pay more, so you don't sell all to the government. You keep a stash, a little stash, for make a ring, a necklace." Brazilian smugglers often paid more because it was worth it to them to get the gold to take back across the border. The currency there was stronger. Venezuelans paid more also. So Waseer sold them—foreign miners—some of the gold.

The rest he used for a different scheme: he would melt it and water it down with other metal. He used a blowtorch and melted nails, tacks, pieces of telephone wire and anything else he could find, and added it to the gold. It was like adding bread crumbs to hamburger.

"You find five pennyweight, you get ten. They don't know you do it," he said. He pretended to hold a blowtorch in one hand and waved it at the other cupped like a crucible. "You got to mix it with copper and so," he said. He melted the imaginary gold.

"Yeah, yeah," Dotson said. He watched the demonstration for too long and the truck fishtailed. It was much worse than the last time. The rear wheels broke loose and the side of the truck lashed against the trees. Waseer's temple hit the door hard, and I fell forward from the toolbox into the windshield.

"Ow."

"Hey, boy," said Waseer, holding his head. The mock blowtorch demonstration ended.

"Okay. Okay."

Dotson regained control and Waseer rested back against the springs of the passenger seat with the vacant look of someone seeing stars. We were silent a minute. Waseer supervised Dotson's driving.

"Yes," said Waseer when Dotson regained proper control of the wheel and the truck had run straight for a few minutes. Dotson leaned intently over the wide steering wheel now with his eyes tight on the road.

"Miss the money," Waseer said when it seemed okay to speak again. He leaned back into the broken seat. "The money good, man. Gold. Diamonds. Lot of gold in this bush, boy."

"Africa got more gold than us," Dotson said.

"Yeah yeah. But it less pure."

"We got the purest gold. This a rich, rich country," Dotson said.

It was true, but I could not avoid thinking that for all the riches, and our destination at a literal gold mine, none of us was particularly comfortable at that moment. We were in a rusty truck on a road from 1930 the country could not afford to pave: not even with gold but with tar. The trail came out of the trees into a bright clearing. The light was enough to make us blink and wince after hours in the trees. Dotson pulled to the side and said he wanted to stop for something. He pulled over, reached under the seat for the cutlass, and leaped out the door through tufts of dead shrub. Waseer and I waited in the cab. Lionel climbed from the back and came forward looking woozy. Across the clearing we could see Dotson hacking at something with long green leaves; he returned to the cab in a moment smiling victoriously and holding a small pineapple. He split the fruit over the fender with the cutlass and passed the slices around.

Lionel wanted to be a gold miner.

"It true you can drive from America to Canada, boy?" he said. "Cross a bridge?"

"Yeah, boy, they got a bridge," Dotson said.

We had been driving through the forest for three days and come eighty miles.

"But you got to pay [to] cross the bridge?"

"Yeah, boy."

"Better go with plane," Lionel observed. "It true you can go with truck to Venezuela?"

"Truck and boat, out the Cuyuni. Go right over [to] Venezuela," Dotson said.

He named the rivers to take. "Cuyuni, Mazaruni, Pomeroon," he said. The Cuyuni was the river that led to El Dorado, Venezuela. It began near Bartica and ran a week's trip west through the jungle to the border. It was still a common route for gold miners because of the closure—the dispute meant there were no formal checkpoints and the patrols couldn't catch everyone.

Lionel digested this. It sounded promising. He was the only one of the three not to have spent time in the mines yet.

The most popular smuggler's route across the border was the Pomeroon River. It was farther north, near the coast. It was a rougher ride but more direct. But the Pomeroon route involved crossing a small cape in the open ocean at night. The waters there were unpredictable and often capsized the launches.

Amazon borders are a bit of a myth generally. It's very easy to lose track of what country you are in from moment to moment. The Amerindians in particular tend to just walk over the lines to visit relatives on the Brazilian border, and no one pays it any mind. In Georgetown a week prior a young attaché with the American embassy had told me the Pomeroon was becoming enough of a drug transshipment point that even he knew about it—the drugs were transferred to cargo ships in Georgetown and brought to the United States and Europe through the Caribbean islands. He was a young man from Illinois just out of college. There was no official effort to cut the trail yet, he'd said, but if much more cocaine went that way than what miners were using themselves, someone would eventually notice and want to do something about it. But for now the gold prospectors could move mostly unmolested across the borders so long as they stuck to smuggling only minor amounts of drugs or guns and concentrated on gold. Only the Guyanese cared about smuggling gold, because it usually was leaving Guyana; no one smuggled gold into Guyana. But Guyana did not have enough soldiers to stop it. Dotson gave a whistling exhale through his two middle teeth. "This the slackest country, man," he said. "We let anyone in, do whatever you want, no papers."

The Venezuelans were less slack.

"Men there, they shoot at you," Dotson said.

"Shoot at you, boy?" Lionel smiled; he had an unnerving habit of smiling at bad news.

"Yeah, man," said Dotson. "And they got a fast boat, faster than your boat."

"What happen when they catch you?"

"They catch you, you go to prison, boy."

Dotson borrowed a pocket knife and whittled unsuccessfully at a damp stick. I asked if he had tried working in Venezuela. He said no. He had thought about it. But it was too dangerous, he decided. The boat trip was also expensive. He thought about it sometimes though when the money wasn't coming fast enough, he said.

We were tired. Dotson more than the rest of us: he had been fixing the truck constantly. We were thirty miles from Mahdia and he was taking a rest on a decayed log. Across the trail and down a bank was a creek and a bridge made of rough planks. Trees hung over the water dropping leaves into the current. The leaves stained it the color of leather. We had slept there the previous night and it was a hot morning. Dotson excused himself down to the creek. It was a small, pretty creek overhung with vines. He squatted on some rocks along the bank, pulled his baseball cap off by the shredded brim, and wet it in the water. With his other palm he spilled more water down the front of his neck and with the bottom of his shirt scrubbed his face clean. Lionel followed after him to the water and did the same, trying to keep cool. It was too far to walk in either direction now but we were stranded all the same.

Across the trail Waseer was mashing a foot pump. Fixing flats was supposedly Dotson's job, but he had ignored Waseer when he called. The sun had been up for an hour. Light came over the treetops.

Waseer wanted out too.

"How much the plane for New York?" he said.

He had fixed the tire and we were almost there. We had started to see a few gold miners walking the road, men with machetes and bags. A few called for rides, but Waseer refused most of them. There was occasional banditry on the road and he did not want to risk anything.

"I paid seven hundred and sixty dollars," I said.

"U.S.?"

Guyanese money is also called dollars, but it's common to buy American greenbacks from street brokers for large purchases. It is necessary to specify what type of dollars you mean—American or local—when talking about money.

"Yeah. Seven-sixty U.S. Three-eighty each way."

"Maybe you can get me paper?" he said, a little too eagerly he realized as he said it. By paper he meant a visa. His face focused self-consciously away to a point in the road. "For go America," he explained. "You need a paper for work. Go America for two month."

"Two months?"

Waseer concentrated on steering through a rutted section of trail. When he had picked the way through he said, "Two months, make two, three thousand U.S. Two, three thousand U.S., [then] come back. I know many [skills] for work. I know [how to] work truck, mechanic, gas weld. Carpenter. But only, I have sponsor, for write a letter."

I told him a visa could take years. He knew that; he wasn't asking for a real visa. If it was possible to fix things even momentarily to get him onto the plane—an invitation to visit me for vacation—he could take care of the rest, he said. He would never get in touch, not even be in the same city. He'd disappear right off the tarmac. If he could avoid deportation for sixty days he could make enough to buy a house in Bartica.

I tried to explain that the penalties for immigration fraud were severe and he was asking me to take a criminal risk. He didn't say much more but kept nosing around the idea as we drove. Every few minutes he would ask some details about American geography, or pay rates for various professions, or where the good jobs were. He had already given the latter some thought. New York and Miami were closest and would be best for finding work, he said. Chicago was possible, but the cold put him off. So Miami or New York would be best. Any job there was better than a miner's or even than a trucker's wage in Guyana.

"No opportunity here," he said.

The closer we got to the gold mine the more he talked about North America as if it were a larger gold mine just out of reach.

"Only for write a letter," he said many times.

"The Road to Mahdia," Dotson said. "The terrible, terrible story of a terrible, terrible truck." He was underneath it again. We were so, so close. Lionel was thinking of walking; it would only take a day now. Waseer and Dotson were arguing. We were hopelessly out of food.

That afternoon I had told Dotson I was there to write about the gold mines and that he was going to be a character in a book if he didn't mind. He had agreed and thereafter teased Waseer every time the truck broke down. Dotson raised the jack to its limit and rolled from underneath the back. It had to go higher but he would not go under again. The jack was too unsteady in the dirt. Waseer told him to get back under. Dotson refused. He waved the tire iron from Waseer to Lionel.

"We only got one black man," Dotson said. "Only black man do this work. Coolie man no good for work." Waseer stood firm with his arms on his hips yelling at Dotson to get back to work. Dotson refused. Waseer fetched Lionel to the cab for the cutlass and pointed to a spot beneath the truck. Everyone was out of patience, but this was a bad time for short tempers. The truck was balanced on a jack the size of a fruit jar, in the middle of the forest, we were out of food, and the sun was going down.

"Dig. There," Waseer said.

Lionel dutifully shinnied beneath the truck.

"Careful, boy," Dotson said. The jack had six tons resting on a spot the size of a quarter, in soft sand, with the boy underneath.

He made chipping little scrapes with the machete.

"You do a lot of gardening work?" Waseer said. "You a gardener?" Even Dotson laughed at the joke and took it up, mangling a few verses of "The Farmer in the Dell."

> *The farmer ring the bell.*
> *The farmer ring the bell.*
> *Hi-ho the merry-O*

They were trying to calm themselves, but Lionel paused for a moment and gave Dotson a look of betrayal the mechanic did not see. Lionel was breathing hard and looked weary and unhappy. He rested on the cutlass gripped in two hands like a shovel: one palm on the handle, the other encircling the blade's unsharpened heel. A trench came into existence around the wheel, and after a moment Lionel pulled himself very fast from beneath the truck.

"It good," he said.

"Just now," said Waseer. He tugged to remove another flat. As he did the truck moaned and the jack's thin shaft snapped like a horse's ankle. The wheel was four feet high and the truck, twelve thousand pounds, crashed onto Waseer. He threw himself backward into the trees.

"Jack break, boy," Lionel said.

Dotson hurled himself behind a tire.

Waseer was all right. He crawled out of the trees and leaned against one looking himself over.

"Jack break," Lionel said again, grinning his grin of trouble.

"We're cursed," Dotson said. For the first time in three days he seemed at a loss. He excavated the jack from the sand. It was in several pieces. "Totally broke. What we going to do?" Kiskadees, yellow birds with sharp white bands like masks around their heads, dove above us and angered everyone.

Dotson sat back down on the spare, reached into his pocket, and took some pills. His malaria was coming on, he said. Waseer wasn't saying anything to anyone and just stared at the six tons of wreckage in the trail.

Dotson said the malaria came and went. He had vomited the previous night while drinking water; that was a usual sign, he said. He took his quinine. The sun was nearly down. Lionel looked at the pieces of the jack and shrugged. I felt myself becoming convinced we were going to abandon the shipment and walk all night.

"No, boy, no worries," Dotson said. He took the pieces of jack from Lionel and brought them to a spare tire dumped in the trail. Waseer came from the far side finally.

We all watched Dotson turn the jack over in his hands two or three times, then begin to reassemble it. It took about an hour and did not look like it had before when he was done, but it worked. Waseer did the jacking this time. His head was under the six tons and he raised it all the way. I am convinced that in my country Dotson would be a mechanical engineer designing jets or bridges. He saved us frequently.

A mile from Mahdia, Waseer stopped to pick up an Amerindian family returning from work in a cassava field and then we drove into town. Most of the family were small children. The rest were a few women and an elderly man who was shirtless. They all had small digging knives. The women lifted the smallest kids to Lionel in the back and then climbed over the tailgate. A girl fifteen years old and about six months pregnant climbed in the cab and rode next to Waseer. Her pregnancy did not dissuade Waseer from trying to set her up with Lionel for the night.

"Boy go back-dam," she said. The baby's father was a miner working outside town in a camp. She wasn't interested. They talked about cooking instead then.

We pulled into Mahdia on a Saturday night. To each side of the street were shacks on stilts. Anemic dogs lay on the steps. Shopkeepers leaned out their windows backlit by candles. A recording of a throaty male voice barked from a disco in what looked like the center of town. It was a few hundred yards away via a saddle in the road. Strings of Christmas lights blinking red and green lit the walls outside the disco. Prostitutes leaned on the wall outside. A few young men came toward us on bicycles. Their adult legs flapped sideways on the tiny cycles. Teenage boys strutted in clumps along the street. Everyone was in town from the mines, Waseer said. Virtually all of the men and boys in town worked in the mines a few miles from town or in related jobs: delivering fuel, fixing tools, driving trucks. There were only a few women in sight besides those by the disco.

The boys affected thuggish poses and had hidden their heads under knit ski caps despite the hot evening. The men on bikes pacing us wore plenty of gaudy, poorly made gold jewelry on each arm. It glinted in the truck's headlights.

Waseer stopped in front of a two-story concrete building. The compound had a spiked fence around it. Dotson leaped off the roof. The boys on the bikes hovered nearby and called up to Lionel asking what was in the truck and who was down from Bartica.

"Stay with the truck," Dotson said from outside the door. Waseer climbed out with him and the two men walked to a gate and called into the building.

"Hey, Nehru."

"Nehru, boy."

"Neh-*ru.*"

A guard dog came to the hurricane fence. The top of its head and part of its jaw were bald from mange and its shoulders mottled with liver spots and scars. Its exposed skull was blue. Behind it four dogs of similar size hung back avoiding the alpha brother. Their heads hung down and they regarded the road beyond the fence with trepidation and sadness. The lead dog's legs looked freshly bloodstained. Each time Waseer and Dotson called out Nehru's name it hurled itself at the fence and growled full of hatred and drooled.

Nehru came from the shop's rear room rubbing his face. He had been stirred from a nap. He was a tall man with a healthy stomach that presented itself like a full moon. He kicked the dogs aside and opened the gate.

The family we had picked up on the outskirts of town were passing the youngest children back over the truck's side and starting toward their homes in the Amerindian section south of town. The teenager who had ridden in the cab the last mile refused a hand down despite her pregnancy and corralled the youngest children. There were enough children to keep everyone occupied. Two stood with their knives beside their temples, yawning and rubbing their eyes with the heels of their palms. Some older ones chased each other in quick sprints: a game of tag. The pregnant girl chased them unsuccessfully and yelled at them to behave themselves. The kids waved their knives and ran.

Waseer climbed back in and started the engine. He eased the truck across the road and into the yard, parting the bikes and the curious miners. Nehru locked the gate behind us. The miners dispersed into clumps of two and three and moved with reluctance up the road toward the dance hall. It was a concrete building and music still pulsed from it, enveloping the entire town.

Dotson stood at the door to the shop's back room looking toward the gate.

I asked if they knew a place to stay.

"You write something about Nehru the kindly shopkeeper," Dotson said: he arranged for me to stay in the shop.

"I'll certainly do that," I said, and so have here.

Nehru laughed and waved Dotson off and called Lionel to follow him into the front of the shop. It was dark inside. The rest of us went in a side door to a gloomy kitchen and met the others carrying a plastic wash bin filled with chicken thighs. They dumped them out on a rough wooden worktable. There was not much refrigeration and he needed to cook everything.

"Go, make food," he said. Everyone was starving.

Prosperity seemed to avoid places with a lot of gold. Living conditions always grew worse the closer the actual stuff was. This caused a sense of cognitive dissonance that had begun in Georgetown, increased on the trail, and continued in Mahdia. It was not a prosperous place even by the standards of a poor, indebted country. Nehru's store was pleasant, however. The store supplied the town beside the mine with groceries and household goods. It was a spare operation. The back room's light came from a bulb hanging from a wire nailed to the concrete wall. Lionel and Dotson were by the table discussing a movie showing in a shack across the road. There was a double feature playing that night for as long as the generator kept going: the town only had electricity for a few hours at a time. Dotson said he thought the show was *Universal Soldier: The Return* (mercenary goes on revenge spree) and *Basic Instinct* (nymphomaniac serial killer falls in love). Weeks later the movie house got hold of *Anaconda*, about a man-eating snake, and *Traffic*, about cocaine smugglers. It chose shows with local resonance.

Lionel said he had already seen *Universal Soldier*.

"No," said Dotson emphatically. "This one *The Return*."

Lionel said he'd think about it. Waseer crossed the tight kitchen with a pot. He thrust it at me.

"Make American chicken. I make Guyanese chicken," he said.

"Sure." It was a friendly challenge and I got to work chopping onions.

Everyone was famished, but Waseer was particular about his cooking. Aromas of spices and vinegar rose from his work. His hand flicked for unlabeled bottles of red liquids on a moldy shelf nailed to the wall. We cooked next to each other over camp stoves attached to propane tanks.

Waseer peered sideways a little furtively at my dish. He snickered. I protested that American chicken was roasted in an oven or barbecued. Dotson and Waseer exchanged some looks.

Waseer's voice peaked into a falsetto to mimic a child's and he danced his hands around in the air.

"You make little, fancy food."

He tipped his pot and showed off his own work in progress. It looked hearty.

"Guyanese chicken." It had several colors and a thick yellow sauce, and there was a lot of it. Mine was a few bits of meat and vegetable in the bottom of a pan.

"Trade?" I suggested.

"No, boy."

The smell of the food had lifted everyone's spirits. Nehru sampled my work, and because he was a thoughtful man pronounced American chicken a charming appetizer. The dogs came to the door; Nehru excused himself to dig into a pot of rice for them. He spooned some white grains into a bowl and dumped it in three piles on the concrete outside the kitchen. They came like a school of piranhas. The evil lead dog claimed all the rice. If the other dogs tried to lick a few grains from the periphery the main dog snarled and bit at them. Its head seemed bluer in the light and hairless as a helmet.

"Is your dog sick?" I asked Nehru.

He, Dotson, and I were sitting on stacks of rice sacks and chairs arranged around a table made of scrap wood, picking at the food in my pot. Nehru said the blue was from a medicine. It was something he'd scared up to fix something wrong with the dog's head. Dotson suggested a bullet might work better. Lionel hovered behind us and grabbed for some food. He and Dotson had decided to wait for dinner and not go to the movies. They watched the dogs fight until Waseer announced dinner was ready.

"Guyanese chicken," Waseer said with far too much grandeur. He waved the pot around and we all lined up with plates from Nehru for rice and Waseer's chicken curry.

He tried some of mine from the pan.

"American chicken not as good."

"Okay, okay," I said. I'd had enough insults but was glad

Waseer let me have some of his food, which was delicious. He really was a very good cook.

Later Waseer and I strung hammocks in Nehru's workroom. It was a narrow garage behind the property. A trench ran alongside, crossed by a footbridge made of an old plank. The room smelled of rat droppings and grease. It was full of camping supplies and spare parts—engines, crates of mosquito coils, ramen noodles, moldy tarps.

Waseer seemed not to notice the stench, and I did not mind either. It had been a long trip. He climbed into his hammock and flicked off the flashlight.

"Have you tried the cassava bread?" he said in the dark. "Amerindians make it. You toast it. It's lovely."

Lovely: the word sounded strange coming from Waseer, who had mostly cursed for the prior four days.

I asked where Lionel and Dotson were. They were sleeping in the truck, he said. They were driving back in the morning if they could get the truck repaired.

"Already?"

"It's my wife's birthday," he said after a moment.

The breakdowns had kept him from getting back in time to Bartica, and he wanted to hurry.

"You marry?" he said.

"No."

"My wife's birthday and I sleeping in a garage," he said.

SAINT ELIZABETH'S
GOLD MINE

The most startling thing about St. Elizabeth's gold mine was its color. It was bright white. The hole was fifty feet down and ran to some trees on the far horizon. It was like looking down from the top of a marble stadium. The ground gave way, sucked away one of my shoes, and I fell. Now covered in mud, my pants were wet and heavy and slipped off partway when I tried to pull myself up. I sat in the heat for a moment wondering what to do until I saw the men in the bottom of the hole covered in what looked like spackle from head to toe. My only mistake had been keeping my clothes on. Most of them were nearly naked, and that seemed to make sense.

St. Elizabeth's was one of three large gold mines located in a partial ring around Mahdia. Adjacent to it was another called White Hole. The two were the largest in the area. The two gold mines were a short distance out of town, but I had not known the road to take. I had walked up the hill from Nehru's that morning to ask directions. A truck for a government agency, the Geology and Mines Commission, had been parked in front of a snack bar called Margaret's. The agency name was stenciled on the door. The driver had agreed to let me ride with him to St. Elizabeth's.

Ten minutes later we took the road from town a short way, turned into the forest and drove up a trail a few hundred yards to the edge of the hole.

Below the rim, perhaps fifty feet down, a team worked with hoses around a wooden platform sunk waist-deep in gray paste. It took several minutes to climb to the bottom and wade through a pond to the men, who turned out to be the wrong ones. A Brazilian and a much taller Guyanese said they were only there to operate a pump which drained a swamp below. The water went by pipes laid in the hole's bottom to water cannons on the other side. The cannons sprayed the water into the walls and brought down tons of mud to sift with mercury and retrieve the gold. Over *there*—the Brazilian pointed, and said to follow the hoses to the other side a few hundred yards away. I stumbled off.

Across the hole, seven men were having lunch under a tarp. Behind them was a cliff leading to a canyon. The cliff fell three stories or so to a sludgy floor where hoses and tools lay discarded in the water. A catwalk made of old planks traversed the cliff to the bottom. Everything was soaking wet despite the sun beating down. There were pipes and hoses leaking into the white sand, creating patches of quicksand. Planks laid over the ground made it possible to walk without sinking.

The wall across the canyon was undermined at the bottom, and the top was loose and unstable. The morning's work of the hoses had left a concave dent in the wall. Above the dent the top of the wall gave way every few minutes. The white sand lent it the look of an avalanche.

A man leaned on a pole holding up the tarp. He wore a red-and-green knit hat holding a lot of hair and a knit shirt, but was not wearing any pants. He said his name was Ron Thompson. He was done with lunch before the others.

I asked if I could watch him work. He was waiting for his

coworkers before heading back down, he said. But another miner named Vilbert Jerry was heading down immediately. He was a short East Indian man, muscular but smaller than Thompson. He had a particular spot he was anxious to sample and said I could come along.

Jerry walked to the edge and pointed to the area he had in mind. Part of the last landslide had just covered part of it.

"Come-come. No worries, man," he said.

Jerry gathered himself a pick and a prospector's pan, a broad steel dish, from a pile of tools near the tarp. He started down the wooden planks into the canyon. It was a steep, long drop. The planks were pushed into the mud along the side of the wall to make it possible to walk without slipping, but it was slow going. Jerry had adapted his gait to the planks. He descended heel-toe like a tightrope walker with his weight never long enough on either foot to make the plank totter. He could do this very quickly and was far below me before long.

After two switchbacks the path stopped at a wood platform built halfway down the wall. It stuck out of the canyon's side as if cantilevered. Jerry waited for me on the platform. He explained: the machinery received the pipes bringing water from the swamp, connected it to the hoses, and pumped the water at high pressure to blast the walls. When the miners had blasted enough of the wall down they reversed the machines and sucked the mud up the canyon wall, where others sifted it and poured in the mercury to get the gold.

The platform was a room-sized deck halfway to the canyon floor with a tin roof above. A ton or so of motors and heavy pipe fittings took up most of the space. It looked noticeably unstable; the platform tilted slightly downhill. It felt pregnant with gravity, like a sled. It was made of tree trunks lashed to oil drums underneath with yellow cords.

The motors weren't switched on. Jerry was only going down to do some testing. It was a large operation to run the hoses and pumps, so before committing to blasting a part of the wall some men went to the bottom with pans and took samples of different parts of the hole. If enough bits of gold showed up in a panful of mud, they would blast that area next. They tried to blast the richest part of the wall first, because their pay was a percentage of the week's take. The idea was to get the largest amount of gold out of the mud fast so the percentage amounted to more money quickly. They would blast the entire wall eventually, but by then a particular miner might be ready to go back to Georgetown, or fall ill, or want some time off. If that miner knew the richest areas had already been worked, and he had gotten paid his percentage, he would have done well and left the less rich areas for others to handle. Jerry confirmed this. We stood on the platform. If you worked for a percentage, he said, you tried to be working the day the rich spots were recovered, and not on the days the poorer deposits came through. It was just as hard work to move dirt that wasn't full of gold as it was to move dirt that was.

Ron Thompson caught up from behind, passed us, danced around the platform, and disappeared off the end. He came back into view at the bottom. There was a plank in the muddy floor of the canyon. The hoses constantly blasting against the walls had made the floor sodden and thick. It was nearly impossible to move through.

Jerry and I headed after Thompson, reached the bottom, and joined him on the plank.

"That the good gravel where the gold is," Thompson said. It was shady in the bottom. The heat was still intense, but the light was no longer directly on us. The canyon wall sheltered us. Thompson pointed at the center of the wall toward something indistinguishable; it was a section of white that looked just like the rest of the wall. I asked how he knew that was the right spot. The spots nearby had shown some good gravel and a little gold, he said. It was a guess. But he seemed satisfied and turned his attention higher up the canyon.

"And this is the overburden."

"Overburden" was anything they had to clear away to get at the gold. The big mines used the same term. It encompassed aspects of the remaining landscape that could not possibly contain gold: the fringe of plants at the pit's top, groves of trees, parts of the dirt trail along the rim, an encampment there. Anything could be considered overburden if the hole decided to expand its way. Jerry said he had his area to go sample, took his pan and pick and headed toward a crag in the sidewall. It was only a few feet away but not easy to reach. He stepped off the plank into the mud like a scuba diver off the back of a boat. He only sank to his hips at first, but even mired only half-deep it was hard to move. To the wall was only the distance across a small room but it took him nearly a minute of wading before he could get to work. He set his wide pan down and took up a pickax.

I would like to say there was something heroic to the gold prospector's swing of the heavy tool—something suggesting rail workers driving golden spikes, lumberjacks, John Henry and the steam engine—but it just wasn't the case. Jerry choked up on his pick and made winsome little raking motions. If he became too enthusiastic in his work he seemed to lose his balance. It was a little disappointing to watch him mine. Jerry was a small man by miner's standards. He did not talk much. He wore a pair of pants and nothing else. He was covered uncomfortably in white sand. It bunched in his black hair and up his bare back. In the canyon's dull shade the sand and water made him look as if he'd been dipped in guano. His hair matted into clumps. The mud at times seemed to be drowning him as he worked. He found an area where he could stand with the mud only reaching his ankles and dug faster for a few minutes. But Thompson finally told him he had collected enough soil and Jerry relented, shoveled a heaping pile into the pan with his hands—not testing exactly the area he wanted, but close enough—and started the long trudge back to the plank. He strained to keep the pan out of the mud. He held it in front of himself with two upturned hands as if carrying a birthday cake. The mud looked as heavy as wet cement. I picked up some from beside the plank—a handful of gold, Thompson tried to convince me, though it looked like a handful of muck. It was dense stuff. A handful seemed indeed to weigh a hundred pounds.

"We make this," Thompson said and indicated the muck.

Beside us was a pool of stagnant water they had made earlier. Thompson seemed satisfied with the work so far and remarked on details I would not have considered important: the puddle's color (dishwater), consistency (runny), and size (roughly a large Jacuzzi). This was a particularly promising batch, he said, and he was looking forward to pumping it out and seeing how they had done that morning. After the rest of the men finished lunch they would fire up the pumps on the raft above and suck the slurry up the canyon wall through the hoses; up top they would strain it, spill the slurry over the metal slides, and wash it down with mercury a few days later to get whatever gold was in it. Then they would dump the leftovers onto the ground to run toward the other side of the pit.

Jerry hauled himself past us with long, tired strides. He had the unsteady steps of a shipwreck survivor dragging ashore. A small landslide fell behind us where he had been working—nothing threatening, but I wondered if it was just the first where

Jerry had been digging. His pickwork seemed likely to have caused it, but Jerry said no, these things just happen when they want to. He put down his pan beside the pool of water.

Sometimes the landslides were dangerous, he said. He'd been buried a few weeks prior and nearly suffocated from the weight of the mud. But these were small slides behind us. Even in one large enough to bury him his coworkers had managed to pull him out, he said.

Thompson had been there when it happened. He agreed it was not serious.

"Two men die this time last year, but no men die recently now," he said. A wall had collapsed and buried the men.

This was impossible to verify. Reports of fatalities or injuries in the mines are almost entirely anecdotal: the government has only scarce occupational safety laws on its books and few officers to enforce them, so no accurate record exists of accidents among the thousands of men working in the interior. The circumstantial evidence was convincing, though. The land around us shifted and fell constantly in even the fifteen or twenty minutes we spent at the bottom. At the top, meanwhile, many of the men were missing fingers.

Jerry eased into the pool of water and Thompson joined him. Thompson's pan was smaller than Jerry's, not much larger than a dinner plate. He cut some mud from the bank with the disc's edge and slipped it a little beneath the surface, then flipped some water backward toward himself, like tossing noodles in a colander. He began to swirl the pan. The two men worked facing each other. Jerry crouched low in the water with his hardwon pile of mud. He dipped his pan's edge more cautiously than Thompson, who played it fast and loose. In a few minutes the mud in both pans had thinned and individual grains of gold became visible—yellow flakes suspended in what looked like sedimented tidewater. The water kept swirling out with each rotation the pan made. The gold was heavy even in small amounts, so it sank to the bottom and clung to the side of the pan. When most of the water had spilled over the edge the gold dust formed a ragged arc that fattened toward the top, like a stroke in a gesture drawing, across one side of the pan.

Jerry brushed the last bits of mud away with slow passes of the back of his hand. He showed Thompson the result. Thompson inspected the pan and shook his head in a manner that could have suggested good news or bad.

"Get a pennyweight?" I said. It was a fraction of an ounce.

"Pennyweight? No, man."

Jerry leveled the pan and climbed with care out of the pool. He stood on the far bank in a sunny patch and tilted the pan to catch the light. The yellow dust clung in the center.

"Maybe a grain," he said.

A grain of gold is not the same as a grain of sand. It's an official measurement—twenty-four grains to the pennyweight, twenty pennyweights to the ounce. The measurement determines how much money the gold is worth. An ounce of gold was worth about three hundred dollars at the time. In the end, Jerry's grain of gold was 1/480 ounce, so would have earned him sixty-two cents if he pocketed it. He was not supposed to; he was supposed to turn the gold over to the man who owned the mine and receive a percentage of the take every few weeks. For every ounce of gold he produced, nearly five hundred times what was in the pan, he earned about seven U.S. dollars. He headed back up the planks to show the others.

Thompson was not sure that part of the hole was worth working. Probably yes, they'd do it anyway, he said. He started the climb up the canyon wall.

———

I had walked back from the mine and came through the gate past the dogs. Waseer and Dotson had spent most of the day taking the vehicle apart. Pieces of it lay around the yard in an indecipherable pattern. They had salvaged the reparable parts and stripped others from a second truck—the carcass parked in front of the store. Their successful return to Bartica depended on getting the repairs finished solidly. A breakdown meant coming back to Mahdia, and then they would just have to spend weeks getting another ride and turning around again with a rescue truck.

Dotson sat against a gasoline drum on the edge of the yard. He and Lionel had just gassed up the truck with a siphon. Dotson looked spent.

"The truck working good, boy," he said. They were leaving that afternoon as hoped.

"Already?"

Yes, said Dotson. They were three days behind schedule and he wanted to go home.

Within an hour he banged on the engine, it started, and Nehru opened the gate. The feral dogs scattered from the hot exhaust. Waseer was already in the cab. He had been gruff with me that morning. He had broached the subject of a letter of invitation for the Immigration and Naturalization Service again the previous night, to get him into the country to work, and I had put him off again. I walked over to the cab and called up to him to say my goodbyes a little reluctantly.

"You stay upstairs now, not alone in the back," he said. He was visible high in the driver's seat but not looking down. He fussed with something beside him in the cab, out of sight.

"It's fine in the back," I said. It was. And it seemed presumptuous to intrude on the rooms above the shop, which were Nehru's home. Waseer nodded negatively.

"You stay in back someone murder you, or thief," he said. Thief is a verb in the patois. He was working toward a last stab at the immigration letter and finally said so. I didn't know what to say. I couldn't help him. I said that sponsoring a fraudulent visa was a serious matter. The penalties with the Immigration Service were severe. Meanwhile an honest one could take years. Waseer listened. He made his case a last time, and I couldn't argue with him. Outsiders came through infrequently, he said. Having happened to cross paths with one who might conceivably get him a visa was something he had to pursue.

The motor idled and warmed. Waseer dropped the topic. He advised staying away from the miners: they were bad men, he said. He revved the engine to work through some misfires and turned back to fiddling with something in the cab.

In the back of the truck Lionel was tying the tarp down. He called from the tailgate when I passed.

"Those nice boots."

A pillow of bloody gauze still covered his fingertip on one hand. He had cut himself on a piece of the truck a week prior and had yet to change the bandage. The wound was not healing, and still tender under the gauze, which by then had bled through. Cuts did not heal well in the tropical climate. He worked avoiding the finger. Exhaust, sulfurous black puffs, poured from underneath the truck.

"Hey boy," Lionel said. "How much for boots like that?" He meant a pair of canvas basketball sneakers I was wearing, which by then were covered in dry mud and held together with frayed laces. I told him I had paid twenty-five dollars U.S. for my shoes, and he whistled and disappeared under the canvas.

Waseer yelled that they were leaving. Dotson pulled himself to the roof. He seemed to have energy again and smiled. He was pleased to be going home. I wished them luck. He waved from the roof, Nehru opened the gate, and they pulled out of the driveway and up the hill with the teenagers on cycles chasing them back north. Two weeks later someone at the Demico in Georgetown claimed to have seen them straggling into the Cool Breeze in Bartica the following week. So they had made it back within the week. Then they would reload the truck and start back down again.

PORK KNOCKERS

That night the plumbing in Nehru's kitchen had a civilizing effect, even knowing the pipes were only shuttling rainwater off the roof to cisterns below the gutters. Nehru filled a pot from the tap and put rice to boil over one of the propane stoves. His next-door neighbor, Prance Wilkie, had come by after work. Prance had been a gold miner a few years prior but given it up for logging. Logs were more profitable and less dangerous. This seemed evident from his appearance: after spending all day with half-naked gold miners, Prance was noticeably well-dressed. His shoes—he had closed-toe shoes, a rarity in the interior—were thick leather loafers with fussy little leather straps decorating the sides. His pants were thick cotton. He'd gotten his hair clipped short after riding his bicycle back from the forest and shaved the edges of his goatee neat. He'd bought a new knit shirt recently as well, trucked down from Georgetown, and had worn it that night, and as he announced its newness he smoothed the sleeves. In the middle of the forest, he looked like a stockbroker after work on a Friday.

He was sitting in the corner of the kitchen with his leg up on an upturned bucket reading aloud from a three-day-old newspaper. The lead story said Omai Gold Mines Ltd. had given up prospecting on Eagle Mountain, a mesa just south of Mahdia, because the price of gold was low that year. Eagle Mountain was a blocky tabletop covered in cloud forest. It was visible from the front of Nehru's store.

"Good," said Prance. He dropped the paper on the table like a dirty rag.

Nehru measured out rice. Outside we could hear crickets and the night's animal noises beginning, and behind that the faint thump from the disco. The light was dim from a few candles in the small room. It bounced off the stone walls. The kitchen was hot and smelled of propane.

"You British?" Prance said.

"American," Nehru answered for me from the other side of the kitchen.

"Ah, American. You know Jimmy Swaggart?"

"I've seen him on television," I said. I sat across the table on bags of rice.

"He is a man of God," said Prance. "I think he got in trouble?"

"Who?"

"Swaggart."

"Yes, he did," I said.

"Yes, yes. Many of them do. But you? You are a Christian?" It wasn't an entirely benign inquiry: a bit presumptive, a friendly challenge.

Swaggart had a bad reputation with some Americans, I said by way of an answer.

"Politics?"

"Mm."

Prance said, "Politics, politics," a few times. Then:

"There used to be a Nazi living in Bartica and another in Kaieteur. They come here after the World War."

After a full day at the mine, and the terse goodbye from Waseer, it was comfortable to be sitting in the kitchen having a calm conversation about televangelists and history. Prance's presence had given dinner the pleasant formality of having guests to the house. (I was more of a boarder, it felt.) He was only in town for one night, having just returned from a logging and mining camp in the forest but due to head back the next day. In the meantime he had treated himself to a shower in rainwater. Logging was his latest job since giving up the mines, he'd told me earlier in the evening.

"A Nazi?" I said.

"Yes. But dead now. Never marry. The one at Kaieteur, I think he did a little pork-knocking," Prance said.

"Pork knocker" was the local term for a gold miner. Guesses as to the term's origin range from the grossly unlikely to the predictably pornographic. It likely has something to do with the salt pork the prospectors used to carry, because it did not rot in the humidity, and their tendency to knock about in the forest. The Nazi pork knocker was another guy with a pan in the trees, it appeared.

"Did you know his name?" I said.

"No one know his real name."

Nehru came from tending the rice and joined us at the table.

"He never marry here," he said. "I think the women, they won't have anything to do with him. You know, no one talk to him. He keep to himself."

The escaped Nazi had been there for forty years, they claimed.

"Forty years of torment," said Prance. He thought about that for a moment. Then: "What you think of Guyana?" he said.

It was a baiting question; Prance seemed to have something he wanted to say. He wanted to answer the question himself. I

said the country seemed like a place where people were chari-
table.

Prance tipped his head side to side, equivocating. He was a
light-skinned man with a lively face. I guessed Amerindian, but
he said no, Portuguese.

"We're . . ." he said. He cut the word off and thought a moment. "How should this be said?"

He moved his feet on the overturned plastic bucket/footrest
and pressed his palms together in a prayerful pose, pointing his
fingertips at me.

"Guyana, this place is a mess," he said.

Nehru checked on the food. It had started to smell as if it was
simmering. He came from the stove and dropped himself in a
metal folding chair, and the men waited for me to respond. I
didn't say anything, though—he was right, but it seemed wrong
to agree—so Nehru changed the subject after an uncomfortable
silence. He reached behind himself, pulled a green coconut from
a burlap sack, and seemed to consider the fruit.

"What you grow in America?" he said.

"Fruits and vegetables mostly. Where I live."

"No coconut?"

"No, I don't think so."

"No palm tree?" Prance asked. It was as if I'd told him there
were no rivers either.

"Yeah, we've got palm trees," I said. "Just no coconuts."

"If you have palm tree, there are coconuts."

"Nope. No coconuts."

Nehru winced at me and said nothing. He looked tired of
contending with an idiot. He put the coconut away.

"No, no, something is unusual then," he said, troubled.

Prance was less bothered by the agricultural details.

"I hear in America if you have gold teeth they don't hire you.

Only people from the street have gold teeth. Criminals. That true?"

"Yeah, that's probably fair to say."

"What is an example?"

I thought for a minute. "For example, if you wanted to keep working in logging, they might not care. But if you wanted to work in a bank they wouldn't like it."

Prance gave a start.

"But it's not clear-cut," I hastened to add.

"You work coconut farmer then," said Nehru, and turned a hand up, as if the solution would appear from it. Prance laughed at the idea across the table, smiled fantastically wide, and said it was decided: he and Nehru and I would all become coconut farmers together in California. The first step was to bring one of Nehru's green coconuts back to the United States and start planting them immediately, which would be my job.

"I don't know the first thing about growing coconuts," I said.

"It's easy. Just leave the husk on and put it in the ground."

I suggested maybe we become gold miners in their country instead.

"No," Nehru said. He frowned, resting his hands on the back of his head, his elbows out.

"Why not?"

Prance made an airplane with his hand, his thumb out, and flew it off his knee. It wasn't a good way to get rich.

"It all leave the country. The gold. Either the Brazilians smuggle it out or Omai takes it."

Prance shook his head slow side to side.

Nehru got up to check on dinner. He was slow-cooking the rest of the chicken from the previous night in a stewpot that teetered over the burner.

"Need a hand?"

"No, no, take some relaxation, man."

Prance was still considering our business future together in Guyana. The political problems were too great. "Burnham. He destroy this country," Prance said. Forbes Burnham was the name of a dictator who had ruled Guyana from its independence in 1966 until his death nearly twenty years later.

Nehru poked at the stew.

"Burnham did not want any white people in the country," he said. "Everyone knows white people run everything." He re-capped the pot.

"Just white people?"

Well, mostly, no outsiders. The men discussed politics.

"Look at what they've done in Barbados," Nehru said. "They have nothing. They're a tiny island. And they're a rich country." It was a common argument; in Georgetown every few days someone had made it in a letter to the *Stabroek News*. Though Guyana was the largest country in the Caribbean by far and had more natural resources than any other, it was the poorest. This was a constant frustration: that with all its riches the vacation is-lands were still better off, despite being scarcely specks in the ocean.

"They have beaches," I said.

"We have beauty here. Mahdia is in a beautiful forest."

Mahdia wasn't beautiful. It was a hole with some shacks around it, I said, and immediately regretted it.

Prance didn't seem offended but said no, Nehru and I both had it wrong: the problem was never politics. The failure was spiritual. "We are not looking to God. We forget God."

The country was a young democracy then after decades of dictatorship.

For most of its history, Mahdia had been about as it is today. The dictator, Forbes Burnham, had come to power in a period of postcolonial confusion and Cold War skullduggery and only let go with his death in 1985. It had been another seven years of confusion before all the dust settled and the country held its first free election in 1992. Even then, and during the second poll in 1997, riots and accusations of corruption shadowed the vote. A vote scheduled for 2001 was starting to bring demonstrations and new accusations already. (The vote ultimately went off without major incident.)

For most of the dictatorship the gold had sat dormant. This too was partially politics. In the 1950s a man named Cheddi Jagan had been the then colony's prime minister. He was a leading voice for independence. He was also a Marxist, and in 1953 the British government had suspended the local constitution and removed him from office in what was then a colony. Race was also significant. Jagan was an East Indian, as were most of his followers; Burnham led the Afro-Guyanese minority. The two groups coexisted uneasily, and a partnership between Jagan and Burnham shortly thereafter had been historic. Both men were politically leftists and both wanted independence from England. It was an imperfect accommodation, but the independence cause moved forward.

But independence, when it came, went badly, and the dictatorship had run the city and the country to ruin. Jagan and Burnham had gotten at each other's throats by then and also the United States had gotten involved. Jagan had attended Howard University in Washington, D.C., and dental school in Illinois at Northwestern and knew North America well. His wife was an American, Janet Rosenberg, a relative of Julius and Ethel Rosenberg and a Marxist also.

Jagan had spent the 1950s giving starkly anti-American speeches and praising Fidel Castro during the run-up to independence. By the 1960s, his activities convinced the Kennedy

White House that Guyana was becoming communism's toehold on the South American continent. If Jagan won an upcoming poll and Guyana became independent under him, went the American scenario, the Soviet Union would have an important domino tipped in the western hemisphere. Kennedy's men decided the Jagans needed to go. The extent of the concern with the little country in Washington seems peculiar now, but the evidence of that concern is fairly unambiguous. Documents from the time seem to confirm Washington's preoccupation with Jagan:

State and CIA are under the impression that a firm decision has been taken to get rid of the Jagan government.... British Guiana has 600,000 inhabitants. Jagan would no doubt be gratified to know that the American and British governments are spending more man-hours per capita on British Guiana than on any other current problem!

—MARCH 8, 1962, MEMO TO PRESIDENT JOHN KENNEDY FROM
SPECIAL ASSISTANT ARTHUR SCHLESINGER, JR.

It is unproven that CIA knows how to manipulate an election in British Guiana without a backfire.... immediate suggestion is that when you have read this, we should have a pretty searching meeting on the details of the tactical plans, in which you can cross-examine those who are really responsible for their development.

—JULY 13, 1962, MEMO FROM
NATIONAL SECURITY ADVISER McGEORGE BUNDY

Does the CIA think that they can carry out a really covert operation, i.e., an operation which, whatever suspicions Jagan might have, will leave no visible traces which he can cite before the world, whether he wins or loses, as evidence of U.S. intervention? If we lose, what then?

—SCHLESINGER IN A JULY 19, 1962, MEMO

Burnham won a pre-independence election presumed to have been rigged; this meant he, not Jagan, brokered the split from England and became the putative father of his country. Unfortunately, after independence all pretense of democracy ended almost immediately.

Burnham was popular with his followers, an impressive orator, and a good politician. But his ego got the better of him and by the seventies he had become nearly a parody of a postcolonial strongman.

He banned bread flour, declaring it a capitalist tool. He managed, by nationalizing and then mismanaging the sugar industry—long a bitter symbol of the colonial plantation system for both the Afro-Guyanese and the East Indians—to make sugar unavailable in a country where cane grew like a weed. Rationing resulted; rationing sugar in the Caribbean is a little like having to ration corn in Iowa.

He tore the national railroad out of the ground and sold it off in pieces, for no apparent reason but a mania for removing any vestiges of the colonial past in the country, even if it meant not having a good way to travel across it. Next, he banned buses.

Newspapers and television fell under state control, and nearly all imports of non-Guyanese goods were prohibited in an attempt to create total self-sufficiency. This instead created a raging black market for everything from lipstick to aspirin, and encouraged smuggling from which local officials often profited.

Guyanese journalist Ovid Abrams writes that the leader soon started calling himself Kabaka or "paramount chief" and "eschewed any notion he could be fallible," then "ostracized anyone he considered as a potential threat to his authority and purged his inner circle of anyone who was not a yes-man." Burnham's finances remain to this day murky, but he is reported to have lived extravagantly amid the increasing misery. Jagan carried on in opposition but made little headway.

By the late seventies the only time anyone outside the region even noticed the peculiar little nation or its hard-pressed citizens was in 1978, when Jim Jones's People's Temple cult, from San Francisco, California, chose Guyana's northwest forests for a utopian commune. The subsequent massacre at Jonestown resulted in the death of over nine hundred and the assassination of U.S. Representative Leo Ryan. The notoriety this brought the country remains a strange footnote to nearly any reference to it. It is not frequently mentioned in the country anymore. The only evidence of a prominent memory of the event is some ill-designed T-shirts sold on the sidewalk outside Fogerty's cafeteria in Georgetown, showing a map of Guyana and its sites of interest. They sometimes note Jonestown's location, ghoulishly, with a small skull.

However, while Burnham isolated the country, the price of gold had also shot up spectacularly from 1972, and the gold rush in nearby Brazil was under way. Burnham's anticapitalist rhetoric seemed not to interfere with his ability to start talking business with foreign mining companies. Golden Star's David Fennell, having retired from professional football the previous year (a star defensive lineman for Canada's Edmonton Eskimos, his nickname was "Doctor Death"), came to the region in 1984, according to Fennell. The Burnham government was willing to talk by then. It was broke.

Burnham continued to censor the newspapers, buy local elections, murder his adversaries, and presumably raid the treasury while he talked with Golden Star. The deal went slowly. First the company had to look into exploration to pick a site to dig, and that exploration would take a few years. But they signed a contract, and then in 1985, Burnham died unexpectedly.

He was not particularly ill at the time. But his isolation of the nation from the world had left Georgetown Public Hospital ill equipped to handle what English writer Matthew Carr, son of a Jagan friend, has noted was a perfectly curable throat infection, allowed to go septic because doctors were forbidden to import basic antibiotics. Taken that way, Burnham's death could be the most elaborate suicide by self-deprivation in history.

The country was so disenchanted with him by then that there were celebrations of his death in crumbled Georgetown. Also in the offices of several overseas mining companies: the forest would be fully open for business before long. The strong-man's political party held on for a few more years after the dictator's fall but soon succumbed to infighting, public fatigue, and pressure for elections from the rest of the world. An election in 1992 installed the by then aged Cheddi Jagan as president, to the delight of the East Indian majority. The deal for the first gold mine was already signed with Golden Star. Jagan let it go forward: the country was flat broke. The Omai mine opened the next year.

In all that time little had changed in Mahdia, Nehru said. Omai had considered digging at Mahdia, which would have effectively wiped out the town. But the local miners wanted to keep working in the soft soil there, and Golden Star didn't want a fight. So nothing had changed in forty years in Mahdia except for the pits getting slowly larger, a blast of hose at a time.

Nehru brought the pot to the table and served up a thin chicken stew.

"Some people say we better off if England comes back," he said.

"No, we look to God," Prance insisted.

Nehru ignored Prance. He spooned some stew onto a white plastic plate for me. The table was unsteady and rocked a little.

"I don't think things will get better here. Maybe if England comes back."

"You really want the English back?" It was a common, usually flip comment I'd already heard a few times in Georgetown.

"Yes. But I don't think they will." Nehru shrugged and left to check on the rice.

MONEY
AND WEALTH

The next day I went back to St. Elizabeth's to see the mines a last time. Ron Thompson and Vilbert Jerry climbed to the top of the canyon and sat on the edge with a miner named Gavin Elder. He was a tall, powerful man. When he smiled it made the corners of his eyes dip skeptically. They were done sampling dirt for the morning. Elder used a plastic bucket as a chair, sitting on its edges with his knees straight out, as if on a toilet, an impression that was hard to shake since he wore only some small red underwear. I asked how they had become miners.

Thompson had started out working on the Essequibo River at seventeen, was now thirty-two, and had worked most of the rivers and that same hole more than a few times by then.

"Fifteen years."

"Good work?"

"It hard. But I like the work. You make more money here than working for the government," he said. "Yes, man. Lot more."

"Like, in a month how much you think you make?"

"In a month? In a month maybe you make four thousand [thirty U.S. dollars]. You don't make much." A short caucus about wages ensued between him and Jerry.

"It all depend," Thompson said.

I had heard similar numbers from other miners in town. It seemed to make sense: some were pork knockers working their own small bits of the hole, but most were employees of people with larger claims who owned the heavy equipment. So they got paid percentages. Thompson, Jerry, and Elder were employees. The usual split, Thompson said (as Dotson also had), was 30 percent of the gold for the crew each week and 70 percent for the owner. The crew split the 30 percent. So in a crew of six, each man got 5 percent of the week's gold, which might be half an ounce. It worked out to a dollar or two U.S. a day, Thompson said.

With one finger he twisted a dreadlock where it fell from his hat. Gavin Elder stayed silent and gave attention to an ingrown toenail, picking at it, his toe raised in a small salute.

Once, Thompson said, working on a nearby river, he'd hit a rich vein and made 200,000 local dollars, about eleven hundred American, in only two months in the hole. The average person in Guyana made a little over seven hundred U.S. dollars for the entire year, so this was a very good haul. When he had worked himself to exhaustion he headed to the market in Georgetown with plans to sell the gold and come back. "Keep working. Come down to town, then come back this side."

But after being in Georgetown a little while, he found he couldn't return to the lucky spot. "Supposed to come back there. But we didn't get the plane." Other prospectors had heard of the spot and rushed in, taking up all the seats on the Cessnas and the boats. He couldn't find a ride back for weeks, and by then it was too late.

"How long ago was that?"

"This was six weeks ago."

"Six weeks?" He'd told the story as if it had happened ten years ago.

"Recently," he agreed. This meant he'd blown a year's wages in a month and a half. It had made sense at the time, he said, a little apologetically, because he was sure there was more gold where that came from. But easy come easy go; he "couldn't get the plane go back there," he said. Pork knockers had a reputation for blowing their gold in spectacular binges, but this was the first evidence I'd seen. After running out of money, he'd come to Mahdia on the new road, via the logging trails from Georgetown. Unlike the cargo route the new road only took a day from Stabroek market, right in the center of town. It wasn't as good as heading down from Bartica, where he had the option to head up other rivers if word of a new discovery came. But it was fast work, at least. He planned to spend two months working in the pit, then return to Georgetown to spend a month with his wife and children, then come back in again for another two months in the jungle. And then again.

Jerry told a similar story, and Gavin Elder as well: a few months in the hole, then back to town. He had a family in Georgetown, two kids, one five years old, the other a new baby, six months old.

"Do you think they'll do this job someday?" I said.

"I don't think so," Elder said. He laughed a little and his eyes dipped.

"Why not?"

He didn't say anything. Thompson interjected himself: his son was too lazy to be a gold miner. "No, no. No hard work for them." I looked over to Jerry.

"Kids will go to college," he said, emphatically.

A few minutes later, Thompson stood at the pit's edge with Elder, looking over the white expanse.

"It's wonderful," he said. "One thing, there no malaria. The trees all chopped down." It was true: for the first time in weeks there were no mosquitoes around, nothing alive at all.

"I get malaria about forty times," Thompson said. There was an odd boastfulness, a machismo, to most malaria stories I heard. He counted out his medical problems on his fingers. "Dengue fever, other fever, malaria, all them diseases." In town the miners called Mahdia "Malaria City," and were fond of saying that you wouldn't find gold if you didn't get malaria. The government required a blood test to leave Mahdia, but no one ever actually got one, because there was no one to enforce the rule. The miners had all had it enough. They talked of malaria the way others talk about a head cold.

"I get tablets. I don't get it for a little while," Thompson said. But he stopped taking them and eventually the shivers and night sweats returned. He was resigned to the disease. It was an occupational hazard: his health would last as long as it did, and then it would fail, and that was out of his control, he said.

This too was something I had heard constantly in town and the city. People boasted about their malaria history. The more times you had it the longer you had spent in the forest. I tended to be considered a curious exception for not having picked up the parasite yet.

The sun was higher in the sky and had begun to beat heavily. I asked if they had ever thought to work at Omai. The men I'd seen there had beds to sleep in, uniforms, boots, hard hats; they were trained to operate machinery and could probably turn that training into a visa without much trouble. Elder said no.

"The country is in development, you know," Elder said. "We make the contribution to the government, they can develop the country."

"What about Omai?"

"Foreign investors?"

"Yeah."

"The foreign investors come in, more jobs for people."

"Would you work for them?"

"Nah. I don't think about that."

"Plenty restrictions," said Thompson. "Omai, you know, you can't walk about the trails. Can't do anything. Small company, you got more freedom."

"Yeah. More freedom," said Elder.

"Even when your pay falls?"

Elder squinted into the sun. Yeah, the freedom was worth the low pay.

Right then wages were unusually low though, he said. In late 1999 the International Monetary Fund, which owns roughly 100 million ounces of gold, considered selling some of it off and using the money to pay the debts of countries like Guyana, what it called "Highly Indebted Poor Countries" (in the acronym-mad world of government argot, these were HIPCs). The gold mining industry, through its lobby the World Gold Council, lobbied the IMF not to do so. The sale would have driven down the price of gold. The lobbying was successful and the deal was restructured in such a way that no gold hit the world's market.

What had in part persuaded the IMF was that when it looked at its list of HIPC countries, many were gold producers. So the countries the program was designed to help would have actually suffered under the gold-for-aid plan. One of these countries was Guyana, and the miners had worried the plan would have lowered the price of gold, which would have cut Ron Thompson's wages, which were already not much more than a dollar a day. The biggest fear from the plan globally, though, was of bankrupting South Africa. It was the world's largest gold producer, and Nelson Mandela's post-Apartheid government had only just begun rebuilding the country at the time. A drop in the gold price could have doomed the South African economy just as the black population had gained access to it. Meanwhile, smaller countries faced similar questions. In Guyana, Omai accounted for about a fifth of the national income. It was a brutal paradox: some of the world's poorest governments were wildly endowed with riches and had become dependent on them. If they stopped digging, their people starved; but while they kept digging, they seemed to starve anyway.

The IMF plan was not the only concern. Many of the world's richest governments were dumping gold as well, because they no longer used it to back their currencies. Even Switzerland, a traditionally conservative country where gold holdings were concerned, planned to sell off much of its reserves. Again the gold industry lobbied and won an agreement to limit gold sales. These were all fairly arcane, if serious, debates about international finance. It was not the sort of news most people have reason to follow. But the miners in the Mahdia pits had paid attention because it affected their wages.

"Australia release some gold on the world market, about two years ago, prices fall," said Thompson. "Yeah, price drops, pay drop. Australia release some gold, prices drop. Sometimes go down, sometimes come up. Right now low, yeah."

"Flood the market," Elder said.

We talked only a short while longer: their thoughts on Vilbert's youngest daughter ("bright, beautiful"), their confusion over the toxicity of mercury ("no, silver no hurt you" ranging to "maybe, maybe"), Mahdia's terrible crime rate (denials: "we all brothers"), and then Jerry and Thompson excused themselves to the shelter of the tarp nearby and Elder stood to leave the pit. It was time to go back to work for Thompson and Jerry, and Elder was heading back to his hammock for a nap. I accompanied him out. He walked easily in long strides, treading over the surface of the mud and never sinking despite his hulking frame. When he reached the edge he turned down a path into the trees where his hammock waited.

"So what happened with Bush? Have they finished the vote in Florida yet?" he said. He was concerned because America ran the world, he said. I told him what I knew, which turned out to be nothing more than he did.

Finally I found some miners working. It was only a few minutes away down a shady path with jungle on each side. I came to a trail and followed it through a camp of hammocks and a kitchen to the edge of the hole. They were firing off the hoses below, the water ribboning into the walls. The pit was called White Hole. It was like a scene from a three-alarm fire. The men leaned their weight into the pressure to hold the stream steady. The hoses strained and curled, the water rearing into swan's necks, arcing over the sand before landing ten yards away with a splash in the wall. A miner I had not met before watched the mud and gold pooling below. He was a short East Indian man with a potbelly. It was impossible to hear him or get his name over the din of the machinery, the pump lacking any sort of muffler. The hole sounded like the world's loudest motorcycle. The miners worked in a line not far below us. The hole was not yet as deep as the one I had just left, but it would be in a few weeks. It had rained the previous night, so there was plenty of water in the swamp to use for blasting that day. Wet days let the miners work longer shifts to recover more gold faster. When the rains slowed they had less water for the hoses. I climbed down into the hole with the East Indian miner. The miner stayed ahead of me so if one of us slipped, presumably me, I wouldn't knock him into the machines below. There were no planks in the mud at White Hole and we slid most of the way down. On the bottom there were some logs to walk on, but we stayed well away from each other as we did. The pumps were beside the logs and we had to be careful to stay away from them. There were two and each was only the size of a car engine, but the flywheels and fans were exposed and spun like saw blades. In the bottom a man took a break leaning against the wall feeling the spray from a hose. It was like standing in a great ashtray, everywhere puffs of dust and debris. The mud turned to talc when it dried and clung to everything from the hoses to the miners. A pump pulled the slurry up, dumped it over the sluice, and drained the waste water onto the ground below. Beyond the rim was a wide white area like a beach, covered with a few inches of dumped swamp water.

We stayed in the bottom sitting in the mud watching the men work. The slurry ran down the walls and toward their legs, pooling in the deepest part. The day drained out and the sky turned darker over the rim of the mine. The more time passed, the more the men seemed to be faltering, straining more and more to stand in the heat, starting to lose their balance, slogging with less success through the slurry with more worry in their faces. In an hour more, most had lost their swagger and confidence. The men nearby were getting more careful as they grew tired. They held their hands in close to their torsos and kept an eye on the blasting water and the landslides. They walked a bit clearer of the machines. Still, their muscles were swollen so much from the work it was impossible to believe they were tiring, and harder to believe the medical reports back in Georgetown, the studies of AIDS and malaria and enlarged livers. They looked like circus strongmen. Then they begin to drop the hoses and call for an end to work. They had seemed, and boasted themselves to be, beyond fatigue. By late afternoon everyone climbed out of the hole and left the hoses sitting for later where they fell.

On the other end of the hole, on the opposite rim, was a

camp. It was nearing dinnertime and the men were heading that way. Multicolored lizards raced over the feet of the cooks in the field kitchens. A Brazilian was making dozens of homemade rolls, while a few more men slept nearby in hammocks. The mine drew an international sample: from Brazil, Venezuela, teenagers from difficult neighborhoods in Trinidad and the islands beyond. The shifts were changing; one group was coming in covered in mud and going to wash off in water from buckets before falling into hammocks. The other group was waking up and heading into the hole.

Down the road half a mile was a store. I was out of water. It was still hot out. I rapped on the steel cage that covered the counter and a man about fifty with long hair and shorts, his skin sun-racked so that he looked like an old potato, came to the counter. After he sold me a bottle of water he asked what I was doing there. I pulled the plastic cap off the bottle and rested at the counter. He turned out to be a man with several claims in the mines nearby. His name was Royston Stuart. I had heard the name. The word in town was that he controlled much of White Hole: he had made some of the first claims and a percentage of the production still went his way. But he had retired from managing his operations full-time and opened the dry-goods store to keep busy. He was from the coast but had come to the interior decades earlier, he said. That was when he had made his wise claims on parts of the hole; if you wanted to mine in most of White Hole you had to talk to him, and pay him for the right. Eventually he had married an Amerindian woman from the interior and settled down.

That seemed like an adventuresome thing to do, I said. Not many people from the coast thought to scratch out a business in the southern jungles.

"They lazy, man," he said. Stuart leaned on his counter and spoke through the bars. "Lazy people. They lazy . . . they don't want to come here and work, they want to go with American visa. They think that they can get a visa, when they can't get a visa. Then they backtrack! They backtrack. They go over there and they idle it up. Enough of them go there to work and idle it up. They living in Brooklyn, idling. I got a brother over there. My brother live in Brooklyn. Or maybe he gone in Queens though."

"What kind of work does he do there?"

"Well, he marry and work a deal. I don't know. It's some custodial work. He was to come with me in the bush, but he find a girl." The woman was an American, so that's why Stuart's brother had moved to New York, he said. They had met in Guyana and she had brought the brother home with her north.

"Lazy, man, they lazy," Stuart said. It frustrated him that his relatives didn't want a stake in White Hole. If true, somewhere in Brooklyn is a custodian whose brother owns a gold mine in the Amazon, and who doesn't want any part of it.

Three days later from the porch outside Nehru's spare room the mist cleared above Eagle Mountain to the southeast. Nehru was on the porch in a hammock hovering low with his belly rising and falling, loosing wet snores. Nearer by in the town's center two goats butted heads in the main square. The smack was audible as a flat echo. It was early morning and I was heading back north. I didn't want to wake Nehru and left him in the hammock. I finished packing my bag and walked out the gate past the dogs.

At the rotunda in the center of town three men stood in the dirt road holding babies, cooing over them. Beside the men was a disco called, a bit stridently, the Desert Storm, the name painted on the wall in someone's unsteady hand. It sat across from a one-story motel. Two women were visible inside getting the older children ready for school.

None of the stalls selling food were open yet. I was early. Two women leaned against the nearest stall, Margaret's snackette, waiting for it to open. The women watched the goats fight and leaned into each other whispering of romantic scandals.

Margaret's was owned by a thirtyish woman with gold teeth—Margaret—who showed up before long. She was slight and usually looked busy behind the counter. She made excellent pastry. After a few minutes she pushed the top of her stand open where it swung from undersized hinges and invited everyone in.

"Morning, white boy," she said. I had been to Margaret's for breakfast most days in Mahdia. I was often called "white boy" in Guyana, sometimes "snow-boy." I liked the frankness. Margaret asked my plans and I said I was heading back to town, meaning Georgetown. She gave me a free coffee to celebrate. She was from the coast herself, she said.

"Not Mahdia?" I'd just assumed anyone who hadn't come for the gold was from Mahdia.

She served up a pastry.

"No, no, only business." She said with some pride that the shop was hers alone. "Few women own shop. Most working up there," she said, and grimaced. She pointed to the rows of shacks past the center of town. "Or down there." She pointed toward another, less conspicuous shack, in the direction of a dark disco called the Cave. "Prostitute," she said, loud enough to be heard outside. The other two women were there talking and eating their pastry by then. They seemed not to notice Margaret. I had spoken to a few of the prostitutes in town but it was always too much of a public spectacle to learn anything interesting: everyone watched the white boy chatting up the Afro-Guyanese girl and it was a self-conscious situation for everyone. Available statistics told much of the story broadly anyway. Guyana had one of South America's fastest rates of HIV infection. Medical reports suggested the disease spread south when gold prospectors, their girlfriends, and prostitutes carried the virus back and forth between the frontier towns and the cities. Many of the younger women in town were runaways from the coast. Efforts to provide general health care, blood tests, and preventive programs in mining areas were laughable, hampered by the remoteness of the sites.

It seemed like a bad place to start a business, I said. Margaret shook a finger at me, no, no she said. It was cheaper to start up in Mahdia than in the capital, and often people asked for credit in Georgetown but not in Mahdia. She could usually count on the miners for payment in cash. And the miners liked to spend: she loved a good gold rush. True, it could be a rough town at times, but the men were not bad to her, she said, though she had friends there who looked out for her "in certain circumstances." Those kinds of circumstances were rare, though—miners were good men, with families, earning money a little at a time, but always with the possibility of a big nugget coming up in the trap and buying their families out of Mahdia, perhaps even out of Guyana, she said.

Another of the women from outside came in and Margaret poured her some coffee.

"Can you tell me someone who struck it rich and left town?" I said.

Margaret thought about it. No, she said, she had not heard of that actually happening recently. The shopkeepers did much better than the miners. Mostly the men just got tired or fell weak with malaria. But a shopkeeper could do well for a few years, prove the business had value, sell it, and live well. She was happy where she was.

"This is where I decided to establish business," she said. "This my home now. Temporary. Maybe. I don't know."

Outside the town was waking up. There were dozens of children arriving on the street. Most of the miners had families up in Georgetown, but there was a permanent population in Mahdia as well. Some kids were from Amerindian families and others were of people who ran stores for the miners. Some were the children of village women and miners who were otherwise married elsewhere. Some were just families that lived nearby farming cassava.

As in every town the school was the best building by far, cared for and built with attention to the details, the joints in the windows and the doorframe just so, always with fresh paint and new wood shutters. Several miners were there seeing their children to class before walking back out to the pits. The men carried their things in buckets and the children carried their supplies in dainty plaid nylon bags or bright backpacks. At the schoolhouse the children gathering in groups with uniforms coded by color for their age, the girls in deep red or yellow school dresses, the oldest in orange, the youngest boys in khaki knickers. The miners and some of the women stopped for a moment and watched their kids play on the grass in front of the school.

It is tempting to believe the men who worked in the pits and women who worked nearby spoke cynically when they claimed, as they often did, that they did so for the sake of their children. Vilbert Jerry said his kids, who lived elsewhere, would go to college. But for kids in Mahdia that was too pat an answer and the mining town's demands too sinister to ignore. The claim seemed absurd on its face: a frontier town where unknown assailants poured kerosene on men and set them alight while they slept in a hammock; where deadly plagues were common; where the water ran poisoned with heavy metal—this was hardly an ideal place to raise a child, and many families were there by choice. There were ways back to the coast if one wanted them, and so many of the miners returned to families there.

And yet, I came to be convinced. Though the children emerged from lean-tos and homes made of raw planks, many seemed exactly what the miners said they were: cared for, attended to. Their uniforms were cleaned and creased and each carried the expensive supplies and tools of primary school; they all had colored pencils in special pockets designed for that purpose, closed-toe shoes with fancy buckles that shone proudly. A few hugged dolls tenaciously; the boys carried cricket bats. In a town of sick men earning a dollar or two a day this procession of a few dozen perfect children seemed impossible. Only one boy, who looked about six, lacked for anything, but that lack seemed more a matter of personal style than deprivation. He strode with great purpose in his uniform carrying only a bundle of scallions. He clutched them tightly in a determined fist. The other children seemed to understand the seriousness of his scallion-related mission and I didn't ask.

Outside the school the mothers and aunts were already in their platform shoes and miniskirts and halter tops, even at eight in the morning. They fussed and put up the children's hair with strips of yarn in hopeful colors that matched the school dresses. The children marched into the schoolhouse for the day and soon enough were audible singing and counting. The parents headed off to work.

A Guyanese businessman with whom I had
chatted in Paramaribo had told me of the long
queues that formed each day outside the
British, American and Canadian embassies.
Students, doctors, nurses, teachers, technicians,
whores—they were all trying to run away.
I was gazing at social collapse; I was
glad I was only in transit.

– FROM **BLACK AND WHITE**, BY SHIVA NAIPAUL

PILES AND PILES
OF JEWELRY

The most direct way back from the forest is a van that leaves when it is full. It's not comfortable but it's fast. I boarded with some gold prospectors and a few women who would not say much or even look at their fellow passengers. By the time we were all loaded we were sitting at various times on, over, or beneath each other on four bench seats. The bus left later than expected. A young woman had delayed it to complete personal errands. She was a pain and a bore to everyone. She wore enough gold bracelets to cover half her forearm. More necklaces hung thickly and tangled around her neck, coils upon coils of gold. Her mouth was a row of gold-capped teeth framed by two lips painted a bloody shade of red. Her departure was a minor event in town. She took a gift from a boyfriend as she boarded. It was a box with a purple bow on top. She beamed with her gold teeth glinting. Once she was aboard and settled her prodigious self near the door, another boyfriend came. He had a gift box also and gave it over to her through the window.

"Baby!" she said.

Her voice squealed and everyone in the bus shuddered, though there was really no room available for shuddering.

The driver tried to leave again but the gilded woman yelled for him to stop once more. A new man came and passed her a bottle of soft drink through the window. After him another muscular man, holding an infant, came for a goodbye kiss. This man was less indulgent. He was tall and wore dreadlocks. Rather than give a gift, he whispered to her through the window something that made her screw up her face and turn away from him. We pulled out.

At the first mining camp down the road—dropping off two men and picking up three—they all knew her; on the banks of the Essequibo, a man driving a small ferry winked at her. She seemed to know him and waved back with excitement.

The driver negotiated the logging road for hours, curling through the forest, following a wildly indirect path, until sometime before nightfall the road widened and emerged from the trees.

In another hour the van reached Georgetown's central bazaar. The air tasted of exhaust. Eager men took turns trying to force the arriving passengers into alleyways. I stepped over the wide canals full of velvety sludge and green tadpoles.

Walking, it was possible to still see traces of the old city. The capital had been one of the most beautiful in the Caribbean. The ditches that were now flooded had been grassy promenades. Most of the buildings had been wood palaces. The national cathedral, in the center of a traffic roundabout downtown, was a grand white structure said to be the largest of its type in the world. The presidential mansion was a vast airy clapboard building surrounded by palms and carefully tended grounds.

But only the public buildings could be maintained like that. Downtown were avenue after avenue lined with rows of similar mansions falling into disrepair. Some had collapsed far enough to be condemned and only squatters stayed in them. There was still detail in the shutters and the knurled posts, but the structures sagged and many did not have paint anymore, so were the color of sodden wood and were rotting. The newer parts of the city were made of stone instead of wood. Professionals lived in concrete houses on the outskirts. The shopping districts were lines of square stalls in painted concrete. These were the busiest places—the new, slapped-together street markets. Hawkers lined the sidewalks and filled them, so that it was difficult to walk without fear of stepping into the sewer canals.

Nothing worked. Sewage flooded the roads. Everywhere in Georgetown were remnants of the failing Dutch canal system. Georgetown sat below sea level behind a dike. This meant rain had to flow uphill to drain from the roads. Sluice gates—great wooden guillotines that hung every few miles along the edge of the ocean—had to open and close in careful sync with the rain and the tides. The gates never worked as they should. To cross a road often required leaping a roiling gap. Concrete bridges placed across the canals were cracked and untrustworthy. Navigating the sidewalks took care. Every few blocks the smaller roadside trenches emptied into broader canals where the poor bathed, a grid of malodorous moats. Washington, D.C., is also a drained swamp, I reminded myself. But Georgetown seemed to need re-draining.

Much of the country was under evacuation. The entire nation was not impoverished, but those with means tended to use those means to leave. Anyone with money or skills or education found ways to better places, slowed only by the outside world's willingness to provide visas. Later, when I spoke to a few local treasury ministry officials, they would whisper that the few hundred thousand people left in the country were living on dollars wired from outside. Without that help, nothing got done, and as it was the country was treading water. Even when some improvement came—a new road, some garbage moved away, crippled stabs at progress—it was often so incremental as to be nearly imperceptible. "I'd settle for some fuckin' sidewalks," an American foreign aid official in Georgetown had growled in an interview before I'd headed to Mahdia. I had asked him to suggest an example of the progress the finance ministry reported. There were said to be rising economic indicators and a steady currency, if still a falling population. The aid official couldn't think of anything. When I mentioned the professionals in suits I saw in the lunchrooms downtown, he dismissed them, and began quoting prostitution and suicide statistics from the rest of the city at me.

A week after returning to Georgetown I rode in the front seat of a taxi to try to find out where the money from the gold had all gone. I took the taxi to a government building near the seawall. I was there to see a man named Satkumar Hemraj. At the time Hemraj was general manager of the Gold Board, the agency through which the government theoretically purchased all the gold the small miners found in the forest. The foreign mines were not his responsibility. The bosses at Mahdia or the smaller teams working on the rivers or in the trees were supposed to sell their production to the Gold Board, and the board would pay them that day's price for the gold. I was going to see him—and I was in Georgetown at all—to try to make some sense of the conditions in the interior and the capital. A country with so much gold was nevertheless very poor. Both the government and many citizens were not able to afford what they needed day to day. Even with the taxes and royalties from Omai the government could not provide most basic services. And even with the option of going a little bit south of town, digging for a month, and returning almost assuredly with a handful of gold, many people could not provide for themselves either. The obvious conclusion seemed to be that gold was not the way the country was going to improve its situation. If that was so, Hemraj was in a position to confirm it.

The taxi was a Japanese car badly in need of repairs. The thing was in tatters, the driver's seat held together with tape and bent aluminum straps twisted together. The engine whined and rattled against the hood. The driver was a young man who sped through the intersections as if he had somewhere important to go, though he said I would likely be his only fare for the day. On the far side of the seawall a half-dozen fishing skiffs lay canted in the muck with their oars shipped, waiting out low tide. The taxi swung through a wide roundabout and passed the dictator Burnham's former home. It was a grand wooden mansion. The resources ministry was just past. It was a campus of low wooden field houses so much like a suburban junior high school in America I half expected to see rows of metal lockers and bright lunch benches when we pulled up. The cab stopped at the gate, beside a wall topped with spiked wire. Outside the wind from the sea had kicked up and another squall seemed imminent.

The cab pulled to the gate and scattered some goats grazing outside. Two security guards, one fat, one thin, in stained brown uniforms and plastic baseball caps played dominos in a narrow sentry house. The thin one penciled something on a clipboard. He was an older man with a white, stubbly beard. He told me to wait outside the gate on the road and went back to his domino game. I exited toward the goats grazing by one of the sewer canals. A half hour passed. It rained and I stood under my umbrella watching the goats. Finally the larger sentry waved me over and the smaller fellow led the way across the compound and up an outdoor stairway. The Gold Board office was a door at the end of a hallway with ratty carpet. An air conditioner and a naked fluorescent made the waiting room feel like a morgue. An assistant at a low desk said Hemraj was at lunch but would be back soon. He offered some copies of the *Stabroek News*.

CAIMAN CHOMPS CHUNK OFF CHILD'S ARM: . . . Stating that it all happened within about two to three minutes, she said she was unable to see the size of the caiman because it was dark.

NEIGHBORS HELP NAB MANGO THIEF: Thirty-two-year-old Fazil Khan confessed.

NO PLAN FOR INSANE VAGRANTS: Some of these wanderers are of unsound mind and they carry weapons with them. I recall that a young lady was bludgeoned to death by an insane man plying the public road in the Crabwood Creek area. What accentuates my concern is the nude presence of an insane woman in front of the Springlands police station. Yours faithfully.

SPOON THIEF SENTENCED TO THREE MONTHS: Edwards, 41, stole 12 spoons from Hazrat Alli's General Store. It was his first offense and said it was triggered by a domestic issue.

Hemraj was a short, bald man with a girthy look to him, in a gray suit and conservative brown tie, who dashed through the anteroom with a bag of leftovers. The secretary waved me inside after a moment. Walking through the door was like stepping into a diorama of what life was like elsewhere. There was a computer on one side of an L-shaped desk and a television financial report streaming into the monitor. Stock ticker symbols skittered along the bottom of the screen like roaches.

Hemraj put his doggy bag away in a top drawer and gave his attention to the stock report. His desk was wide and heavy.

He offered a chair but the video screen kept distracting him.

After a moment he folded his hands on his desk blotter. There was a generous gold ring on one finger. He apologized for lunch running late and asked what questions he could answer.

I wanted to know why the plumbing did not work in Georgetown; they could have made new pipes out of gold. But I asked how long he'd held his job.

He shrugged.

"I hope not much longer."

I waited.

"Personally I am more free-enterprise-trained. I don't think government should be involved in commerce."

He checked the stock ticker again.

"We had a dictator who ruined the country, [and] we had some currency problems, so the government sought to use gold, which at the time, less now, was money. . . . Last year, we bought one hundred and ten ounces." He tilted his head to one side, unimpressed, then back straight.

I did the math. "Thirty million dollars?"

"Yes," he said. "We are a poor country, and as you know, we have this gold barely holding its value." He ran through some discouraging statistics. Eight, nine, maybe ten thousand Guyanese prospectors worked in the forest so far as his office was aware, but only seven hundred did business with him. That wasn't counting the Brazilians and the Venezuelans there illegally. Most prospectors avoided him and sold their gold on the street. So most of the gold was leaving the country, either by smuggling or as black market jewelry. By his reckoning a quarter million ounces of gold went outside the country with smugglers, over to Venezuela, out to Brazil, across to the islands, or to jewelers directly, and the country never saw a penny from it.

"Some of it, we lose in fuel buys, supplies, this we know. The miners use it as a currency."

Shrug.

"We can't do much about that. But the jewelry is the problem. Pork knockers sell to the jewelers directly, or they bring it to Barbados. Ninety-nine percent of the jewelry [in Georgetown] is illegal."

He leaned back in his office chair. It squeaked like a toy, the back broken. It reclined too far. A look of alarm came over his face before he reached an equilibrium in the chair. He relaxed. He threw up a hand.

"You go to Temerhi [the airport], you can hit Forty-seventh Street in twenty-four hours."

Forty-seventh Street is New York City's jewelry district. Gold fetched American dollars there. Over his shoulder the afternoon business report kept playing. Hemraj obviously still wished to be watching it. The reporter on the computer monitor said something about cellular phones; a picture of a phone hovered behind her. Hemraj and I watched the news together for a moment. The cell phone report ended and he said he was impressed.

"We are seeing a more stable world," he said. "The G-8 countries [the world's largest industrialized nations and Russia] are doing a fantastic job creating stability." Gold had not mattered for decades; only currencies and government bonds were relevant, he said. Perception had not yet caught up to reality, that was all it was. People did not realize gold was no longer valuable. But they would, and Guyana would be doomed to rely on its riches no matter how much they had in the forest. "I believe we will see in twenty years, gold will end up like silver. Silver was money once too."

This was a common argument. By the late 1990s the price of gold had been steadily decreasing for twenty years. At the time it was worth less than three hundred dollars for one ounce. This was one of the lowest prices in history when adjusted for inflation. If the decline continued, the essential nature of gold would change for the first time in five thousand years. Rather than money, it would be a commodity exchangeable for money. This was a subtle but important distinction. If gold became a commodity, like hay or soybeans, then Guyana wasn't sitting on a pile of cash anymore. It was sitting on a yellow metal that might or might not be worth something in the future.

"So what will you do?"

"Nothing, there is nothing you can do. Even Mr. Alan Greenspan. There is nothing even he could do." Hemraj laughed, a pitiful sort of laugh deep in his generous stomach, and rocked in his chair some more. He dropped names of other famous international bankers he respected and said again that there was nothing even powerful men and women in Geneva and New York and Tokyo could do to make Guyana's treasure valuable.

"It's the future. You cannot fight that. I think they are right, those that say gold will hold forty, fifty percent of its value. There are people, technical people, who'll say thirty percent."

"One hundred dollars for an ounce of gold?"

"Yes."

"You'll go broke."

But of course they were already broke. Hemraj flipped a hand, dismissive, as if tossing away a wrapper. Even Omai would be worthless in the end. The air conditioner hummed and rattled in its mount. The director's office was more aggressively climate-controlled than even the anteroom had been. The business report was still on the computer monitor. I wondered how he managed such good video reception in a country with such terrible phone lines.

I asked about Omai. It flew its gold directly to North America, up the Essequibo, and over the Gold Board manager's head.

Did this benefit the country as much as the company, or was it mercantilism? Hemraj thought about mercantilism for a moment. He tented his fingers together. The cuffs of his dress shirt were starched and bone white around his thick wrists.

"You have to take the deal. You must. If you don't take it, okay, but in the meantime you'd have been waiting with a bowl."

He leaned across the desk blotter and cupped his hands like a bowl. He shook them to show it empty.

"We benefited a lot. We learned a lot from Omai. But it would have been much, much more. It provided a global presence. It put us on the map. But when you have a major find, and you become the center of attention, you have to capitalize on it. And we failed."

"How so?"

He wagged a finger, an elbow on his desk. "It isn't the gold only. It was about the deals," he said. He meant exploration. Governments often charge mining companies millions of dollars just for the right to come into the country and look around for gold. And there had been plenty of possible customers after the big find at Omai, he said. Americans, Canadians, South Africans. This was at the beginning of the gold rush when there were dozens of mining companies looking for gold—foreign companies with good credit and backing from their government trade agencies, venture capitalists buying in, and stock offerings. "Whether we find another Omai or not, you get geological surveys. You bring in exploration money even if you don't find anything." But they hadn't done it. "We would have had dozens of foreign exploration companies here. Peru attracted two billion in exploration. But we did not pursue it."

"Why not?"

The politics had been too muddled. Burnham had died, his

successor was barely holding on to power. They had missed their chance squabbling, he said, and now the moment was passed.

"It's over," he said. "As soon as the gold price fell, no one came to explore. We had a window that was one or two decades. It's like a black hole. You have to do it now, because in twenty years, it will be in the ground and no one will want it."

The business report was over. He had missed that too. He offered a handshake and directed the way from his chilly corner of the compound back into the heat. The thin guard snapped the plastic credential back and pointed toward the corner. But no buses or cabs passed. The walk back downtown was not long. A few of the goats fell in with me as we went. They bayed for snacks and I tossed them crackers from a box in my bag. They were companionable creatures.

Two months later, newspaper reports alleged Hemraj's involvement in a scheme to steal gold from the Gold Board. The prime minister granted Hemraj his wish soon after and removed the general manager from his office, ending the poor man's government job.

The miners who were supposed to be selling their gold to Hemraj were instead selling it to jewelers on the street, who made cheap rings and necklaces out of it and sold it off to locals. There were plenty of customers. This was not always vanity, though of course it was sometimes. In a country with plenty of gold that is nevertheless poor, buying jewelry is often one of the few reliable ways to make an investment to better one's lot. In Georgetown, for example, bank accounts are hard to get for many and deposits shakily insured, and mechanisms like pensions all but unheard of. So a small-scale gold standard applies in many cases. A gold ring made of watered-down gold alloy costs as little as a few dollars. By comparison, the minimum balance for a bank account was fifty, sometimes a hundred U.S. dollars at the country's few banks. This is a lot of money when the average person earns seven hundred dollars a year. A gold ring is a more accessible kind of savings account. It holds its value better than a small country's currency. No bankers are necessary to do business, just a local gold supply, which the forest and the miners provide. Even when the ring isn't bought strictly as an investment, over time it still acts like one.

The metal's popularity among Guyanese women had an additional dimension. A woman can sell her gold, providing her husband has not appropriated it, to a jeweler or a money changer for whatever its weight brings that day. This provides a degree of autonomy. There was no substitute for cheap gold jewelry in this role. Gemstones like diamonds are nearly impossible to sell for what they were originally worth, and rarely increase in value. Gold is not so subjective; the money changer just puts it on the scale. A culture of adornment thrives. The women who sold potato chips from wooden trays on the side of the road for ten cents a bag, near my apartment, often wore elegant gold ropes as they did so. They earned barely a dollar a day, but their teeth were gold-plated. Georgetown often looked like El Dorado, the citizens strolling the capital with thick gold cuffs on their arms. Jewelry shops were as common in parts of Georgetown as doughnut shops are in North America. But it was a city of gilded paupers.

Men depended differently on gold. Many wore as much as the women did. But for those without professional skills or a job in the city, the dependency was about employment, not savings. As many as thirty thousand men worked just over the line in Venezuela, many of them Guyanese there illegally. To the south, Brazil had by some estimates a hundred thousand miners still working. These men were all in addition to the eight or ten thousand Guyanese in the country's own forests. In Stabroek Market, men with three rings on each finger and bracelets all the way up their arms strolled the aisles. In the back I looked over the rings in the case and drew a small crowd. The expensive ones cost sixty dollars U.S. or so. In the aisle behind me a seller held out his jeweled arm and asked me to make him an offer. He was a man in his late twenties with bracelets pushed up to each elbow and rings on all his fingers. They were not to my liking. They had been made very badly. Each looked like a pat of butter mixed with some aluminum foil. I asked to photograph his rings instead of buying them and he looked understandably skeptical. I explained why I wanted the picture.

"What you pay?" he said. Two friends flanking him encouraged the bargaining.

"Nothing."

"Nothing, boy?"

"No."

"So this how it works? You take a picture, put it in a book, sell this book, and don't got to pay me nothing?"

"That's the convention."

"Hah."

"So, no?"

"All right. Take your picture, boy." He took a seat on a stool behind him and made two fists.

More formal gold shops lay at the end of the aisle, a row of glass cases lit with naked bulbs. Some were pawn shops labeled jewelry shops. The light glinted off the jewelry and bounced around the glass cases. The cases had a jaundiced glow. Behind them the sellers stood, and the light hit them too. Their gold teeth would catch the light's glint if the seller smiled. There were dozens of gold sellers in the market. Each had a few showcases, each showcase a few feet long. Around every case was a cage made of rebar painted white with hurried, streaky strokes. The jewelry was garish and bulky. The rings all had cameos done in an unsteady hand or with a bad mold. Most were obvious icons: a shoe company logo, a tracing of Africa, a pair of dice, a heart, two hearts, a cracked heart, a Star of David, an outline of Guyana, the Guyanese flag, the American flag, a cricket bat and ball in miniature, the letters NY superimposed as on a New York Yankees cap, the crest of the Manchester United soccer team, a pistol, an eagle with arrows in its claws, a pair of lips.

Gold is soft. This is one of the reasons it is ideal for jewelry. It is easy to bend and mold. This is also the reason there is a lot of cheap jewelry in the world. Almost anyone can make a gold ring with a blowtorch, some gold, and a little practice.

Gold was not, however, always the standard. It has been less valuable in places where it is more plentiful. In roughly the tenth century B.C., copper was coveted in sub-Saharan Africa, and iron was highly sought in Greece. Aristocrats in the 1700s thought it the height of nobility to eat off aluminum plates. Pearls were universally desired in most cultures. At the turn of the first millennium A.D., Roman citizens wore bone and grass rings; senators and soldiers wore iron. In ancient China, rings were often jade; in Syria it was agate.

Gold's rise to prominence almost certainly has much to do with its scarcity in Europe. Among Europeans, Roman diplomats and ambassadors were among the first to wear gold. When eventually Rome lessened strictures on adornment, soldiers and eventually all freeborn males wore gold rings, previously the symbol of high office. Servants who won their freedom were permitted to wear silver rings, and those that hadn't wore iron, which became the mark of a slave. Roman gods had no shortage of gold in their depictions: golden chariots, slippers, lyres, bows.

It was a sign of power. But there is evidence that Roman society also had its own versions of tacky guys in gold necklaces. "Criticism of gold through to the Middle Ages was to focus on the same question of the inappropriate use, or overuse, of gold," writes historian Dominic James.

The origin of women's use of gold is a surprisingly shadowy topic, and the history of wedding rings even sketchier. Gold rings for betrothal are not strictly a western convention, though the exact manner of their use has varied a lot over time. It's fair to say that no one really knows with any definitiveness where or when the link between gold and marriage started. Art historians have made a pastime of looking at what finger a wedding ring is on in ancient portraits, and debating whether these rings are wedding bands at all. There is some evidence ancient Romans married each other by exchanging rings of some sort, but the gold ring surfaces in a western marriage ceremony clearly only a thousand years later, in fifteenth-century Greece. If you had happened to be at a wedding presided over by the archbishop of Thessalonica in 1453 you would have seen two rings on the altar, one gold and one iron. The bride and groom would exchange rings three times in the ceremony, for the Christian Trinity, and would end up with the man holding the gold ring and the woman the iron.

The central place gold rings have come to hold in wedding ceremonies centuries later has been good news for gold miners. In much of the world you just can't get married if you don't buy their product. In India the ring is supplemented with bracelets and chains and necklaces; Indian brides wear as much gold as possible. But the gold is often a low purity—there is less gold in each piece of jewelry. Other kinds of marriage ceremonies may not culminate in the exchange of rings at all, or have other equally important symbolic moments. Some Hindus traditionally tie a knot in a piece of fabric. Many cultures decorate the brides in henna. The Taureg people in the Sahara slaughter a camel. But exchanging a gold ring is the central moment in hundreds of millions of weddings, and gold jewelry is so common now it is difficult to recall it was once a sign of aristocracy. The world's largest consumer of gold today is India, followed by the United States: respectively the world's largest democracy and its wealthiest.

This is currently changing, however. In America, at the end of the twentieth century something odd happened. Jewelry remained wildly popular, but gold was no longer the most coveted kind. Americans had money to spend on themselves during boom years at the end of the century. In 1999, with the American economy roaring and American consumption of virtually all goods nearly overheating (a friend once noted the sight of "toast tongs" for sale in an American shop as an early sign of impending recession; he was right), sales of gold jewelry rose a respectable 10 percent. But jewelry made from platinum, a more valuable metal, rose 700 percent. Brands and logos were also becoming more important than materials to Americans. If you bought a gold bracelet in a souk in Kuwait in 1999, the jeweler still put it on the scale and weighed it to determine the price; by comparison, if you bought the same bracelet in the United States, the jeweler looked inside the band for the brand name and set the price by the reputation of the producer. This was not a matter of a brand standing for quality. Gold produced at large mines tended to be exported to a few widely known mints that refined it and certified its purity; the Canadian Mint was the certifier for most Guyanese gold. A jewelry producer would then buy its gold from one of the mints or a middleman. Most jewelers got their gold from the same place and used the same purity of gold. (There are, of course, plenty of shady gold dealers in the world, but for the most part jewelers claiming eighteen-karat gold in any legitimate business really are selling objects with eighteen parts of gold in them for every twenty-four of metal.)

So in the United States, the brand on a piece of jewelry increased the price strictly on the basis of fashionable reputation. In the past the maker's name at least guaranteed the metal's purity. Today the word "Cartier" or "Tiffany" is itself the purity: the mark can have more to do with a piece of gold jewelry's value than the gold itself does. A lot more. Two ounces of gold contained in perfectly good but unbranded necklaces priced by their weight, found in a middle-class shopping mall in Malaysia or India, costs roughly eight hundred dollars. That's two ounces of gold at three hundred dollars or so an ounce, plus a markup for the jeweler. A single necklace containing less gold, but made by Cartier and sold in a boutique, easily costs ten times more. Brands have had this sort of influence for a long time with most consumer goods. But the word "gold" is arguably the world's oldest brand. The influence of a random manufacturer's name on the metal's price suggests gold doesn't mean what it once did. "Good as gold" is a fairly meaningless expression today.

But if the cost of a bracelet is in the brand and not the weight, then the brand can leave the metal behind and float wherever it wants. This happened. By 2000, handbags and cocktail dresses easily sold for as much as gold necklaces and offered more cachet.

For miners, there was no easy response. They were traditionally loath to associate their elegant final product, costume jewelry, with their less elegant business, strip mining. But the sales figures and the risk of gold's being less valuable than brands caused them to attempt to raise their profile. They had seen the fur industry all but die, though mink coats had once been a widely accepted status symbol. The jewelry sellers themselves— the people with glass cases and rings on velvet fingers—did not care whether they sold gold, platinum, or silver so long as they sold something.

More and more American couples were marrying with platinum rings, even titanium, a boring industrial metal.

"Anything you don't promote becomes a commodity," a spokesman for the World Gold Council, one of several Washington, D.C., industry lobbies, told me by phone after I returned from Guyana. Rick Banerot's title was marketing manager; his job was to persuade people to buy gold. That someone had to do this at all is surprising. "Instead of jewelry a woman can choose to buy a pair of [fancy] slings." What centuries of alchemy had failed to accomplish, advertising had done in a few years: spun silk or linen into virtual gold.

The gold lobby commissioned a promotional campaign. "People are successfully promoting such common products as milk, or you know, pork, the other white meat," Banerot said. Full-page advertisements appeared in American magazines targeted at wealthy shoppers encouraging them to purchase as much gold jewelry as possible. Darcy Bussel, a dancer in London's Royal Ballet Company, posed as the campaign's first model in her ballerina costume wearing an expensive gold necklace. The idea was to convince shoppers that gold jewelry was the equal of platinum or diamonds or even some nice shoes.

But at the same time, the gold industry was trying to sell as many pieces of cheap, tinny jewelry as possible. Gold had to avoid losing its elitist associations while simultaneously placing its product in as many stores as possible. They failed at the former, but succeeded at the latter. Across the United States, teenagers bought ninety-nine-dollar necklaces with their baby-sitting money in shopping malls, at chain jewelers advertised with circulars in the Sunday paper and plugs on drive-time radio. Wholesalers shoveling out cut-rate gold from cookie-cutter boutiques were already a fixture of the American retail landscape, led by shopping mall outlets like Zales. By the end of the twentieth century, virtually every American family had the means to acquire some gold—a necklace, a ring—if they wanted it, for the price of a good kitchen appliance.

"Target, Kmart, Wal-Mart are all now vendors in gold, at price points that were never available before," Banerot said. These "new distribution streams" were opening even wider overseas. "England is a nine-karat market. South Africa is a nine-karat market"—a culture where it's socially acceptable to buy jewelry with only nine parts gold in every twenty-four of metal, without being considered a cheapskate. Americans prefer fourteen- or eighteen-karat gold for jewelry, which is very pure gold. China's markets represented another billion potential customers for cheap rings, and India continued to increase its gold buying. Sales of gold jewelry rose every year in the United States as well through 2000 and 2001. But as it did it became more common, and the metal's appeal seemed only to dilute more. It was no longer the case that wearing gold was literally to wear money.

None of this was true in places like Guyana, though. The jewelry there was cheap and black-market. The miners avoided selling to the government and sold straight to the jewelers to avoid hassles and paperwork. This is why a Guyanese gold ring the size of a pair of dice—perhaps actually cast in the likeness of a pair of dice—could cost thirty dollars: there were probably more bits of copper wire and carpet tacks in the ring than gold. I went to see one of the local jewelers work. There was one right around the corner from the apartment. There was one on nearly every major block in the city.

The woman who lived on the landing was still asleep at noon. Past her, over a flooded canal, and around two scrapping dogs, the projectionist set up the movie theater next door for the day. Middle-aged men and orphans stood in front of the theater engaging in small, failing acts of deception, the men exchanging drugs, the boys money, both waiting to sneak into the day's first show. That week it was a vampire film followed by a karate movie. Entertainment was hit-or-miss in Guyana. There was no real money to be made distributing movies, so the theaters showed whatever the proprietors could manage to acquire through back channels: Nixon-era Asian kung fu extravaganzas (*Shao-Lin Master* was one); third-rate thrillers, featuring Hollywood stars' worst roles and earliest, regretted scenes; the most schizophrenic of the Indian musicals; southern Mediterranean pornography (one called *Panty Girls* played frequently). I waved to the theater owner, a cheery man busy pushing a broom, and at a gap in the minibus traffic crossed the road with the dogs. The animals led the way along the canal downtown.

Imperial Jewelry was actually one of four gold shops within a block of the apartment. The shop was locked and the glass door covered in a sheet of opaque tint like a car window. I rang, knocked, then pounded. The proprietor, a woman in her forties, came to the door lazily. A key turned and the door opened a few inches. Cold air puffed out.

"Yes?"

We engaged in a ridiculous parley, like entering a speakeasy. I stood on a narrow plank across the sewage canal trying to talk my way into the jewelry shop. A pile of white sand sat beside it, dumped in front of the store, another pubic works job that had started months ago but not quite gotten finished. It took some wrangling before the woman agreed to let me inside. There were a lot of robberies and she vetted strangers before letting them into the store.

"No, the owner is not here. My husband is the owner. Well,

yes, I am the owner too. You are shopping for yourself? You are getting married? No? Well, what can I do for you then?"

The shop was the size of a walk-in closet and filled almost to the white walls with two glass cases arranged in an L shape. A towerlike display in the corner turned on a loud electric motor. Inside were shelves with rings placed on purple velvet fingers. The store walls were unpainted plasterboard that revealed a two-way mirror in the back of the room. The woman who had let me in said her name was Sandra.

I asked her where the jewelry came from. Sandra disappeared into the back office, visible faintly through the trick mirror, and returned with a catalog printed in Chinese. She flipped to a page.

"They come from these," she said. She spun the catalog toward me on the counter. The page showed rows of what looked like small salt shakers, the paper kind for picnic baskets. They were ceramic molds. Each was a cylinder a few inches high with a hole in one end to pour in melted gold. Below each was a picture of a golden dragon or a heart or an abstract shape, whatever the mold would cast.

"Come," she said.

She led around the jewelry case into the office and pushed on a section of plasterboard cut out behind the office desk. One side of the wall flipped open into a tight room where three young men worked back to back in welding masks. Slender red and green tanks of oxygen and acetylene with hoses snaking to blowtorches leaned against the walls. Pliers and hammers lay haphazardly across worktables. Above the worktables were smaller shelves holding vials of chemicals in glass flasks. The jewelry workshop smelled of ignition, and the jet-engine sound of the torches bounced around the narrow room. It felt like a ship's boiler room, squeezed and hot.

The jeweler closest by was named Vijay. He was a short, very young man, perhaps seventeen, and friendly when he raised his mask. Sandra made a shoveling motion of her hand toward him and told him to show what he put in the rings. The young man held up one of the white cylinders from the catalog. It was the size of his thumb with a recess at one end, a shallow dimple.

From below a worktable he produced a block of wood perhaps four inches on a side with two sides blackened. It looked like a piece of used firewood. In the center of one of the charred sides was a small depression. It was a cheap crucible.

He reached for some square tins on a shelf above his workbench, took a tangle of copper telephone wire from one, and dropped it into the dimple in the wood. Next he added a few shavings of silver from a petri dish, pinching his fingers from a low height like a chef salting a turkey. The last addition was the gold, two tiny asymmetrical beads from a margarine tub on the worktable. He showed me the bowl. It looked like gum wrappers in an ashtray. Very fast, he grabbed a torch and the sparker, gave an authoritative whack of his thumb against the spring to strike the flint against an inch of file, and the torch flashed on. It was a cold yellow flame and juked around until Vijay reached across the room and spun the dials on the tanks behind him. The jet sound increased and the torch narrowed into a blue cone with a white core. He used this like a pen and turned it on the metal shavings.

The gold melted immediately, then the wire, then the silver, and then he set the torch aside on the workbench and poured the gold mixture into the mold. When the metal was all poured he reached for a plastic bowl filled with black putty and pressed the mold into the putty hard with his hand clamped tightly over it. We waited.

Sandra's gold shop had done badly that Christmas, she said.

"Ech." It was a bad year. At least the gold was cheap. "We buy from the miners. You buy from the Gold Board, you have to tell them what you're using it for." She looked as if she had tasted something bitter. "I don't know. They have forms to fill out, all these things. Easier just to buy from the miner."

When the mold was cool, Vijay cracked it with an undersized hammer and scraped the ceramic shell away with his thumbnail. Inside was nothing recognizable. It was a hard gray lump, like a piece of concrete chipped from a sidewalk. He ran it under water from a spout beside him, picked at it with his thumbnail, and scrubbed it with a dirty toothbrush until all the ash was off and six dull yellow rings appeared attached to a center spar. Each had a setting for a gem in the center. The tree of rings looked like something oddly practical, a hinge, or a piece of circuitry, more than items for decoration. Vijay snapped a tear of excess gold from the tree's bottom, twisted off each ring, and dropped them in Sandra's palm like a fistful of coins. The gold from the central spar went back in the margarine tub with other excess to melt down later. The container of gold ingots sat on the shelf like a tin of loose screws. The gold in it had been reused several times already, and there was more telephone wire and less gold in each teardrop each time. Eventually all the gold would end up in more wedding rings that would come later.

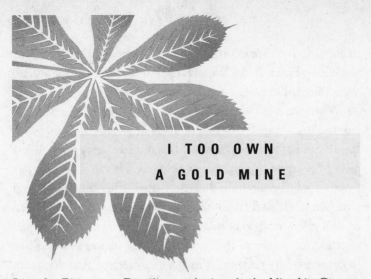

I TOO OWN
A GOLD MINE

Leandro Pires was a Brazilian geologist who had lived in Guyana for thirteen years. A man at the treasury ministry had given me his number. He had acquired a gold mine in the northwest after working on some of the foreign mines farther south. I was speaking to him to learn what had happened to bankrupt the mines he had helped discover, and why he would want to get into the business now. He had been one of the first geologists to come to the country and had worked at Omai, and his new operation was his first as the person in charge.

His office was also his residence. Camp Street was one of Georgetown's better avenues, and his house was large and had a gate with a security guard, who led me up the steps. Pires met me at the door dressed like a tourist, in running shoes without socks and a fanny pack around his waist. He was thirty-eight years old. Piles of maps and rolls of surveys sat on his desk in a pile, with a laptop computer humming alongside. Nearby a fax machine dominated an old table made of nibi thatch. The furnishings were Old World stuff, but it was a modern home office, cooled with the consistent symbol of tropical prosperity, a window air-conditioning unit.

Companies he had worked with were getting clobbered toward the end of the twentieth century. Gold prices rise in times of distress; it's an industry that thrives on bad news. People invest in gold during times of uncertainty, so, for example, wars are good for gold prices. So are stock market crashes and inflation. Good news has the opposite effect, and the 1990s had been a time of good news in the industrialized world. By the end of that decade, gold was at its lowest value in twenty years.

Not that Pires was in such bad shape: he was a big shot among the local gold miners. He was in line for international development money to open his gold mine—basically a cheap loan from the British government in exchange for doing business in a troubled economy. And he was not a smuggler or a guy with a hose on his shoulder working out in the trees in a pit. He was a middle-class man.

Still, he was no millionaire, despite knowing where billions in gold was buried, owning a stake in some of it, and having already helped dig a few million ounces out of the ground over the past decade. His plan made no sense: Omai wasn't breaking even and most of the gold was gone; Las Cristinas, the mine just over the border in Venezuela, wasn't going to open after a planned $600 million development, and back in North America most smaller prospectors were getting thrown off the stock listings as worthless investments. If Guyana was not benefiting from its gold because outsiders were taking it all—if Omai was just sixteenth-century mercantilism promoted as twenty-first-century globalism—then at least the foreign robber barons should be rich. But they weren't; somehow gold was turning to smoke. Pires had nevertheless decided this was the moment to go into the business for himself.

He offered a seat and took his tall black chair. A mural on the wall behind him distracted me. It was done in what looked like blue finger paint and showed bulldozers digging a hole. The painting was unusually two-dimensional, with badly flawed perspective, like ancient paintings that show people in heaven by having them stand on the heads of the living. The bulldozer in the painting looked a little bent in the middle.

"Is that your mine?"

"This?" He grinned and shook his head ruefully. "This must have been what Omai looked like." A previous company had painted it. It was out of business now. I wondered if that gave him pause. He swiveled in his expensive black desk chair from the mural and toward me.

"No, no." He brushed away the concerns with the back of his hand. Digging up some gold while everyone else got out was the best idea he'd had in a while. The business was just undergoing a transformation from a stock scam to a legitimate business, and people like him were the ones poised to become rich off the shift.

"They left behind lots of two, three, five hundred thousand that can be very profitable." He was talking about ounces of gold. He played with a pen on his desk, watching his hands as he did. "It's . . . man, there's a lot of them out there. Look around, some stupid Canadian has spent three million and found gold but left it because he wanted a million ounces. It's stock, man, stock. The only explanation."

The gold mines that he claimed were everywhere for the taking—he unfurled some maps at my request and showed some locations marked with colored dots—were the debris left over from what was basically a stock market fiasco. When gold prices peaked in the early 1980s, dozens of small, start-up mineral exploration outfits sprang up to exploit the enthusiasm. They had staffs of only a few people and budgets considered tiny by corporate standards. The companies were called, with a kicky diminutive, junior mining companies or juniors. Pires had worked for several. They had reached their heyday in the early 1990s, a few years before a virtually identical structure showed up in the high-technology industry and gave rise to the dot-com.

The idea of a junior was to make money first by finding gold but not digging it up. Instead the owners would just announce the discovery and take the company public on the stock market. When a junior announced a discovery, its stock would rise fast and steeply. The profits would come on the stock and not from the gold. Then they would sell out to a larger mining company and move on to the next discovery.

Juniors were often slippery enterprises, and their claims, if not boldly exaggerated, at least erred toward the optimistic. Most traded on marginal stock exchanges known for their lax policing, the most infamous of which in the 1980s and 1990s was the stock exchange in Vancouver, British Columbia. The companies' success, or at least the amount of success they enjoyed, often rested more on public relations—creating a sense of possibility and opportunity about themselves—than on economics or geology. Among investors, owners of such small gold exploration firms weren't called "prospectors," "gold miners," or even "developers," but most often "promoters." They often worked within the law but at the outer ranges of good taste. At an industry conference I attended after returning from Guyana in 2000, the audience was overwhelmingly composed of senior citizens bused from Florida retirement communities to hear gold stock promotions. Brokers would greet them in the lobby with handshakes, and each retiree received a twenty-four-karat rose. Afterward they would get a chatting-up from the brokers about the prospects of some mineral deposit in the Solomon Islands or a far corner of Alaska.

Often it turned out later the gold could not be recovered profitably. With that the stock crashed and the public was left holding the bag. It was a classic pump-and-dump scheme and nothing new. That sort of thing went back to the California gold rush and the Comstock Lode. Remarkably, the same old scams, called "dirt-pile scams," still worked.

Outright fraud was uncommon, but when it occurred it was spectacular. Anyone with a pile of dirt could claim it was full of gold. Telephone solicitation of tiny gold stocks became enough of a nuisance in the 1990s that the National Association of Securities Dealers, which regulates the Nasdaq stock market, published a list of guidelines to avoid false claims of rich soil. In most cases, crooked stockbrokers would call people's homes and offer shares in a gold mine discovered in some faraway place that was hard to verify. The scams were comparable to telephone solicitations for allegedly valuable coins or real estate deals for swampland in Florida.

But short of such outright deception, even the legitimate discoveries—the ones Pires was looking to acquire—were still often based on generous assumptions. Exploration companies had to somehow convince investors that gold in the ground would become valuable as gold in the hand. When they had convinced enough people for a moment, they sold off and left.

"They didn't want to produce gold. They wanted to double their stock, sell, and get out," Pires said. "Lots of them are left behind, two hundred, five hundred thousand ounces," Pires said. He said this more than once. "I can name you twelve around here."

Part of the scheme rested on gold's sentimental value. The United States only went off the gold standard in 1972. Fort Knox is still a place most Americans have heard of, if not as much as it used to be, and is still shorthand for American solidity (though most of the national gold is actually in New York City, in a vault under the Federal Reserve Bank). Prior generations used jewelry as a store of family wealth. Gold jewelry was an insurance policy in bad times. The attachment to an object that offers security is hard to lose even with evidence to the contrary.

In many cases there is also the matter of distrusting the government. Gold, as miners are heard to say, is no one's liability. The dollar is: it's the U.S. government's currency and subject to the government's whims and actions. No one sets a preferred value for gold, adjusts the gold supply after a meeting of a committee, or alters gold's value against the yen and the euro to reach some economic result. Gold is purely a matter of supply and demand. So miners argue that gold is not only still money, and a bulwark against uncertainty, but a guarantee against excesses of governments. It's an appealing sentiment: if the government makes bad judgments and your economy goes to the dogs, the gold under the bed will only become more valuable.

But this lingering sentiment can cloud some important choices. The distinction between owning a piece of gold and owning a piece of a gold mine is a fairly subtle one, for example, but it makes an enormous difference. Gold holds its value over time, has at least *some* value even in down times. But a thousand dollars' worth of stock in a gold mining company can go from three bucks a share down to eleven cents a share pretty fast.

Still, when the gold price rises, stock in gold companies goes with it. Though the phrases "good as gold" or "that place is a gold mine" aren't actually used much anymore, and have a bit of a Tin Pan Alley ring when they are, there is still plenty of money going into gold when the right conditions arise. It's understandable. Of all the products a company can produce—shoes, chemicals, sitcoms—bars of gold seem like a sure bet to always have customers, or at least to rise fast and profitably when a company announces its latest discovery. Striking gold is exciting in ways most things aren't. A restaurant with a line out the door is called a gold mine; no one ever calls a successful gold mine a restaurant.

Pires, though, was not a sentimentalist. He was a geologist trying to make money in a rain forest, which is about the least sentimental sort of person one may meet. His plan was simple: he would go back to these deposits of gold that had been left behind as insufficient to pump stock prices, dig the gold up, and sell it to the government of Guyana—sell it to Satkumar Hemraj. He wasn't even going to take his company public on the stock market. He waved his hand again, swatting an invisible fly. "That million-ounce shit is over."

A million ounces had been the key number during the stock promotion days. Omai had four million, and Golden Star Resources' stock had gone from two or three dollars a share to over twenty when it announced a deal to develop Omai.

But Omai was also an example of a typical failure. Its expenses were always high. Though gold was everywhere in the forest, it was not always evenly distributed. There were costs involved in getting gold out of the ground, and those costs had a threshold. Below the threshold the amount of gold was not worth digging up and recovering. That meant miners had either to find a spot where there was a lot of gold in every ton of dirt they processed, or to be very efficient with their work and spend very little on processing the dirt. But the amounts of gold in every shovelful were small even under the best circumstances. Seven or eight grams of gold in every ton of dirt was considered extraordinarily promising soil. Seven or eight grams is seven or eight cigarettes. A ton is two thousand pounds; a small car weighs about a ton. Omai never got close. There was often less than two grams of gold in each ton of rock there. Costs also changed as the miners dug through the layers of earth. The softer clays at the surface gave up their gold more easily than the harder, rockier earth deeper down. Harder rock meant more processing. More processing meant slower work and more expense.

All these costs affected profits, and profits were important to investors. So most announcements of gold discoveries from the time include a prediction of the "cost per ounce" to dig up the gold. Often these ranged from as low as one hundred dollars. But in many cases, such as Omai, they could get as high as between two and three hundred. These numbers were slippery too, though. The "cost per ounce" was the gold miner's production costs: the price of blasting, sifting, milling, chemically treating, and transporting earth until a gold bar was sitting on the table. But it did not usually include other expenses like fees paid to the host government, insurance, taxes, legal fees, and all the other costs of running a business. It also did not usually take into account changes in the geology as they dug for months at a time, until another financial quarter ended and the company reported its finances again. Companies often predicted their digging costs based on the first, easy soils and then saw them climb. I had asked Seeta Mohamed, the Omai spokeswoman, about costs once. She avoided mentioning just how much it cost her company to dig up one ounce of gold. She started at $260, dropped that to $220, then she decided it was not in her interest to answer and claimed not to know. Whatever the number, across the industry profit margins were already slim even before gold prices fell below three hundred dollars per ounce at the end of the 1990s. Today, Golden Star Resources does not expect to make any money from the Omai gold mine, and its partner Cambior is emerging from near bankruptcy, despite producing well over a quarter million ounces of gold a year from its hole.

After returning from Guyana I spoke with one of Pires's old bosses, David Fennell. The pit at Omai was named the Fennell Pit; he'd discovered the mine and run Golden Star Resources for most of the company's history. He is now the president of another junior mining company called Hope Bay. His version of events confirmed Pires's.

"People were making the assumption that the gold price was going to rise," he said. "So the game was to put together ounces. You're putting very low-grade deposits"—places with very little gold in every shovel of dirt—"into production. And your concern wasn't cost of production. It was saying you had five hundred thousand ounces in production, and eight hundred thousand next year, and a million the next." The stock rose on the promises, attracting quick money for quick returns; the companies rose and crashed within a few years. "Dramatically," said Fennell. " 'Ninety-six was the big year. You saw five, six billion dollars floating around when the U.S. mutual funds decided they needed to get in. Hey, call me a dot-com and I'm a hero."

The ride ended with a scandal in 1997. Gold mines had been settings for astounding frauds going back centuries. But in the late 1990s no one expected one of the oldest, most obvious scams there is to become one of the largest stock market messes in history. The deal that finally blew up in everyone's face was Wall Street's Bre-X disaster. Bre-X, a junior gold company based in Calgary, Alberta, Canada, had lied extravagantly about the amount of gold it had found at a hidden site in the forests of Indonesian Borneo, promising an Asian El Dorado while having virtually nothing. Their drilling program—the procedure which provided tests of the amount of gold in the land—was a fraud rigged by a dishonest geologist.

After Bre-X ran its stock values up many thousand percent on the false claims, with pension programs and even some of the most vanilla, allegedly low-risk American mutual funds rushing to get in on the opportunity, the deception came out and the company's stock crashed to worthlessness. Investors from large institutions to mom-and-pop retirement accounts lost billions, and the scandal put the tiny gold exploration industry on the front page of newspapers around the world. It was like something out of a Hollywood movie: gold, deceit, high-wire finance, fugitives, tropical explorers. And death: the geologist alleged to be responsible for the lie subsequently leaped out of a helicopter over the forests of Borneo, or got pushed, or faked his suicide, depending on who tells the story (Canadian reporter Jennifer Wells makes an interesting case for a faked death in *Fever: The Dark History of the Bre-X Gold Rush*). Another partner in the company may or may not have fled to the Cayman Islands, a popular location for mining company financing, where he presumably remains with his numbered bank account, laughing on the beach with a Mai-Tai. The effect on the world's economy was probably negligible, but the incident did expose the enduring tendency among presumably careful investors to get caught up in a gold rush and lose their shirts. The industry also became a pariah. Bre-X has gone down as one of the grander stock market bamboozles in the history of business. It was also, for a very few who sold their stock at the right time, the most successful gold promotion ever.

Pires sat at his mess of a desk and recalled the period. "It was always a promotion. Every press release, from '92 on or so, you go through them, they end with 'excellent potential for a million ounces.' You go there, do some trenches, drill some holes, boost the stock two, three, four times, and get out."

But after Bre-X the gold rush ebbed. Gold miners got a black eye out of the incident—bankers no longer lent them money. Then European central banks sold off tons more gold. This made it more difficult for miners to convince investors that their discoveries were worth something; the market was already flooding. Then more bad news: in March 2000, an annual ranking of industrial pollution, published by the U.S. Environmental Protection Agency, found the mining industry created more waste for every bit of its product it made than any other business in the United States. This suggested the possibility of liability lawsuits for environmental damage, and that could make it even harder to get loans. Nevada, a big mining state, led the list of American pollution worries that year. Cleaning up old mines would cost more than the industry could afford, and the presumption was the holes, particularly in the lesser-regulated developing countries like Guyana, would end up abandoned toxic pits when the gold was done. The troubles gold miners had started to cause everyone were magnitudes greater than their contributions to the overall economy or any notion of general prosperity. It became difficult to like these guys if you weren't a gold miner yourself. By the end of the 1990s, even greedy people didn't like them, Fennell lamented later. "Right now there is a lack of access to capital. The Street is very careful these days about who gets money. But all things are cyclical. Put the price at five hundred dollars and they'll come rushing in . . ."

This is probably true. Evidence of continued faith emerged within months of our conversation. In early 2002, uncertainty over terrorism, war in the Middle East, a lingering American recession, and questions over the strength of the U.S. dollar drove the price of gold above three hundred dollars per ounce for the first time in two years. Stocks in gold mining companies outperformed virtually every other business in the country for the period. Mutual funds focusing on precious metals saw healthy returns, and financial pundits began talking about gold stocks in language not heard since the promoters were busy. This encouraged Fennell; there were still people willing to give him money. "If I find another high-grade deposit I'll have your grandkids farting through silk," he promised.

Others—chiefly financial analysts—have suggested that in 2001–2002, as American political and economic conditions began to mirror those of the 1970s, the price of gold should have done in 2002 what it did in the 1970s too, and shot up. If gold was the world's financial refuge in bad times, and times were getting particularly bad, then gold's value should have risen to four hundred, six hundred, a thousand dollars an ounce. That didn't happen. War, recession, a stock market decline, and political uncertainty sent the metal to a modest recovery of its value, but adjusted for inflation it was still dirt cheap, historically speaking. That may suggest gold is an anachronism in any part of the world that has other stores of wealth available—that it's just a pretty commodity now, a fancy soybean. The process, following the title of an investment bank report, is sometimes called "reverse alchemy," turning gold into straw. Whether this is actually occurring is unknown. It will take more time to sense a trend, and gold could always recover its value over time. People like Fennell and Pires insist it will, and have staked their livelihoods on it. Many smaller countries with gold reserves continue to make the same bet, as the northern Amazon did in the 1990s. There has been little evidence to support this faith over the past twenty years. Discounting the usual brief spikes and slides, stocks in gold-mining companies—and the value of the metal itself—have fallen steadily through much of the late-twentieth century and the beginning of the twenty-first. Gold investors have often referred to a twenty-year slump in the value of their holdings. The returns have been so bad at times that conspiracy theories, most alleging price fixing by the world's largest bankers, have become common in the small corner of the investing world reserved for precious metals obsessives, nick-named "gold bugs."

Pires said the quick stock market buck wasn't his plan. "We are going to find gold, get gold, and sell gold." He would produce small amounts of gold very inexpensively, sell them to the Gold Board, and pocket the money, and that would be that.

"It's still not worth much, is it?" I was thinking of Hemraj's comment that gold was becoming silver.

"That's bullshit, man," Pires said. "Bullshit, bullshit. We're just at the beginning now. The million-ounce days, those are over. But we can still . . . these medium-size mines are still very profitable. With our technology, we are going to be very profitable, man." His technology was nothing spectacular: he was going to put a lot of soft earth in a big box and shake it through a massive screen, essentially. Then sift it a little. Then float it in some water until the gold fell to the bottom. No mercury, no cyanide, no problem. The Omai guys had tried to dig in rock that was too hard. His spot would work, he said.

He was heading back to the forest at the end of the week. He owned the mine, but that still meant getting dirty, going into the hole and handling tools. It also meant mosquitoes. He sorted some packets of malaria pills with his index finger on the desk. "I have it [malaria] seven, eight times," he said. He fingered the medicine packets. "But I've got a new one I'm trying now, a Chinese one, herbs."

I said I'd just been to Mahdia and the malaria was bad there. He nodded.

"White Hole, Red Hole, St. Elizabeth's. They're fucked, those places. Totally fucked. People, guys getting killed down there." He said he simply couldn't understand it. The locals took risks for nothing, and the outsiders found millions in treasure and just left it lying there.

———

I stopped at a bank on my way back to the apartment. I always went to the Globe Trust on Middle Street to change my U.S. dollars into orange and green Guyanese bills.

"So you changing more money, you must like it here," the teller, a tall woman with a thin gold necklace, would usually say. She filled out the exchange form. Often in Guyana people would ask what I thought of the country. It was part of many small transactions. The cashier at Fogerty's cafeteria would ask how I liked the food and by extension the country. Even Mrs. Persaud, my landlady, who loved to ask me about California and visiting her sister's in New York, always stressed her dislike of the cold there compared to the good weather in Guyana; didn't I prefer the added heat?

Often I would answer with white lies or small omissions. "Thanks for recommending the restaurant. The one near the park," I said to the teller. A partially naked man had been waving a shovel and declaiming loudly about some perceived slight from beyond the patio much of the time I was at the recommended restaurant. But I left that part out. I took my money and left in a good mood.

I walked up Main Street along the side of the road. When I stopped to look in a furniture store window a man covered in dust who looked to have just pulled himself out of the canal walked up to me. I looked over in time to see him pull a machine gun from the back of his sagging pants, aim at my chest, and pull the trigger.

"Pah, pah, pah," he said.

By the time I recognized what was happening it was obvious the gun was a plastic toy. By then the man seemed ready to shoot again. He kept the toy trained a few inches from my head and looked seriously at me. His left eye was badly infected and full of white matter along its edge. In his other hand was a piece of steel he'd fashioned into a long, sharp poker. He seemed to have forgotten about that for the moment. He tugged at his dirty pants a little and looked in my eyes for signs of life. I was against the furniture store window, and either fleeing or attacking him seemed likely to just get me jabbed with the piece of metal in his hand. I stood still and hoped my appearance fit his idea of how the standing dead might look. He did not speak to me, so I stayed silent also. After a moment he holstered the pop gun in the back of his pants and continued down the street. He held his metal poker stiffly vertical as he went for a few steps. Near the national bank he rediscovered it and began to swing it low right to left as if cutting weeds. The crowd parted around him.

By then I had given up my room at the Rima Guest House and rented an apartment above a beautician's shop, the His and Hers Beauty Salon on Waterloo Street. The shopping district on Regent Street was only a few blocks away and the botanical garden the same distance in the other direction. I liked living there. Mrs. Persaud, the landlady and chief beautician, seemed to do very little paying business, but the shop was usually abuzz with women chatting about their relatives in North America and happily doing each other's hair anyway. It was a neighborly place. Mrs. Persaud's daughter Praveena often hung around and minded a small five-and-dime the Persauds ran opposite a concrete landing. She was twelve. She liked to talk about her plans to attend Fordham Law School in New York City. A law degree seemed like the best way to ensure that her father, who sold reconditioned cargo truck parts, would triumph in business disputes, she said. She was a no-nonsense girl and hovered near the top of her class most years, Mrs. Persaud said. It was Praveena's intention to leave Guyana, for school and perhaps a job, when she was old enough, but perhaps come back. Perhaps.

Living over the shop was a good arrangement, but the neigh-
borhood had a bad reputation. Across the road was a pornographic theater and a crack house. But it was a wide street and
most of the trouble seemed to stay on the other side. Only one
woman on our side seemed affected by the local blight personally. She was a nervous woman who struck me as likely to be a
cocaine addict. She never agreed to tell me her name. At night,
after the Persauds left for the day, she would sleep on a wooden
bench on the landing of the salon, in a torn shirt, her head
shaved nearly bald, so that ropy scars stood out on her skull.
Once she accepted some food, but anything more I gave was usually gone from her possession within a day.

That evening, after meeting Pires, I went to a popular nightclub
called the Sheriff. The dance hall was filled with flailing dancers
and furious thumps of soca. A DJ was onstage dancing behind
his turntables waving his hands high. He wore a high bright knit
hat pulled tight over his assiduously matted hair. It was late on a
Thursday night. Above my table on the stage, two white men in
their fifties danced with two young prostitutes. The women were
dressed in what appeared to be once-fine dresses ravaged by
jaguars. They were hardly dresses at all, more like small cargo
nets. Their bodies leaked out unflatteringly. The quartet danced
in the corner. The men were in khaki pants and short sleeves,
as if for a round of Sunday golf. They were not good dancers
but they did not lack enthusiasm. One wiggled gamely, if
grotesquely, swirling his belly independently of the rest of his
torso. The other performed an unlikely can-can. For their part
the women with them danced much more slowly and mostly
with each other. At a signal they would swing their butts around
and with great purpose settle themselves backward into their
dates' waists right around the belt buckle. Each time they did this

it caused the men to panic. This seemed to be the desired effect. The women would swirl their hips around heatedly, then look with manufactured interest over their shoulders before turning back to each other and laughing at their clients.

I could not decide which way this tipped the scale, so I looked away. Two East Indian teenagers were dancing nearby. The boy was dancing an obligatory two-step. But the woman was having more fun. She spun in unpredictable bursts. She had dressed more modestly and less showily than any of the other dancers in the room, in what could have been a store clerk's uniform, but before long the others looked over their partners' shoulder to watch her. After another few moments even the DJ looked up from his records to watch too. Over protests and irritated looks from the whole room, for only this one young woman the Afro-Guyanese DJ pulled the needle across the grooves sharply—the rending sound seemed intentional, but still jarring—and shifted to an Indian song on a second turntable. The room, which was a plywood stage spray-painted black under a roof made from tent tarps, filled with trilling Hindi pop that had somehow found its way to South America from a movie studio in Bombay.

The young woman's mouth curled into the slightest pleased grin. She sped up the dips she was making with one knee and gathered her hand at her waist; her thumb met her fingertip as if to pinch a handful of fabric and hold a dress off the floor while she danced. She wore no such dress, just her grey clerk's skirt. But with her hand in that odd punctilio you could picture something grander and colorful that should have been billowing around her.

Everyone in the hall was watching the young woman. She seemed indifferent to the eyes on her, though I don't imagine she was.

The next day I walked from the apartment to the sound of drums. The woman with the cocaine habit came out the front gate and walked to the corner with me. A parade of no clear purpose filled the street. At the head of the crowd a man in a fine black suit high-stepped like a drum major. He played a xylophone shaped like a musical clef. Following behind were drummers in pressed white shirts and slacks. Three boys beat on bass drums, and one made a fast staccato like a military march on the rim of a snare. It was slung from his narrow waist with a cord. Most of the marchers were Afro-Guyanese, with only a few East Indian people here and there. It did not seem like a political matter, but there was no holiday. It was a Friday around noon. Behind the drum corps a dozen young men in dark suits danced in a line. It looked more like an American step than a Caribbean one. They dipped a shoulder halfway to the road, snapped it back, slid a rear leg forward, then the other. After a few repetitions they would stop, tip a finger to their black fedoras, adjust their dark glasses, and turn their heads so everyone watching could see the gold studs in their ears. They had practiced this; it looked good. Behind them was a group of older church women. One needed a cane and two friends to help her walk. They wore gaudy brooches and elaborate hats piled high with white and purple flowers sewn to the hatbands.

A few street boys seven or eight years old had come from the abandoned truck parked in the median in front of the flat where I lived. One claimed he could do a backflip, and did. The woman from the landing watched the parade and for the first and last time in my experience smiled, and laughed in the direction of the boy doing acrobatic tricks for coins. What was this? She pointed her chin toward the parade's rear, where more men danced and others carried a coffin. The song the leader played on the xylophone was familiar then, "You Can't Take It With You When You Go."

The parade passed the pornographic theater, and another boy, not more than twelve, dashed inside to catch a few glimpses of *Panty Girls.*

A few weeks later I came out of the apartment with some clothes I intended to give to the boys across the street. They lived in the abandoned delivery truck. There were between five and eight boys living in the truck at any one time. The oldest was a one-armed seventeen-year-old. The youngest appeared to be about four. They did odd jobs in the movie theater and for the vendors in Lacytown a few blocks away. I had a tired pair of shoes, a few shirts, and some short pants to offer them. The seams were still solid and the stains from the forest mostly small. One of the smaller boys saw me first, and I handed him the bag. The rest of the boys leaped out of the truck and began to chase their friend. Halfway down the block they tackled him in the road, tore the bag from him, took one of the shirts off his arms, and began beating him to give up one of the shoes. A group of men by the side of the road leaned on the side of a building and did not move to stop the beating. They had taken everything from him in a few seconds. The largest boy put my shirt on his one arm.

I am describing all this in the hope that it is clear that the gold mines and the statistics I have presented were not the country. Those were things that affected the country. They were the part North Americans could access and had reasons to involve ourselves in and form opinions about; it was the part in which I had involved myself. But I do not think I ever saw the country as it was beyond occasional glimpses, like those brief moments on those two days.

THINGS
GET IMPOLITE

As gold mines continued to open around the world in places few had heard of, several environmental lobbies made it their business to oppose them. In the United States the leading role went to a Washington, D.C., organization called the Mineral Policy Center and a second group called Project Underground. The more recognizable political names associated with environmental causes—Greenpeace, the Sierra Club—were less visible on the issue in part because it is a niche concern taking place far away from any obvious constituency.

The Mineral Policy Center was the establishment group. It had an office on K Street, Washington's lobbying corridor (right around the corner from a gold miners' lobby, the Gold Institute). The group worked primarily lobbying the American government to pass or enforce laws regulating gold mines in the United States, but eventually followed the gold overseas as well. It played generally by the rules: it went to Senate offices, testified at hearings, curried influence.

The Project Underground people, by comparison, concentrated their efforts on organizing villages, most overseas, to oppose mining projects. It was an operation of about a dozen people working out of a bunker behind a pizza place in, perhaps inevitably, Berkeley, California. "The Mohawk of Kanesatake Resist Niobium Mining!" was a typical Project Underground announcement in the 1990s. "Help Resist Niobium Mining!" (Niobium is used in rocket engines, Kanesatake is in the American Northeast, and there are today's fun facts.) A former Greenpeace employee dismayed with the larger group's inattention to gold mining and oil drilling, an Australian named Danny Kennedy, had founded Project Underground in the early 1990s. Kennedy soon became an important figure in a decidedly small part of international environmental politics, and Project Underground became an unlikely nexus of facts on the world's least-known locations and the people who lived there: Amungme village chiefs in Indonesia, Andean potato farmers, Guyanese Amerindians. I knew of Project Underground primarily because it could provide e-mail addresses for people who preferred to live in huts in the forest. The Mineral Policy group, meanwhile, continued its work in Washington. Most of its efforts concentrated on opposing subsidies for the mining industry and reforming American mining laws, some of which date from the late 1800s but remain in effect. The founder of the Mineral Policy Center, a man named Phillip Hocker, had been an adviser to the Guyanese government following the cyanide spill at Omai. Both groups, Underground and the Mineral Policy Center, gained incremental amounts of influence as the gold rush continued over the decade. They managed to seed stories in respected publications now and then, and to influence agendas at the relevant meetings of the UN, the EPA, or foreign governments.

Gold mining remained a fairly marginal political matter anyway, of course. And the debate between the environmental groups and mining companies—also represented by lobbies—over time grew fairly tense and bitter. The increased criticism brought a response. There were few shared goals or efforts toward solutions. They just fought. The interests the groups represented could not have been farther apart.

"Sure, they get in your face," a geologist named Bill Yoemans, who had worked in Guyana with Migrate Mining, told me at a gold industry conference in San Francisco. "There was this one lady, what the hell was her name, real environmentalist bitch." The statement was typical of the debate's tone for most of the 1990s: dismissive and mean. In North America the 1990s had seen a trend toward third-party arbitration in environmental disputes—basically a way to avoid lawsuits. There was some effort to get environmentalists, loggers, farmers, and industrialists to tables together to hash out compromises. This rarely occurred with much success in gold mining. The two sides utterly detested each other.

"It's the communists," David Fennell had guessed by phone to me once. "They got their ass kicked in the nineties. They morphed themselves, and now they're environmentalists." A common acronym for mining critics at two industry conferences I attended was BANANAS, for "Don't Build Anything Near Anyone or Near Anything." Critics of the mines meanwhile often thought nothing of terming their opponents "rapists." A biologist in Guyana had said with horror that he'd heard of one gold miner who kept a harpy eagle, a particularly majestic, rare bird from the Kunuku Mountains, chained up in his office to annoy environmentalists. He wasn't sure who.

Eventually the environmentalists began to succeed. Governments enforced more restrictions on miners, and gold miners—who generally don't even trust the idea of paper money—confirmed their abiding hatred of governments. From there the entire matter grew more hopelessly confrontational.

"As far as I'm concerned the EPA got their heads so far up

their ass they can only see brown," David Fennell said by phone. He meant the U.S. Environmental Protection Agency, not the Guyanese. "I got an EPA scientist in his class-four contamination suit, telling me I need concrete lining [a protective structure for a toxic waste pond]. I just wonder, what fucking planet was he from?"

In part, the planet he was from was one in which environmental debate was shifting noticeably from a discussion of plants and animals to one about people and money. By the end of the decade, particularly in the international arena, environmental discussions had become in many cases a human rights discussion. If you wanted to open a gold mine in a forest, increasingly you had to make clear either to a government or at least a local newspaper that you weren't going to affect local fishing businesses or harm the drinking water. Whereas American environmental debate often found itself, in the 1990s, caught up in a hopeless public scrum over the rights of spotted owls versus those of loggers, or the value of a salmon's life to a hydroelectric plant's, mining critics undertook a discussion of human rights. This was significant. Mining critics were some of the first in the United States to recognize that the rich world had different environmental debates than the rest of the world, and that the rest of the world often offered better descriptions of the matters at hand: land ownership laws, public health concerns near industrial sites, and the environmental costs and benefits of economic development to the people who lived near the impact sites.

Poverty was not a large part of American environmental discussion in the early 1990s. Opposing a gold mine, however, demanded some thought to it. Arguing against recovering treasure in a cash-strapped country is a tough sell, and requires not simply describing the obvious destruction of digging, but working environmental, humanitarian, and economic agendas into a coherent critique. North American mining critics never succeeded in finding that critique or articulating it in any publicly compelling way. They made brief stabs at a response. Several organizations that sprang up around the world in the 1990s—Project Underground in the United States, Minewatch in the U.K. and Canada, and another in Australia called the Mineral Policy Institute—began addressing their concerns almost entirely in the language of public health or civil rights rather than as discussions of trees or animals. Though at times shrill as these groups presented it—they were typically run by very, very angry people—the discussion anticipated a shift in global politics that occurred later in the decade. How to balance economic progress, human rights, and environmental destruction has only become a central issue of public debate since the early 1990s, the undercurrent to discussions of the globalization of markets. Financial agencies, most publicly the World Bank, only recently had to begin defending their environmental practices regularly to the general public. Debates over gold mines were one of the places where this broader, arguably more useful discussion began, and where blind spots in existing environmental thinking appeared starkly in the early 1990s. But it was an obscure debate at the time.

And redefining the problem did not lead to a solution. Business continued more or less as usual on the ground. There were still no solutions to the concerns that were primary there. The American logger I had met at the Palm—the man who cut down rain forests for a living—said he only paid attention to environmental debates for the entertainment value. "People tell me they want to promote 'ecotourism' in these places and then we won't have to log or mine anything." He had been into his third beer at the time. "And I always want to say, what the hell is 'ecotourism'? Are you going to *fly* to the rain forest? Do you have any idea how much pollution it takes to build an airplane, and get an airplane off the ground, just so you can see a parrot?" Things had to come from somewhere, and environmentalists ignored that, he said.

It was a fair criticism in Guyana. If not mining, what then? This was particularly true where the small miners were concerned. Most foreign environmental opposition to gold mining focused on transnational corporations. The small miners were causing the same problems—disruption, poisoning food supplies, stealing land from local villages.

Even concentrating on the big mines, the environmental camp had not offered solutions. Income from Omai accounted for 20 percent of the national income every year. Guyana was using that to pay down its debts and run the government. Critiques of the mine never suggested a way to replace one-fifth of the national economy. Obviously there was still an enormous incentive to mine in places with no other obvious paths to wealth. Incentives to do other, better activities rarely entered the discussion.

It was a huge oversight. In Guyana, whether someone mined or not—the government or an individual—often boiled down to a matter of being able to afford food and medicine. It was an immediate concern. No matter how destructive gold mining was, it's hard to tell people to stop doing what may be the only job available to them in their entire country. Particularly if you are denying them the papers to leave: visas were the other common discussion. There were few jobs in Georgetown and no hope of a visa to a better market for the unskilled. That left mining. Without the mines, life would become insupportable for thousands of people.

"I acknowledge the destruction," the miner who called himself Ricky had told me in El Dorado three years before. "We have to be aware of this because this is where our children will live.

But this is my work, this is how I provide for a family." It was a common sentiment.

Solutions used for other environmental problems were not viable. If efforts began to persuade people to stop buying jewelry tomorrow, the way we have stopped buying mink stoles for the sake of minks and tuna caught with badly designed nets that trap dolphins, thousands would lose their livelihoods in already unstable countries and whole towns would become ghost towns.

In the case of El Dorado or Mahdia, it's unlikely anyone would miss living there. The miners themselves were already moving on to areas north and west. But when they get there they are starting new mines. There's nothing else to do there.

Prohibition had its own difficulties. If the Guyanese government stepped in, shut down Mahdia as the environmental and public health debacle it is, and declared the practice illegal, then Margaret's snack bar would close and her primary professional option in town would be prostitution, which she would not choose, particularly in a country with a rate of AIDS infection approaching Haiti's and central Africa's.

The foreign miner's model doesn't present a solution either. Golden Star had prospected at Mahdia and found hundreds of thousands of ounces. If the Guyanese government outlawed the small miners and handed the land over to the Denver company (no one is actually proposing this; this is hypothetical), there would be jobs for only a minority of the men currently working in those pits. History suggested the others would wind up in armed standoffs over their right to work like the one I saw in El Dorado. And then a big mine would appear and not solve the country's shortfalls anyway before running out of gold within a decade. "One Omai isn't enough. You need twenty Omais to really see anything change in these countries," Fennell had told me. I multiplied by twenty and the picture was not any clearer.

There were some people suggesting solutions. Several tiers of environmental effort existed, and some were more attuned to the situation on the ground than others. David Singh, a Guyanese environmental scientist at the crumbling university in George-town, had called the Omai accident a disguised blessing that jarred the country into writing its first environmental protection laws. He was preparing the first study of mercury pollution in the rivers east of Bartica. An American group called the World Resources Institute had studied the gold mines in southern Venezuela with the intention of lessening their environmental impacts in ways that would not be too financially difficult. An-other organization, the Environmental Law Institute, wrote a legal framework for writing and enforcing such regulations.

But at the time in Mahdia and El Dorado, much less Georgetown, there were still thousands of people looking for something to do, and no one had offered a better option than digging up the backyard.

And finally, there were the people unlucky enough to live near large deposits of gold. Most of the gold was located in rural areas, so most of the people living nearby were Amerindians. Foreign environmentalists advocated almost entirely on behalf of these villagers, whom much of the world had come to call collectively, perhaps preciously, "indigenous people." In Guyana the Amer-indian population was about 10 percent of the country, but most lived in small, often remote locations, while the bulk of Guyanese hugged the coast. Their political aims were usually a matter of discretion over their land and beyond that an apparent desire to be left alone. The local miners and the corporate miners were the same thing in those cases: they were interlopers.

Both historically and by population the Amerindians had the least political muscle in the country. But they were also the group with the greatest likelihood of having their daily lives affected, for both better and worse, by land deals, and many of the land deals had to do with developing new mines. Still, it was rare to include their representatives in the bargaining in Georgetown or Toronto or Denver for new projects.

For this reason and others, the Amerindians had formed an association: the Amerindian People's Association. It was a lobby claiming to represent just fewer than half of the villages in the interior. The group was known around town.

So these are the people I went to see last in Georgetown, when it seemed no one else had any kind of solutions to the problems the gold failed to solve. If nothing else, they were the only people in the country who didn't seem to particularly care that there was treasure lying around everywhere.

The APA office was on the top floor of an old wooden mansion by the botanical garden. It was a quick walk from the apartment on Waterloo Street. It was early afternoon. The sun was behind some low clouds that threatened a squall. Across the street, men played basketball in the national park on a court named for Forbes Burnham; all the men were unusually tall and talented. It was one of the local club teams drilling before a tournament with Barbados, one of the bench players said. Behind the court the rest of the park amounted to a scrubby field with a few horses grazing in the center. Along the edge, children on recess from an elementary school played cricket and mobbed a cart where a man sold shaved ice.

Across from the park an outdoor stairwell led to a door cut high by the roof like a hayloft. Inside, the APA's leader, Tony James, sat at a wooden table fingering the clasp of a knife and another man sat backward in a chair with his arms draped over the back.

James was a compact man with a buzz haircut. A shortwave radio chattered in the back room; the villages rarely had phones, so the shortwave was useful for medical emergencies and to book flights. He offered me a seat. I had arranged the meeting through his son, whom I had met at a party a few nights prior. On the other side of the table from James was Ivor Marslow, a younger man from the northwest I had also met at the party. Tony James's son Kid James wandered into the room and then out a hallway without a hello.

As I sat, a fourth man walked into the room behind me. "Sorry, sorry, sorry," he said, walking fast around the table. Tony James laughed. A teenage couple followed behind the new man and wandered off toward the radio room.

This new man was full of energy. His name was Tony Melville. He was the captain of the village of Chenapau. He was a sight: a clothes horse. He wore a tight sleeveless lavender shirt and a choker necklace. His hair was worn longish with tight curls that spilled over his neck. He wore a goatee, a massive diamond ring, and a choker necklace, and his sunglasses were bulbous yellow Bausch & Lombs like a highway patrol officer's.

"Tony Melville." He reached across the table to shake hands. "Sorry, sorry. I was in a meeting." He slung a tote bag from a science conference on the table. He was an Amerindian representative.

James was the leader of the APA but Melville was its most successful politician. He lived in the highlands above Mahdia. Chenapau village had five hundred residents, and he had become captain—basically mayor and judge—five years ago at age thirty-four. He was now thirty-nine and slowly becoming a national figure as Amerindians went. This was because Chenapau was close to the country's best hope for tourism, the waterfall at Kaieteur, and foreigners had begun showing interest in seeing the village nearby. But Kaieteur was also a mining region. I had hoped to ask him about this. There were rumors of the waterfall turning colors from the mines. Melville said no. The river was not turning colors at the falls but the water upriver was suspect.

"They have heavy mining above there, above the Potaro [River]," he said. He sat across the table. He fussed with his canvas tote bag. "So we get the shitty part of the water. You can't wash clothes, can't drink. So we talk to EPA, talk to GGMC [the Geology and Mines Commission], but they do nothing. So we getting tired of this."

That morning I had also read, however, that the previous year Melville had managed to delay a twelve-million-dollar World Bank program to expand Kaieteur Park until his village was exempted from its boundaries. Mining was to be made illegal inside the park, and many people in Chenapau made their money mining. He had won the concession on a land rights argument: it wasn't that he particularly loved being a gold or a diamond miner, but he did not want outsiders—a mining company, an international environmental group, or a government—determining what would happen there.

"The only income is a little mining. In some areas, you stop it you have big problems."

Melville was himself a miner. His diamond-and-gold ring was from Kaieteur. He held it out like a proud bride. It was a family diamond found in a river near the village. The gold was from nearby there too. Most of his family had worked as miners, as had his father-in-law. They did not expect to stop anytime soon.

The foreign miners were coming as well. Two businessmen had brought him to Georgetown, he claimed, wined and dined him and asked for him to sign a contract granting permission for the company to explore for gold and diamonds near the village. "Last year, a South African and a Canadian. They ask me to the

Pegasus Poolside." But he would not give a name. The Pegasus was the international hotel in Georgetown, a round tower that looked like a prison from the outside but was all clean tile and cloth napkins past the entrance and the sunny central atrium. Prince Charles stayed there once, the brochures noted. The Poolside was the hotel's outdoor café, one of the best places to eat in Georgetown.

"They say you get a nice job, whatever you need. Engine, nice house," Melville claimed. He hung one arm over his chair and leaned lazily. "I say, if I was the landowner okay. But I have a lot of people. I'm speaking for the whole group. Not because, as coastlanders say, 'Amerindians all love nature.' I say this because where they want to go, this is the area where you get things. It's a small place, it's a village, five hundred people. There's no supermarket to go and get food. We have to go and get the food, understand me?"

I more or less understood him: he wanted the land rights. But certainly some of the villages, if they had those rights, would have taken the deal Melville had turned down.

Ivor Marslow, the young man in the chair next to me, nodded disagreement.

"For a short time, it is profitable," he said. "Shops come in. But when they leave, you got twenty shops, no people, and the money runs out. It's well and fine getting paid a percentage. But the deals are bad. We could do a lot better. I think what we need to do is try and get something out of this," he said.

Kid James wandered into the room and then out a hallway again.

"We've got a Logging Act. We've got a Mining Act," Marslow said. "We've got an Amerindian Act. But there's no enforcement. EPA has said they don't have the resources or staff to enforce anything." Tony James continued to sharpen his knife with deliberate strokes, on a stone resting against the side of his shoe. "As a whole I say they shouldn't do it [gold mining]. But if they are going to do it, we should get a better deal. But I think they shouldn't do it."

James hadn't looked up from the knife.

"They believe the activity will bring money to the country, though so far that has yet to happen." Marslow was leaning back against the wall. "Yeah, they get a little cash. Then they spend it and go back into the mines."

The position of the Guyanese government at the time was that any company that came onto its land to prospect or dig mines would first have to sit down with the people in the nearby villages and strike a deal. But the situation did not always work out that way, Marslow claimed. In many cases the Amerindian village councils did not have formal land rights, and when they did, the government enforced those rights unevenly. No one in the villages could say with confidence that he would not get run off his land someday, if someone happened to prospect nearby. This was the APA claim, at least.

James stopped sharpening his knife.

"You talk to Migrate?" he said. He resumed dragging the knife on the stone. Migrate Mining was a South African mining company surveying across parts of southern Guyana. "Somebody say they have an eight-million-acre concession. We don't know. We have been trying to get the attention of the prime minister. But we are talking to him one day, and he says there is no concession, and the next day, we hear he makes an agreement [with Migrate Mining]. We still don't know. We've been trying to find out."

"It sounds like you knew something."

"Somebody knew this guy, and he whisper it to me," he said.

"Which guy?"

"A guy."

"Fine, fine."

"So I hear some things about a company coming in, and I bring it up at a conference, and the president say no, there's no company. Then I get a map of the concession. And I had to go to another conference in Brazil. The media, the cameras, and all that were there, and I hold up the map there. Then, after that, they say there is a concession."

James was wary of local miners as well. The gold rush in Brazil, ten years prior, had been a disaster for the Amerindian populations along the border. There had been skirmishes and smuggling near Aishalton, his village. These were Brazilian problems, and James had watched most of this from the sidelines, from nearby in Guyana. But he wanted to keep it that way, he said. Crime was a concern, he said, primarily assaults on women from the villages.

"Six, seven years ago, we have some miners come. Guyanese miners. They were interfering. Interfering, you know, with our womenfolk. And these guys had to put them out. I never seen Amerindians so angry. They had to come with the bows and arrows, and the police of course, and put them out."

"Bows and arrows?"

He pointed up toward a small fishing bow on the wall: a decoration. "They haven't come back since." He thought a moment. Actually they had, he said. The particular men from six years ago hadn't come back, but others had.

But the presence of gold and diamonds in a cash-poor place made any decisions murky. The miners offered jobs in the villages, which appealed. Often the miners intermarried. When that happened, the gold became a different sort of parley, because the miners married into not only the village but the land rights—they could make claims to the land as Amerindians now.

"Yes, there is money, but they take advantage. They hire men to carry things, so the men walk in with the supplies." James rocked his shoulders under his T-shirt as if hefting a pack. The Amerindians hired themselves out as porters for the miners carrying the gear. "The men walk with their families, because they go for several days. They stay down there. And that's when [the miners] start interfering and there's a problem. They make a lot of problems with the women. You know. And there were two years where one of the creeks, from the land dredge, was changing colors."

"Where was this?"

"This was a place called Toto Creek. My worry is the hunting and fishing mainly."

Ironically, these were the kinds of stories foreign mining company officers embraced as well. Foreigners seeking to strike deals for land concessions in the interior still compared themselves to the pork knockers. Their facilities, it could be argued, were preferable to the local mines, because they imposed order. They did not cause the kinds of crime and pollution problems tens of thousands of miners did—the anarchy of a gold rush. The big facilities, like Omai, could defend their territory and had to meet environmental standards.

Ivor didn't buy it. "They've been honoring the agreements, because it's in the spotlight," he said. It was? Compared to previous years, yes, he insisted. "They can't afford to screw up. There is international attention now. But a lot of verbal promises are made. A lot of the time the communities don't understand what they're signing."

Tony James had gotten up to walk to the back, and stood with the teenage couple listening to a message in the radio room. He returned, sat back down at the end of the table, and began snapping and undoing the clasp on the knife's leather sheath again.

"You British?" he said.

"American."

"America? I been there."

"Yeah?"

"Yes, I've been to California." He crinkled his forehead, thought for a moment. "Malakoff diggings."

It was an obscure monument, an old mine from the last days of the California gold rush. In the 1880s a group of California farmers had sued the last of the gold rush miners, by making basically the same argument biologists are making now in the Amazon: the mines were poisoning the water and killing any chance for anyone else to make some money. Silt from gold mining had plugged up the Golden Gate so badly it nearly shut down shipping into San Francisco Bay and halted navigation up the river to Sacramento. California's gold mines looked a lot like Mahdia at the time; the waste from the high-pressure hoses was making the irrigation water too dirty to use for crops. So the farmers had sued and won.

They probably just replaced the mining chemicals with farming chemicals in the long run: cyanide with pesticide. But the lawsuit ended gold mining in the foothills where everyone had rushed from San Francisco. Then California went ahead and got rich anyway. James had been brought there by Project Underground for a conference. He recalled being impressed driving through San Jose, where there were miles of good roads and endless rows of houses. It seemed like a good model, he said: Stop looking for gold and move on to something else. He could not say what, however.

THE END

Once a friend mentioned to me a marginal but intriguing theory that gold was a product of intelligent design. The theory says God salted the world with gold at Creation. Eventually humans discovered there was gold all over the world and contrived the idea of currency, and from that came trade. This had been God's intention all along. I don't subscribe to the theory—I am skeptical enough of a God without making Him an economist—but I do like the conceit a lot. It suggests a rare intersection between the time scales used by historians and the ones used by geologists. For a while my friend's comment used to occur to me when I looked at world maps. If you look at the Atlantic Ocean's edges on a map it is possible to see where the Amazon fits into the crux of West Africa. Viewed as a puzzle, the world can, from the right angle, seem intentionally thrust apart to spread the wealth, and the wealth located like a magnet to draw people toward each other. When the first caravels passed Ghana they called it the Gold Coast, and that brought them back. And that led to a series of barbaric choices. And that, in South America at least, jump-starts much of history. In North America as well: the gold rush creates California, the Spaniards' Utopia.

For this reason, if I were to hazard a guess after all this time as to the location of El Dorado, I would point to the center of the fissure where Africa and South America met before the continents split. Of course, that place is the floor of the Atlantic. But a remnant should be located roughly in Guyana.

Why we are still searching is a harder thing to explain. The evidence suggests it isn't something rational. Contrary to cliché, people who own gold mines or invest in them do not often get rich. At least they do not get rich by the nearest standard. The pork knockers are among the poorest people in Guyana, one of the poorest countries in the Western Hemisphere. Most of the foreign miners are hardly successes by the standards of other sorts of captains of industry. It is a difficult, volatile business with low margins. You make more money owning a soap factory or a video game company than a gold mine; you make more money mining sand than gold.

And production of new mines is mostly a fetish. Enough gold already exists for decades upon decades of our use. After five centuries of looking and digging, more gold sits above the earth's surface, in vaults and jewelry boxes, than is known to exist beneath it. It's somewhat of an affront to common sense that we even pursue more digging if we have gold sitting by the tens of thousands of tons easily accessible to us. Particularly when the new gold we mine is so often found in fragile, rare places. Knocking down a forest to produce a virtually useless commodity, of which we already have plenty, makes little sense.

It all looks worse when the industry doing the work is considered. Gold mining is one of the dirtiest human activities in the world. Mines release more chemical waste into their surroundings than any other industry in the United States (according to EPA statistics for the year 2000). Statistics are not available for similar regions in Guyana. Mining is responsible for one of the largest stock market frauds in history (Bre-X), and one of the largest toxic waste accidents in a century (Omai); and is not even a particularly good way to make money in the end. A reputation for corruption has shadowed the industry for years; Mark Twain, who covered the gold rush as a reporter after failing as a prospector, allegedly called a gold mine "a hole in the ground owned by a liar" 150 years ago. Few benefit; the corporate offices hire only a small number of employees, and the mining outposts themselves have been miserable places to live for as long as such outposts have existed. In Guyana, Omai has failed to turn a profit. They found a billion dollars in gold and did not make a dime.

And yet, faith in the metal persists. It still seems impossible to think of a gold mine as worthless. Even in Guyana, where the poverty is often obvious, the gold made it seem the country should have been really, secretly, wildly rich. In Georgetown it seemed there had to be something missing—an administrative mistake somewhere or a clue proving mismanagement. The story is supposed to be that you strike gold and get rich. If you strike oil you get rich. If you strike treasure you get rich. If you strike gold . . . you stay poor.

After several weeks more in Georgetown without an explanation for this, I went back to the forest one last time. I figured I would get as close to an accurate answer as was possible if I asked people with diamonds in their pockets and gold rings on their hands, but no money to their names, what the problem was.

When I got there, somewhat to my surprise, everybody talked about my friend's theory. They said faith was the nation's wealth and the gold was just a talisman. This seemed a bit precious to me, and I said so. But they kept repeating it over and over.

This was at a place called Kaieteur Falls. It is a park in the center of the country, on the edge of the Pakaraima Mountains.

There are no roads there. It is necessary to fly. Like many parts of the country's south, it is remote and beautiful beyond easy description. The plane left from Georgetown in late morning.

Ogle was the secondary airstrip. It was reserved for small planes, and everything seemed small there. Its control tower was not a tower at all but a stunted glass booth barely higher than the office beside it. No one was inside. This was no matter—the pilot loaded the passengers onto the air taxi a few minutes late, granted himself permission to take off, and turned the props. In addition to the pilot and me there were two other passengers aboard: a thirtyish woman named Sandy, who ran the shop in Tony Melville's village of Chenapau, and an aged Amerindian man who pointed out rivers and clumps of trees once the plane was airborne. He was hard to understand; there was something wrong with his throat.

The route from Georgetown to Kaieteur Falls heads over the sugarcane fields and the muddy shore beside the seawall. The narrowness of the coastal plain is striking from the air: dull brown, mossy land cut into rectangles by a lattice of irrigation canals. There is very little space for people to live on in the country. From the air, what little there was lay in a discouraging swamp.

East of the airfield the Demerara River is the color of chocolate milk, and a freighter sits grounded on a sandbar in the center. Within a few moments the jungle begins and the only points of reference are a few curls of river, tight hairpins that bend nearly all the way back on themselves; and scattered clearings, unnatural rectangles of white sand. These are gouges where gold and diamond miners have cleared work spaces and wildcat loggers have made raids. There are no roads apparent after some thin trails. The clearings sit in the trees without any way to reach them. Engines and equipment appear in the forest inexplicably, surrounded by rain forest on all sides, like little atolls.

The plane climbed not so much by flying as by lurching upward—in my jump seat the grim ascent felt more like a funicular's progress than an airplane's. There was a storm over the Essequibo, and when we crossed the river the small plane began to prance and twist while rain spat on the windshield. The pilot was a large man with gray hair, cramped into his seat with his elbows tight, so that the showy epaulets on his flying shirt folded like decks of playing cards. His headset slipped around on his head. He wrestled with the controls and we bounced along with occasional sickening drops, but he was a good pilot and kept us tending west. Soon over his shoulder the flat tabletops of the Pakaraimas appeared hovering above a wall of mist.

We came out of the storm at the mouth of a deep fjord. It was a ridiculous setting, too laughably ideal to ever convince a painter to risk the clichés. The engines whined and we dropped below the lip of a canyon with the cliffs rising high past the wingtips. The man with the problematic larynx pointed down through the window. Below us a river fringed with a band of greenery ran white in the canyon's bottom. Above it a second band appeared from a distance as thin green filigree but as we flew closer was revealed as sizable trees in a band of cloud forest. Above and below it, a few hundred yards to either side of the airplane the canyon walls were sheets of gray stone angled slightly away from us. At the top of the cliffs, creeks atomized into the chasm, leaving a puff of cloud where the water had been. At the end of the fjord was Kaieteur, the main cascade, and as the pilot banked its full measure came into view.

Kaieteur Falls is either the highest or second-highest cataract on earth. It is two and a half times as high as Victoria Falls in

Africa and four times as high as Niagara Falls in North America. Some call it a few feet lower than Angel Falls in Venezuela—the waterfall near the town of El Dorado, on the other side of the Pakaraima Mountains. But Angel Falls has a stone ledge that interrupts the unbroken drop; this has led to predictably nationalist arguments between the Guyanese and the Venezuelans about who has the better waterfall. Venezuela's is probably higher, but Kaieteur has the advantage of isolation. It is set in an obscure corner of a rain-forest plateau and is among the least-known of the world's natural wonders. The United Nations seeks to designate it a World Heritage Site, which confers priority to preservation efforts, and yet no one has heard of it. The chasm ended at the edge of this plateau where a broad, black river, the Potaro, bent to the rim and hurled itself into the air. The pilot banked sharply to give us a broader panorama.

For a seventy-story waterfall, Kaieteur is peculiarly lacking in drama. The river approaches the edge slowly and with a sense of resignation. The drop itself looks like an intentional edit in the river and has a ruler-perfect crease at the edge. It's lovely rather than overwhelming; where waterfalls often seem a bit overblown, full of pretensions about their own power and majesty, Kaieteur seems oddly dutiful. The water forms a nearly perfect rectangle against the canyon wall, and the end of the canyon itself is symmetrical to the point of distraction. It looks like a fifteenth-century painting of the edge of the world. The only flourish is the water itself, which is black and red like printer's ink, sanguine, from turbidity and rotted leaves from upriver. A sheet of this red-black water disappears strikingly into a white column of mist before hitting the pool below, the center of which no one has ever seen, of course. The distance from the top to the bottom is almost 750 feet. Two stone ledges—balconies—frame each side.

The pilot climbed out of the canyon, pitched the plane's nose over with a roll of the controls and landed at an airstrip beside the river. The edge of the plateau was a cream-colored stone plain. Other than some distant trees, nothing was visible but savannah and thin clouds far away over the mesas. The sun was behind the mesas and blackened them in silhouette.

The plateau was only a few thousand feet high but felt cool after the swamp heat in Georgetown. Rain forest had sprouted in irregular spots across the top. It seemed incongruous for there to be forest on the rocky top of the plateau, but the mist from the falls was enough to maintain patches along the rim of the canyon. A path of white stones led into a grove, and the air grew cold enough to produce the distant memory of what it was like to feel a chill. The mist was touching the tops of the trees and falling through the canopy slow enough to watch the sun refract through it. At the end of the forest grove the path came out to a clearing very close to the chasm's edge—the roar was loud now, but it was still not visible beyond some shrubs surviving on wet air. At the end of the path was the park warden's house: a low wooden bungalow on stilts with a haphazard yard and laundry lines tied to hanging branches. A few white shirts hung from the lines.

Three thin dogs with the faces of bats—awful, spindly creatures with short white coats—raced barking from beneath the porch as soon as the path rounded the last meander from the trees. They looked furious, but their rage and sense of mission faltered the closer they got to me. Soon the dogs proved to be cowards and retreated onto their haunches. By then the warden had emerged from the house shirtless and stood on the front porch. He came to sit on a tree stump in the yard.

The warden was a short, broadly built Amerindian man in his mid-thirties with short hair and new boots. The bat-dogs cowered behind him turning mincing, pathetic circles around their tails.

I had come unannounced—the mail came with the plane only rarely, and there were no phones—and was quick to introduce myself and state my intentions: to stay a week only and talk to the prospectors nearby. The warden did not say anything, just waited.

"I just need to string up a hammock," I said, to fill the silence.

"You walk with hammock?" His voice was soft and calm.

In the patois, nothing was ever carried. You "walked with" your burdens as if they were companions.

"Yes, yes." I walked with food, water, a hammock, I said, and presented my bag for inspection.

He waved me off and said he was actually the assistant warden. The head warden was away for ranger training, and would not be back during the week. It was not usually legal for people to just show up at the park, he said. There were permits and papers to sign. I presented a letter from an agency in Georgetown. It was fake, from a travel agent with nice stationery. It takes months to get through the Guyanese government. Of course, I said. The assistant warden saw it was fake but now it wouldn't be his fault I was there.

"Come-come, you sleep in the guesthouse. No worries."

He said his name was Alwyn Garcia. "I go get the key."

He disappeared into his house, leaving the dogs turning their tails to me and checking my perhaps suspicious movements over their shoulders. They seemed still hesitant to step forward toward me, so I stepped their way to introduce myself. They were too bony to pet. It felt like touching something unlike a dog: a more fragile animal, like a bird. Alwyn returned a moment later and led the way toward the falls. The three dogs crept ahead, unsure of my intentions.

A second wood house on stilts emerged hidden below the main dwelling. It was larger than the warden's house and sat in a clearing amid a patch of rain forest. It overlooked a scrubby field filled with chickens, which pecked at each other and searched for edible debris in a muddy field. Stairs led to a broad deck overlooking the trees. Alwyn had to lean into the door to open it, forcing the wood a little. It gave a squeal and a puff of stale air emerged. Inside was a wooden hall ringed with tall slatted windows, a table, and a kitchen with fixtures and a refrigerator but no water or electricity. The appliances sat useless, but suggested a certain ambition.

Alwyn cast his arm around the room and said to tie up anywhere. Across the room, nylon ropes hung from the roof beams. I strung my hammock and took out some tins of food. Alwyn waved and drifted from the hall to the patio. He had traded his boots and was shuffling in the standard flip-flops. I opened whatever windows would open and tried to get the air to move. A photo of Prime Minister Hinds hung on the wall. The guesthouse smelled as if it had not been used in some time. Alwyn was on the porch outside.

I went outside with a package of chocolate cookies.

"Yes, man," he said and took several. We leaned on the porch railing and could see the path to the falls just below. The white smoke rose and curved over a line of trees.

"They pork-knocking upriver?"

"You pork knocker?" he said.

"No."

"Yes, yes, they up at the landing," he said. "Not this area." The area where the houses stood was off limits to everything but picture-taking.

I asked some details about the mines in the park. From the plane we had seen sandy beaches along the banks of the Potaro where dredges were working. Alwyn said yes, this was so, he'd worked on them not long ago. So Alwyn too was a miner.

"I do this work also, mining. My other profession was boat building."

"Yeah?"

He bobbed his head side to side—little of this, little of that.

"How did you do?" I had another cookie. They were stale and hard.

"We find some," said Alwyn. "Enough to keep the pot boiling as they say."

"Here?"

"Four years in the Mazaruni." It was a river to the north. "Then the Potaro. It what bring me to this area."

He'd left the job because the rivers were all worked out, and he was all worked out too by then. "We go sometimes, walk for days and days, way up in the Pakaraimas." He pointed over his shoulder in the direction of the mesas. "One time we walk for days, work a little in an area, test this area, then we run out of food and some men have to walk back." All the way back out four days to get more food, then back up into the mountains.

"And it cold, cold up on the top there," he said. He laughed. "You work in this cold."

"How'd you do?" I said again.

"Ah, we get a little. Some gold. Little diamond. Only little. So we walk out."

It was late afternoon. Alwyn showed the way to the edge of the river and the falls, then a narrow path along the cliffside to overlooks at points along the rim. Bird-of-paradise grew along each side of the trail, red and orange, and nearby were spiderwebs of a size to encircle low trees in their entirety. It seemed like a wise spider that thought of that one. Entire bushes had become white balls encircled in walls of thick silk, like Christmas trees covered in fake snow. After showing the way to the trail, Alwyn said it was time for a nap, and advised me to look out for the swifts, small birds, if he was not back by three o'clock. They would mass over the falls in the predusk hours, a spectacle. He said his goodbyes and left for his house, walking in slow, long strides up the trail.

I sat on the edge of the falls. A few Brazilian miners came by for a bath and seemed startled to find me there. I said the swifts had been recommended to me, so I was waiting, and they said yes, it was a good idea. The birds lived in a hollow behind the drop where predators could not disturb their nests. They were small birds, finch-sized. Within half an hour they arrived by the thousands, a screeching black cloud that juked over the chasm. It looked like a smudge of charcoal in the air. The birds turned tight circles in the void only a few yards from the water. As the sun got lower they began to break off and in turn an individual bird would throw itself suicidally into the falling water and disappear. Alwyn had not overstated the oddity of it, the eight-ounce birds hurling themselves into water falling with the weight of concrete blocks.

At last light I took a bath in an eddy a few yards from the fall's edge but with water as still as a mirror. The river was so warm that I did not feel myself stepping into it. Were it not for the constant roar it would have been possible to stand looking upriver, turned away from the edge, and have no sense of the river's slow progress over the side. The only hint was a lack of fish. They must know about the drop; I made a note to ask a biologist back home. One of the dogs, the middle sister, sat a few feet away from me on the bank staring with its black eyes. I had given it some peanut butter before coming to the river and it had subsequently, with mercenary abruptness, shifted its loyalties from Alwyn to me. It had since followed me everywhere: up the path on the rim, to the cliff's edge, through parts of the forest off the trail looking for a particular plant I wanted to photograph. Now the starving animal looked on walleyed as I bathed, desperately waiting for some opportunity to demonstrate loyalty and perhaps earn more peanut butter. It had lived its whole canine life a cup of rice at a time. I liked the dog, but it had been close on my heels for hours, and now I turned on it and suggested it call forth what small remnant of wolf it might still harbor—go eat one of the nearby chickens. It returned my stare uncomprehending but chastened, the thin black diamond of its lips pressed tightly together, its ears rotating like radar. I got mad; I splashed water at it and said it needed to get itself together. I immediately regretted the tantrum. It looked at me so crestfallen and betrayed—the manipulative beast—that with a pang of regret I realized it had won, and I would have to give it more of my scarce food back at the guesthouse. I finished my bath in a fit of selfish remorse.

The dark came quickly and the dog led the way back to the guesthouse. The roar from the falls bounced off the trees and the chasm's rock walls. It was difficult to find my steps along the rapidly darkening cliffside. I followed the dog; I'm sure if it hadn't been heading straight for the peanut butter in the guesthouse I would have walked, cartoonishly, right off the chasm's edge. I did not see where we were until I had nearly walked into the wall. The dog scattered the chickens and led the way up the stairs, and I made us a couple of sandwiches. In the dog's half I mixed a few bits of canned tuna with the peanut butter, and in its face was such a sense of the sublime it quivered as it ate, and then it fled down the stairs without so much as a bark or a look back.

A flock of birds across the clearing screamed as Alwyn approached a few hours later. It was a beastly grackling, like rusty hinges. I was making myself another sandwich and made two.

"The birds don't like you," I said.

"No."

We could see them in the trees still, vague rustling. Before the sun had set they were visible clearly, large animals, black with white wingtips. He knew all about them; they were famous for cackling at people, there were myths about them. "A man killed a woman, let us say his girlfriend or his wife," Alwyn said. "So the others in the village chase him, you know, to get him and tie him up."

"Tie him up?"

"Yes."

"You mean hang him?"

"Let us say tie him up."

"Okay."

"But after they get him he get away. So now this man uses the birds, and they help him. If he wants to take a rest under a tree, they go to the tree and watch for him, and if people come they wake him up."

We cut the bread in half with a pocketknife. I did not quite get the moral of the story. Were the birds evil then, accomplices to a murderer?

"This is a myth as they say," Alwyn said. "For the older Amerindians, you know." He said to forget he'd said anything about it, not to worry about the birds, they were just some noisy animals. He took the sandwich; he'd not shared dinner with anyone much recently, he said. His wife was in Georgetown with their two children; their kids were finishing their vaccinations at Georgetown Public. I had heard other children around the house too. Those were his stepchildren, Alwyn said, from his wife's first marriage. He had married her after her first husband was murdered.

"He was shot by the notorious bandit Blackie," Alwyn said.

The only light was his flashlight resting on the rail and a white candle on the far corner. "He was only called Blackie here, but after he shot these men he went to town and began to become a bandit. He was not right in his head," Alwyn said.

"You knew him?"

"Yes, yes. He was not dangerous-seeming. He was good to me. Very quiet. But he was the sort of man, you know, you did not want to make him angry."

"Mm."

"But he is dead now." In addition to the murders the notorious bandit Blackie had assaulted and likely raped a young girl near the village upriver, Chenapau. The men there had run him out of the area. "After this he went to town and became a thief." But Alwyn had held no personal beef with him. "He never rob the little guy. Mostly he smuggled."

"What sort of smuggling?"

"All things," he said. "Some say he had an agent. He stole Guyana dollars, American, pounds, diamond." Alwyn took a bite of sandwich. The wind was coming up and a rain felt imminent. "They shot him February eleventh. Police surround the house with him inside."

"Why?"

"What do you mean?"

"Why'd they shoot him? Why didn't he give himself up?"

"No, no. He could not give up, because he had a great quantity of weapons and so."

"Mm."

"After that everything got peaceful again," Alwyn said.

For most of the night, rain barraged the plateau and the next morning the falls had widened. Puddles of coppery water pocked the trail.

Alwyn said the pork knockers were at Menzie's Landing, the last boat dock before the falls. It was only half an hour's walk away on the far side of the airstrip. With the rain breaking he offered to show the way.

He led the way back up the path, then veered through a stand of trees into a meadow beside the airstrip. A weather station was there in a clearing. It was a thin pole with instruments spinning on top. Some wires heading to a box of electronics. The little box of technology looked incongruous, like something left behind by visitors from the future. The attendant's house behind it was a square built on stilts like a guard tower, with laundry lines guyed out on a tentpole, from which damp sheets, rewetted in the previous night's rain, dragged along the ground. Under the laundry lines two young girls were staging a tea party and a second two a splash fight with buckets.

"Yes," Alwyn said.

This was his standard greeting. He yelled it at the top of the tower. Above on the stairs, a woman in a green dress came from inside and called back.

"Hey, Alwyn!"

Could he bring her some sugar from the landing? He climbed the stairway and spoke with her. A young man sporting a bushy black hairdo—he seemed to have expended a lot of attention on it—emerged from the house holding a smaller child, a boy about two years old.

"Just now," Alwyn said to me, making a pressing motion toward me with his hand. I agreed to wait.

He mounted the stairs and talked with his neighbor on the porch above. The house was neatly appointed. White drapes swayed out of the windows in the wind. Below the sun was already high and the ground felt hot. I waited with the children until one of the girls, perhaps eight, nine, a few teeth missing, seemed tired of the tea party and marched off from her sister toward the airstrip. The airstrip doubled as the local playground, and she liked to run on the concrete.

Alwyn descended the stairs from the tower pocketing the money for the sugar and waved us on. Past the weather station a tree had fallen into the trail, and Alwyn took a detour that was difficult to discern in the underbrush. The forest ended with abruptness. White pebbles and shards of crystal were scattered here and there thinly across a wide plain of stone. There were veins of milky quartz. The river was across it. Alwyn picked a spot in the trees to point himself toward, a mile across the odd stone savannah, and set off.

Though from the air the forest looks like a green skein over the land, the northern edge changes abruptly from sagebrush to forest to mountains. Here and there was evidence of humans: bits of plastic or a discarded bottle cap. Beside the airstrip was a stack of blue plastic crates, empty glass bottles: the town recycling. It seemed unlikely anyone would devote the airplane fuel to fly the glass back to Georgetown for redemptions; the bottles were stranded on the edge of the Amazon forever. That anyone had carried them from the landing to the middle of the savannah seemed strange. The bottles waited hopefully. After passing the odd blue column in the middle of the plain I looked back toward Alwyn walking ahead of me, and he seemed again to be crossing a prehistoric world.

At the far side of the stone patch was a muddy creek bed. A falcon watched Alwyn pass. There was a slight rise and a drop into the landing. A shack with Dutch doors and shutters along one side sat beside the trail where it emerged from some trees. It was a boardinghouse that looked more like a paddock than a place for humans to live. A young man and two young women lazed on a bench nearby beneath a broad tree like an oak. The man stroked both women's hair, one resting her head on his lap, the other sitting beside him.

"White boy," he said.

"Hey."

"You come buy diamonds?"

"No, not today." He had a cloth with some rough diamonds in his pocket. He could have been selling me broken pieces of a beer bottle for all I could tell.

"Come-come," he urged.

Menzie's Landing was fifty yards long. It sat on either side of a footpath that ended at the river. There were two more boardinghouses and two shops, and that was the town. A tall shirtless miner was across from the shop passed out on the steps of a wood shack. Beside him were three Brazilians I'd met at the falls, one a man with a tooth missing wearing a jersey that said "Petrobas," Brazil's large oil company and sponsor of a popular soccer team. He gave a wave from a stoop next door. He sat in front of a dry-goods shop with two friends drinking rum at ten in the morning. Alwyn opened a gate and climbed some cracked stairs into the shop. Above the counter someone had painted a warning that "Mr. Credit has been murdered by a crooked paymaster," but Alwyn was already planning to pay cash—seven dollars from the woman at the weather station for seven pounds of sugar. An intense young man scooped the sugar from a barrel and weighed it on a floor scale. There was no cane in the interior, and the sugar had come by plane. It cost, absurdly, five times as much as it would in an American supermarket. Alwyn added a soft drink to the bill and sat and drank, hot from the walk. Outside a dog slept on the stairs, twisted across two steps uncomfortably as if boneless. Like Mahdia, the town was surrounded by millions in gold and diamonds and yet was all shacks.

I walked outside and sat on the stoop near the dog. A teenage boy pushed a plastic fuel tank with pain and deliberateness down the path. It was gasoline for an outboard motor. He struggled to slide it through the dirt. It must have weighed a hundred pounds, nearly as much as the boy. He bent his shoulder into the container and shoved it grimly through the sand a few feet with each heave. It was like watching a beetle push a brick. Following behind him was a man with upswept dreadlocks wearing a pistol on his hip. Alwyn finished his transaction, emerged from the store knotting the top of the fat bag of brown sugar, and waved me along. We could talk to this man: he was a diamond miner, Alwyn said. His name was Neil James.

The dreadlocked man pulled his shirt hem over the gun. But the tip still poked out and the pistol-shaped bulge under his jersey only drew more attention to the weapon.

"You go back-dam?" Alwyn said.

"Just one night. Go collect some production," said Neil James.

"Gold?" I said. James seemed startled by me.

"No man. Gold not profitable. Diamond."

The boy had wrestled the boat fuel the rest of the way down the path to the river. Neil apologized and walked after him. They were heading upriver for a few minutes. At the end of the path was a skiff tied to a tree root sticking out of the bank; there was no pier. The boy stopped and stretched his back. He looked from the barrel to the water, judging the slope of the embankment, and began to plan how to lower the tank the few feet into the boat without dropping it and losing it into the current and over the falls. James made his way to the end of the path toward the young assistant, who sat down on the riverbank defeated and vexed.

The town was dead. It was normally dead, though. Alwyn said we would head back and try again later perhaps.

Later was that night. A party was under way. A group of miners had come from upriver and were drinking at the landing. A few yards up the trail was a dark clearing. The clearing and the surrounding savannahs left a wide view of the stars, and with a thin moon the equatorial sky put on a show: more stars than black space between them, the occasional meteor trail. Only the Christmas lights hanging off the rum shop distracted from the sky. There was some yelling through the shop wall, a few wide planks of splintery plywood that looked cut with a dull saw. The party was going well.

A few yards up the path a group of miners sat in the dark on a log.

"White boy," said the nearest man. He was only a few feet away, but it was difficult to see anything in the dark. The man introduced himself as Nigel Lett, offered a seat, and helped to locate it. I offered some rum from a bottle I was dragging in one hand. He refused. "All these wicked things going on. Drinking, fornication," he said. He didn't drink. The party bothered him. Nigel sat with his friend Roger, who did not share the concern and asked for the rum bottle without hesitation. Both men were from Georgetown. Lett chastised his friend for taking the rum.

"You must have faith," he said. He seemed to speechify a bit, a show for the outsider.

"Being a diamond seeker is all about faith," he said. His friend nodded but seemed to have heard it all before and took another drink from the bottle. Lett proselytized some more. Perhaps he was drunk after all. I asked him what he meant about faith. It was a matter of personal safety for one thing, he said.

"You see many, many miracles working in this back-dam. I myself see miracles. I have experienced miracles," he said. He said God had saved his life from a waterfall in the jungle.

"Kaieteur?"

"No, this in another back-dam, on the Mazaruni. Boat come untied in the night. And I wake up, the boat going onto the falls, and I going over." He had been asleep in the boat. "And then, boom, tree branch save me. But I know, it not the tree branch doing this. Hand of God save me."

"What happened to your boat?"

"I get on this tree branch," he said. "Then it go under." Lett waved his hand in a corkscrew, arcing it toward the ground, a boat sinking.

His friend, Roger, agreed.

"I think, yes, faith," he said, and took another drink. "I have some experiences also."

"Miracles?"

He wasn't sure. "One time my partner and I—this was in a different back-dam though, not this place—my partner and I, we come upon a bushmaster, size like me." The bushmaster was a terrifying, deadly snake, venomous enough to cause sudden heart attacks in grown men; in some cases the victim shivered for three days first, then fell dead. Roger held his arms far apart to show the viper's length: six feet, more, he said. "And it get around my partner. But it not squeezing. No bite. None of these things. Snake just do nothing, nothing. Come up close, this bushmaster, but it do nothing, and my partner does not die."

They had both found some gold and plenty of diamonds that week, in an otherwise enigmatic forest. Was that not proof as well? Lett said. A diamond buried in the middle of the jungle, in sand full of gold: that a human could find these things at a random spot in a jungle, this showed divine presence, he said. Otherwise what were the odds, a forest filled with treasure where a poor man could find deliverance from his lot? And God was strongest in Kaieteur. "Mahdia, that back-dam dirty. Got malaria," Nigel said. "This is a cleaner back-dam. You go this back-dam, you see a paradise there." He pointed toward the river, his hand giving a flip. "You go over that side, you find a diamond lying like so." He put out his hands, palms up, as if a diamond lay on the ground between us. "You go with faith and to do this work is to know God." Roger nodded along and took another drink from the bottle of rum.

Late that night I left the house beside the falls and walked toward the airstrip. There was a hut there where I decided to spend the night. A tour group of English teenagers had shown up from the Volunteer Service Organization, and their leader was snoring profoundly. I hauled my hammock out of my bag and headed up the trail into the trees. Out of the trees the path crossed a meadow, and then there was the shelter, lacking walls but with a grass roof made of tight straw bundles. A rain had started. I ducked inside.

It was too dark to see as far as the floor. Someone said, "Good night." He was to the right. The man took a pull of a cigarette. His forehead and the tip of his nose were visible in the glow of the tip. A flashlight came on. He was sitting on a bench beside a hammock.

"Sorry. Didn't see you there," I said.

"Don't apologize, man. Tie up, get some sleep if you want."

He rested with one leg folded frogwise on the bench and an arm over it. His voice was slow and wet. He was smoking a joint the size of a boutonnière. His breath was audible. The straw roof of the hut was quiet in the rain, a softer sound than in the trees, and less intrusive than the ping of the drops on the tin roof at the guesthouse. The man shined his flashlight so that I could see to tie the hammock from the hut's roof beams, and inhaled more smoke.

"White man," he said, coughing.

"Yeah."

"English?"

"American."

"American," he said. "I don't like so much America."

"Mm." I fussed with my bed.

"Yes, man. Not so much." He paused to smoke some more, and asked, with a wary air, if Henry Kissinger was still involved in the government.

"Not that I'm aware of," I said.

"That's good."

He rambled a little while I arranged myself. There was a bit of eagerness to his talking, too many opinions for so late at night. "I a diamond seeker," he said. "Gold? Nah. Omai, they robbing this country," he said. His name was Physic, because he was skilled in electronics, he said. He'd thought of going to school in that field. "I first come into the bush in 1980, make money to go to school. I was supposed to go to the Tuskegee Institute. I'm interested in engineering. I spend four years, get the money, come back out. When I got the money the cost go up, no longer twenty thousand dollars U.S."

"Mm."

"Yes man. I could have gotten a government scholarship, but that would have been only to go to school in Eastern Europe, and the situation there was not so good at that time. I also got Cuba, but the technology in Cuba is not at a very high level, you know. Maybe I get a shop. I like electronics, I do something with that. It true I can sell my production with computers? Otherwise, in Georgetown, they give a bad price."

It rained all night. The next morning the plane came late owing to the weather.

Not long after dawn the man with the pistol, Neil James, came to the door of the hut to gather up Physic and go to work at a diamond mine upriver. He was full of apologies about the other day. "I get a little nervous yesterday when you see me with the gun on my hip," he said.

"It's fine."

"But you never know, this jungle."

"Right, right."

Neil James waited while Physic brushed his teeth outside the hut. He sat on a wooden bench along the wall.

I asked why he lived in the forest looking for treasure.

"See, it like this," James said. He was twenty years younger than Physic but more successful: he ran his own mine. "When I was ten years old I lived in Georgetown. And I thiefing anything I could thief, because a boy's got to eat. Do that five years, and then I first come into the bush, fifteen, part-time. And it work out good." He sat himself on a bench in the hut's rear, waiting out the rain. "After that I had several choices. I could go Suriname, they pay better there. I could go Venezuela or Brazil, because the borders here, you can go there easily. Or I can go to the interior. So I decide to go interior. Because you see, you stay in Georgetown, you make no money. You start down roads, you understand? And you don't want to do bad. You want to do good. So I decide to stay in the bush, because I can do this, you learn what you can do with your own hands. And I don't mind outsiders. Only thing, once they work these areas, we done. All the gold, diamonds, gone, they go back to the other countries, what we got? This interior is what we got. They don't, them people up in Georgetown, they don't make anything. We got gold, diamonds, timber. That's what this place has."

Physic spit out his toothpaste and came back inside the hut.

"Look what happened in the United States," James said. "You cut down all them forests, do the mining. The way I'm thinking, that's what make you rich. This country want to be rich too."

I asked if it would make him rich. He said he was doing okay, sure.

We waited for the plane and for the rain to end. Neil and Physic sat in the hut talking about the election to come, and some rumors about things on the river, gossip. Someone had been registering Brazilians to vote. They laughed a little about that, and then James said it was time to go back to the landing with the rain slackening, to check on "a few things," maybe head upriver again.

"I got one last question to ask," he said. "Ah, just now I forget it." He laughed.

Physic teased him, called him a few names. James put his fingers to his temples, smiled at his forgetfulness, and in another moment remembered his thought and looked up.

"What I want to ask you is when, or, how long do you think, for civilization? That is, when you think there is going to be a Rapture?"

The rain was ending. Physic heard the propeller first, approaching in the fog. When the plane had landed, Alwyn's children emerged with bandages on their arms, the older child holding a doll and looking airsick. The passengers back to Georgetown forced themselves into the wet seats, where water had leaked in through the plane's loose windows in the storm.

"Why do you ask?"

"I don't know. I just think about it," James said. He laughed again.

SOURCES

Guyana is not yet a well-documented place, and many of the statistics that do exist concerning Guyanese society and the Guyanese natural environment are outdated or unreliable. As a result, much of the information in this book is from my own observations and interviews, and of necessity anecdotal.

There were some concrete sources available, of course. Among those used for this book were the following. Bibliographical information is incomplete in a very few cases, owing to books out of print, missing their title pages, or found in photocopy in Guyana.

MODERN GUYANA

Economic and public health statistics for Guyana came from the Guyana state statistical service's 2000 summary report; from the Pan American Health Organization in both Washington, D.C., and Georgetown, Guyana; and from the Inter-American Development Bank's annual economic summary, *Economic and Social Progress in Latin America,* for 1999 and 2000. The *CIA World Factbook* provided geographic and population figures. Commercial and trade details are from the *Country Commercial Guide Guyana, Fiscal Year 2000,* provided by the American embassy, Georgetown.

THE GOLD MINING INDUSTRY

Vivian Danielson and James Whyte's *Mining Explained* (Don Mills, Ont., Canada: Northern Miner, 1998) provided technical explanations of large-scale mining operations and some information on how these operations are financed. Timothy Green's *The New World of Gold,* 2nd ed. (New York: Walker, 1984) provided a less technical but broader picture of the gold industry's global dimensions and architecture. For the history of junior mining companies I referenced Canadian reporter Jennifer Wells's *Fever: the Dark Mystery of the Bre-X Gold Rush* (Penguin Books Canada, Ltd., 1998) and her earlier *Pez: the Manic Life of the Ultimate Promoter* (Toronto: Macfarlane, Walter & Ross, 1991). Brian Hutchinson's *Fool's Gold: The Making of a Global Market Fraud* (Toronto: Knopf Canada, 1998) was a secondary text on juniors.

Among the gold industry professionals who discussed their work with me are Richard Scott-Ram of the World Gold Council; geologist Michael Cartright, a former employee of the Placer Dome and Franco-Nevada mining companies; Patrick Sheridan of Guyana Goldfields Inc., R. Greg McKnight, Director of Mining and Metals for HSBC Securities; and Michael Thomsen, Director of Exploration Acquisitions for the Newmont Mining Corporation.

FINANCE

Peter Bernstein's *The Power of Gold* (New York: Wiley, 2000) and Green's *The New World of Gold,* cited above, provided background on gold's role as a financial instrument from antiquity to the present. John E. Young's *Gold: At What Price?*, a proposal for liquidating government gold reserves prepared for American mining opponents Project Underground, the Mineral Policy Center, and the Western Organization of Resource Councils, provided the environmentalist critique of gold's role in international finance. Young is an economist with the WorldWatch Institute. The Gold Institute's Paul Bateman, the organization's president, provided the gold industry point of view on the same topic in a conversation at his office and by phone. I also consulted a transcript of Columbia University economist and Nobel Prize recipient Robert A. Mundell's March 12, 1997, lecture at St. Vincent College, Latrobe, Penn., "The International System in the 21st Century: *Could Gold Make a Comeback?*"

THE SEARCH FOR EL DORADO
The primary texts I relied on for my summary of the search for El Dorado and the Spanish Conquest were John Hemming's *The Search for El Dorado* (New York: Dutton, 1979) and Michael Woods's *The Spanish Conquest* (Berkeley: University of California Press, 2000). Woods retraced some of the Orellana route, even building a raft at one point, for a BBC documentary. For information on Raleigh I relied on V. S. Naipaul's *The Loss of El Dorado*, (Harmondsworth, U.K.: Penguin, 1969), on Hemming, and on two primary texts: Sir Walter Raleigh's *The Discoverie of the Large, Beautiful and Riche Land of Guiana* and Lawrence Keymis's *A Relation of the Second Voyage to Guiana.* Professor David Browman, an Andean specialist in the archaeology department of Washington University, St. Louis; and Gene Savoy, Reno, Nevada, discoverer of the lost city of Vilcabamba among other things, offered their insights by phone.

GUYANESE HISTORY
For the colonial history of British Guiana, of pork-knocking, and of slavery and indenture I consulted Vere T. Daly's *A Short History of the Guyanese People* (London: Macmillan, 1975); Ron Ramdin's *Arising From Bondage: A History of the Indo-Caribbean People* (New York: New York University Press, 2000); and Ovid

Abrams' *Metegee: The History and Culture of Guyana* (New York: Ashanti Books, 1998). The last two were my source on the country's twentieth-century political history, particularly the stories of Forbes Burnham, Cheddi Jagan, and the American influence on Guyanese politics. *Metegee* was a constant reference on virtually all aspects of daily Guyanese life and culture and contains perhaps the world's only detailed primer on Guyanese Creole.

Matthew French Young's *Guyana, the Lost El Dorado* (Leeds, U.K.: Peepal Tree Press, 1998), Evelyn Waugh's *92 Days* (Focus, 1987), V. S. Naipaul's *The Middle Passage* (New York: Random House, 1981), and Michael Swan's *The Marches of El Dorado* (Boston: Beacon, 1958), all travelogues of time spent in colonial British Guiana, provided firsthand accounts of the Guyanese interior and Georgetown from the 1920s to the 1960s. Shiva Naipaul's *Black and White* (London: H. Hamilton, 1980) and Matthew Carr's memoir *My Father's House* (London: Penguin, 1998) provided context for the Burnham period.

I consulted two works of fiction. Wilson Harris's *The Guyana Quartet* (London: Faber & Faber, 1985) was essential perspective on the interior forests. Will Kirkland's translation of Romulo Gallegos's *Canaima* (Pittsburgh: University of Pittsburgh Press, 1996) provided similar perspective on Venezuelan history and myth.

Documents from the Kennedy administration relating to Cheddi Jagan and Guyanese independence were provided by a website, Guyana.org, and their authenticity confirmed by the reference desk of the Kennedy Library, Boston.

BRAZILIAN MINERS

At the End of the Rainbow: Gold, Land and People in the Brazilian Amazon by Gordon McMillan (New York: Columbia University Press, 1995) and *Anatomy of the Amazon Gold Rush* by David

Cleary (Iowa City: University of Iowa Press, 1990), both studies of alluvial gold miners by anthropologists, were my sources for the history of the 1979–1990 Brazilian gold rush and in particular its effects on Amerindian populations.

GEOLOGY

Several geologists with experience in the region spoke with me, including Rickford Viera of the Guyana Geology and Mines Commission, David Fennell, formerly of Golden Star Resources, and Floyd Gray, a research geologist with the United States Geological Survey. Fred Peschke and Paul Matysek, respectively President and Exploration Manager of Vannessa Ventures, Ltd., a mining company active in Guyana, added their experience in two later conversations.

ENVIRONMENTAL POLITICS

The history of North American environmentalist response to the Amazon gold rush came principally from conversations with Stephen D'Esposito, President of the Mineral Policy Center, Washington, D.C.; Danny Kennedy, founder of Project Underground, currently working for Greenpeace; and David Cassells, Director of the Iwokrama Rainforest Program, Georgetown.

CYANIDE USE

Technical information on cyanide leaching and the operating of mine waste impoundments came from the United States Environmental Protection Agency's September 1994 report *Treatment of Cyanide Heap Leaches and Tailings* and from *Mining Explained*, Danielson and Whyte, cited above.

Corby Anderson, Director of the Center for Advanced Mineral and Metallurgical Processing at Montana Tech University, Butte, Montana, provided technical insight on mine waste storage and institutional memory on the debate over cyanide gold mines in a telephone interview. A transcript of the Minerals, Metals and Materials Society's February 2001 "roundtable discussion," "Cyanide, Where Do We Go from Here?" provided a comprehensive overview of the debate over cyanide. Anderson moderated the discussion. The Mineral Policy Center's reports *Cyanide Uncertainties* and *More Cyanide Uncertainties* and a transcript of the organization's remarks before the April 9, 2001, international conference on "Finance, Mining and Sustainability" provided the environmentalist critique.

Latest estimates of the costs and difficulty of cleaning up abandoned mines were reported in "Abandoned Mines Said Gigantic Environment Problem," Reuters, May 14, 2002. The story quotes Sir Robert Wilson, chairman of the Rio Tinto Plc, estimating the mining industry as a whole faces cleanup costs in excess of a trillion dollars.

CYANIDE ACCIDENTS

Details on the Omai cyanide waste spill are from "Preliminary Report on Technical Causation of the Omai Tailings Dam Failure," drafted for the Guyana Geology and Mines Commission by its Dam Review Team, November 16, 1995. Additional information came from Cambior, Inc., majority owner of the mine, and the International Commission on Large Dams/United Nations Environment Program, Bulletin 121, *Tailings Dams*, 2001. An overview of the local response to the disaster came from the August 20–27 editions of the *Stabroek News* and *Guyana Chronicle*, the two leading daily newspapers of Georgetown, Guyana.

MERCURY

The Guyana Environmental Protection Agency provided information on mercury use among Guyanese gold miners. Evidence of mercury poisoning in Guyanese mining is contained in a survey of the Mazaruni River, "Identification of the Sources and Assessment of the Levels of Mercury Contamination in the Mazaruni Basin in Guyana, in order to Recommend Mitigation Measures," by David Singh, Cynthia Watson, and Simone Mangal. A draft of the report was not yet released at the time of this publication.

"Remote Villagers Poisoned," Reuters, February 3, 1999, confirmed the presence of Minamata disease in the Brazilian Amazon. Maszumi Harada of Kumamoto University and Junko Nakanishi of Yokohama National University, Japan, conducted the study cited in the report and released their findings in the February 1999 edition of *New Scientist* magazine.

Information on the historical impact of mercury in California came from *Mercury Contamination from Historic Gold Mining in California,* U.S. Geological Survey Fact Sheet FS–061–00, by Charles N. Alpers and Michael P. Hunerlach.

GOLD PRODUCTION

Statistics on global central bank gold holdings and production are from the United States Geological Survey's 2001 Mineral Commodity Survey, an annual report of global mine output by material. USGS reported that 33,300 tons of gold existed aboveground as "official stocks held by central banks and about 77,200 tons is privately held as coin, bullion and jewelry" in 2001. The report confirmed there is more gold aboveground, about 110,000 tons, than known to exist in situ, 100,000 tons.

Additional statistics came from *The Millennium in Gold 1000–1999* by Timothy Green, the Gold Institute.

GOLD AND NATIONAL DEVELOPMENT

Prime Minister Samuel Hinds of Guyana spoke with me at his office about gold's role in Guyana's national development scheme and the country's economic prospects generally. Rod Lever of Canada's Export Development Corporation discussed the effects of antiglobalization protests on external credit agencies, in an interview at a mining industry conference in San Francisco.

For statistics on the environmental impact of mining in southern Venezuela I consulted *All That Glitters Is Not Gold: Balancing Conservation and Development in Venezuela's Frontier Forests* by Marta Miranda et al. (Washington, D.C.: World Resources Institute, 1998).

Details of the International Monetary Fund's gold sale program came from the IMF press office.

JEWELRY

The history of gold wedding rings came from *An Illustrated Dictionary of Jewellery* by Anita Mason (New York: Harper & Row, 1974) and from the Jewelry Information Center, a trade association located in New York. The center also provided recent sales statistics for gold and platinum. Additional information on gold history came from *God and Gold in Late Antiquity* by Dominic Janes (Cambridge, U.K., and New York: Cambridge University Press, 1998).

Jewelry sales' relationship to gold production and commodity prices in the late 1990s were found in "Gold Slide Splits Analysts: Worries on Jewelry Demand" by David Bogoslaw, Dow Jones Newswires, January 11, 2001; and "World Gold Council Launches $3 Million National Ad Campaign; First Gold Jewelry Ad Push in Almost Five Years," Business Wire, November 8, 2000.

ACKNOWLEDGMENTS

The information on hammocks previously appeared in a different form, under the title "Balance," in *Open Letters,* an online magazine. Descriptions of El Dorado, Venezuela, and explanations of the gold industry appeared in *Civilization Magazine.* The story of the frozen cabin appeared in *McSweeney's.*

Hundreds of people in Guyana spoke with me over the years with candor and patience for an outsider's questions. It is a country of overwhelming generosity. The residents of El Dorado, Venezuela, and outlying regions abided my presence from time to time in Estado Bolivar. Thank you to Omai Gold Mines, Ltd., which granted me access to its facility, and to the Honorable Samuel Hinds, Prime Minister of Guyana, who offered his time and insight in an interview at his office. Matt Falloon and Amanda Wilson were good friends to me on Waterloo Street. The Persaud family were gracious hosts.

Many thanks to International Investment Conferences for allowing me to attend their functions, and to the dozens of members of the gold mining industry who spoke with me there and by phone.

Jill Grinberg's role in this project is difficult to overstate. Her encouragement, generosity, editorial eye, professional wisdom, and above all, her belief in the stories she makes it possible to tell are why this book came into existence. Though any mistakes are mine, the book has always been a partnership, in which I am by far the greater beneficiary. Meeting Jill and becoming her friend has been one of the story's great joys.

Sean McDonald, my editor, took an interest in a story that would have been far easier to ignore, then proceeded to save it from death at the hands of its author. He did this with infallible clarity and confidence. He also managed to seem convincingly unsurprised once it all worked out, suggesting a suppressed talent for acting. I'd been warned that often editors don't actually read the books they publish these days. Sean read a bit closer than I'd have even hoped, to the book's benefit and my happy exhaustion.

I owe an enormous debt of gratitude to Nan A. Talese for trusting the story and for trusting me with it.

Sara Sklaroff ignored the inexperience and overenthusiasm of an unknown quantity and commissioned the magazine article from which this book grew.

Nancy Ford, of the Art Institute of Chicago library, provided research on the history of jewelry.

Terence Mulligan deciphered a corporate financial statement for me.

David "Grue" DeBry provided the computer I used to write much of this book.

Tom Zoellner offered the anecdote about God and gold, and a constant example of what it is to be a good reporter.

Dena Slothower and Lilya Kaganovsky each sheltered me more times than I can count; Lark Park and Jimmy Evans did so without hesitation at a crucial time late in the game. Then Ms.

Slothower hosted me again at the very end. I currently maintain my own residence.

Seth Masket, Jonathan Bourne, and Steve Mockus read early drafts of this book. K. C. Swanson read later drafts, several times each, and offered essential insight throughout the process.

And thank you to my sister, Staci Herman, and to my friends Robert Rushing, Jennifer Shreve, Alan Rapp, and Jill Shallenberger, for everything.

My mother, Ann Herman, has offered her unconditional encouragement for years.

My father, David Herman, traveled widely during his life as part of his job. He was an example to me, and he is missed.